museum guide book

MUSÉE DU QUAI BRANLY

Stéphane Martin
President

Pierre Hanotaux
Managing Director

Jean-Pierre Mohen
Director of the Heritage
and Collections Department

Anne-Christine Taylor
Director of the Research
and Education Department

Hélène Cerutti
Director of the Department of Cultural
Development and the Public

Danielle Brault
Director of the Department
of Administrative Services and Human Resources

Nadim Callabe
Director of the Department
of Operations and Maintenance

★ museum guide book

musée du quai Branly

PATRONAGE SUPPORT

Major Patrons

Pernod Ricard

AXA

Schneider Electric

Caisse des Dépôts

Fondation d'entreprise Gaz de France

Fondation EDF

Ixis - Corporate & Investment Bank - Groupe Caisse d'Épargne

Patrons

Euro RSCG

Sony France

Sony Europa Foundation

Issey Miyake

Saint-Gobain

Atos Consulting

JCDecaux

Martine and Bruno Roger

Friends of the Australia Project: the Australian Government, through the Australia Council for the Arts and the Harold Mitchell Foundation; the French Foreign Ministry, through the Permanent Secretariat for the Pacific Region; Martine and Bruno Roger; Veolia Environnement, AM Conseil.

DONATIONS

Since 1997, the Musée du quai Branly collections have been enriched by donations of works of art from:

Mr. Benoît Aubenas

Mrs. Patricia Aubenas

Mr. Rémy Audouin

Axis Gallery Inc.

Mrs. de Baillencourt

Mr. Jean Paul Barbier-Mueller

Mrs. Monique Barbier-Mueller

Mrs. Marie-Claire Bataille-Benguigui

Mr. Georges Benguigui

Mrs. Janine Claude Berge

Mrs. Marie-Thérèse Berger

Mr. and Mrs. Jacques Blazy

Mrs. Jacqueline Bocquet

Mr. and Mrs. Gérard Boëly

Mr. and Mrs. Samir Borro

Mr. and Mrs. Cayetana & Anthony JP Meyer

Mrs. Mireille Clausse

Mrs. Catherine Clément

Father Michel Convers

Mr. Pierre Dartevelle

Mr. Sebastian Dass

Mrs. Angelina Dass

Mrs. Catherine Dass

Mrs. Aube and Mrs. Oona Elléouët

Mr. Asher Eskenazy

Mrs. Claudine Foulon

Mr. Léonard Giannada

Mr. Hubert Goldet

Mr. Olivier Goldet

Mrs. Véronique Guérin

Mrs. Fernand Haïm

Mr. Georges Halphen

Mr. Udo Horstmann

Mr. Michel Huguenin

Mr. and Mrs. Jean-Charles Humbert

Mrs. Hélène Joubert

Mr. Guy Joussemet

Mr. Jacques Kerchache

Mrs. Anne Kerchache

Mr. and Mrs. Marcel Korolnik

Mr. Guy Ladrière

Mr. and Mrs. Pierre Langlois

Chief Laukalbi (Tanna tribe, Vanuatu)

Mr. and Mrs. Jean Mansion

Mr. Daniel Marchesseau in memory of André Fourquet

Mr. Louis Jean-Pierre Mathieu

Mr. Pierre Messmer de l'Institut de France

Mr. Alain de Monbrison

Mr. Christophe Niemoller

Mr. Douglas Newton

Mrs. Patricia Oyelola

Mr. Arthur Papadimitriou

Mr. Marc Petit

Mr. and Mrs. Pierre Pinson

Radio France

Mrs. Marie-Hélène Reichlen

Mr. and Mrs. Jeffrey A. Rosen, American donors in honour of Martine Aublet and Bruno Roger

Mrs. Rueff-Pigeat

Mr. Alain Schoffel

Mr. and Mrs. Guy Stresser Péan

Mrs. Pierrette Tapie

Mr. and Mrs. Claude Vérité

Mr. de Vertenelle

Mr. Marcel Wislin

The AXA Group for the acquisition of a masterpiece of African art within the framework of France's law on patronage of the arts.

CONTRIBUTORS, MUSÉE DU QUAI BRANLY

Germain Viatte
Scientific Advisor

Yves Le Fur
Deputy Director responsible
for Permanent Collections

Oceania
Philippe Peltier, P.P.
Head of the Oceania Heritage and
Collections Unit

Constance de Monbrison, C.M.
Head of Insulindia Collections

Magali Mélandri, M.M.
Oceania Collections Department

Asia
Christine Hemmet, C.H.
Head of the Asia Heritage
and Collections Unit

Hana Chidiac, H.C.
Head of the Middle East Collections

Daria Cevoli, D.C.
Asia Collections Department

Africa
Hélène Joubert, H.J.
Head of the Africa Heritage
and Collections Unit

Marie-France Vivier, M.-F.V.
Head of North African Collections

Gaëlle Beaujean-Baltzer, G.B.-B.
African Collections Department

Aurélien Gaborit, A.G.
African Collections Department

Americas
André Delpuech, A.D.
Head of the Americas Heritage
and Collections Unit

Fabienne de Pierrebourg, F.P.
Head of the Americas Collections

Paz Nuñez-Regueiro
Head of the Americas Collections

Françoise Cousin, F.C.
Head of the Textiles Heritage and
Collections Unit

Christine Barthe, Ch.B.
Scientific Head of the National Heritage
Unit for Photographic Collections

Madeleine Leclair, M.L.
Head of the National Heritage Unit of
the Musical Instrument Collections

Nanette Snoep, N.S.
Head of the National Heritage
Unit of the History Collections

Marine Degli, M.D.
Documentary Study Department

Emmanuel Désveaux, E.D.
Research Department

Marina Weill
Chief Librarian

OUTSIDE CONTRIBUTORS

Claude Baudez, C.B.
Honorary Director of Research, CNRS
Jean-François Bouchard, J.-F.B.
Director of Research, CNRS
Pascal Bouchery, P.B.
Senior Lecturer, University of Poitiers
Jean-Pierre Chaumeil, J.-P.C.
Director of Research, CNRS
Mathieu Claveyrolas, M.C.
Doctor of Ethnology, Centre d'études
de l'Inde, EHESS/CNRS
Sophie Desrosiers, S.D.
Senior Lecturer, EHESS
Svetlana Jacquesson, S.J.
Doctor of Ethnology, INALCO/EHESS
Jean-Luc Lambert, J.-L.L.
Senior Lecturer, EPHE
Jean Michaud, J.M.
Professor, University of Montreal
Louis Perrois, L.P.
Ethnologist, Honorary Head of Research,
ORSTOM (IRD)
Gaetano Speranza, G.S.
Ethnological Society, University
of Paris X, Nanterre

The original idea behind the new Musée du quai Branly,
which is devoted entirely to the arts and civilisations of Africa,
Asia, Oceania and the Americas, stemmed from the political
will to see justice rendered to non-European cultures.
This means not only recognising the influence their art has had
on our cultural heritage, but also acknowledging the debt
we owe to the peoples and countries that produced it, many
of which have particularly close ties with France.

In bringing to an end a long history of neglect, arts
and civilisations that have long been ignored or underrated
are being given their rightful place, and dignity is being
restored to peoples who were too often humiliated, oppressed
or even destroyed by arrogance, ignorance, stupidity
and blindness.

The Musée du quai Branly represents a new type of cultural
and research institution that is a museum, a cultural centre
and a research and teaching facility rolled into one.
It repudiates the concept of artistic or racial hierarchy,
and celebrates the universality of human genius in the
dazzling range of cultural expression shown in its collections.

In the Musée du Louvre's Pavillon des Sessions, masterpieces
from Africa, Asia, Oceania and the Americas have a permanent
home under the same roof as some of the major masterpieces
of European art in the heart of the world's greatest museum.
With his unerring eye, vast knowledge, energy, passion and
generous humanity, my late friend Jacques Kerchache selected
items of exceptional quality, which are displayed with
a restraint that allows the impact of their beauty to speak
for itself. Here, it is the exhibits that are the main focus,
rich in history and cloaked in mystery, laying claim to their
strangeness and unfamiliarity that nevertheless strike
a deeply resonant chord within us.

In the building on the quai Branly, designed by the architect Jean Nouvel, the museum is an invitation for us to embrace the full complexity of the art works and the cultures they come from. Its diagonal approach encourages us to deepen our understanding, challenges us to raise our levels of expectation, and makes us look from different angles to see in the unfolding sequence of exhibits a testimony to the constantly evolving artistic genius of non-European civilisations. A melting-pot of diversity, the Musée du quai Branly sets itself the moral standard of looking at other civilisations with greater insight, more respect and last but not least, a more open mind.

The museum sees itself at the heart of a dialogue between cultures and civilisations. This dialogue is made possible by the universal element common to us all, enriched by the individual singularity each one has to offer. This dialogue between cultures and civilisations is essential at a time when humanity is finally becoming aware of what unites it, but where cultural identities are under threat from encroaching standardization that can sometimes create divisions and conflict.

Throughout its history, France has always seen itself as a harbinger of universal values, but it has also advocated the value of otherness. Bringing together different cultures and civilisations is therefore a natural progression for a country that is fully aware of its responsibilities on global and historical levels to promote communication between peoples and cultures in order to counteract the unacceptable face of contempt, hostility and hatred that exists in the world. The Musée du quai Branly also sees its role, perhaps above all else, as championing this cause.

Jacques CHIRAC
President of the French republic

Now that the Musée du quai Branly has opened its doors to the public, this guide will serve to accompany visitors in their discovery of the new institution. Designed by Jean Nouvel, the museum has been built around the collections entrusted to it – a remarkable piece of architecture that perfectly achieves our ambition to celebrate, here in Paris, the arts of Africa, Asia, Oceania and the Americas.

A walkway encased in wood and suspended in the midst of tall trees, the main museum building is made up of a single space. Protected by a high glass wall, it is hidden from sight by a garden that visitors have to cross to get to the museum entrance hall. Greeted by a great Wet'suwet'en pole, visitors then follow a gently sloping ramp that leads them into the heart of the collections. The main gallery is a vast unpartitioned area, its northern part enriched by a series of scenographies mounted in coloured "boxes" projecting out over the garden. It is complemented by two suspended galleries accommodating anthropological presentations and special theme exhibitions drawing upon the museum collections.

Out of the 300,000 works that make up the collections, some 3,500 are on permanent exhibition, shaping the museum's identity in visitors' eyes. Their journey of discovery is organised into four geographical regions, Africa, Asia, Oceania and the Americas, connected by "contact zones" such as the Caribbean and Insulindia, and also takes in major themes common to all. Each continent is introduced by a "take-off area" in which a number of particularly emblematic and spectacular works are grouped together. There is, then, a definite logic to exploring this vast area, although visitors have total freedom of choice as to how they approach it.

The great masterpieces on permanent exhibition were selected for their beauty, rarity and power of expression, for their ethnological interest and technique of composition, or for what they tell us of the minds and genius of the peoples that created them. Thanks to the various types of commentary available – stencilled texts, notices, and multimedia programmes – the visitor can situate the items before him both historically and geographically, and acquaint themselves with their context and use in the societies that produced them.

Additional works are presented to the public through temporary exhibitions, enabling systematic exploration of the collections brought together in the museum. These events bring fresh perspectives to their beauty and their meaning, bearing witness to the diversity of their origins and forms, and of the customs they express.

The Musée du quai Branly is therefore an institution devoted to the enhancement and preservation of the collections entrusted to it. It is also a centre of research and learning, of cooperation and creation. With its theatre, mediatheque, reading room and classrooms, it is an interdisciplinary meeting place for academics, curators, students and visitors. Programming a wide variety of presentations, it accords major importance to music, dance, theatre and cinema, and its cafés, restaurants and walkways also provide opportunities for encounters and enjoyment of leisure time.

This guide has been designed with the museum's many areas of activity in mind. An invitation to discovery or to further exploration, passport or souvenir, foretasting or reliving the pleasure, it is a reference work to be used in countless ways. Before a visit, it familiarises readers with the museum, and helps them to understand its aims and get a feeling for what it wishes to achieve. During the visit, it offers directions and advice, accompanying visitors throughout their journey. And when the visit is over, it spurs them to deepen their knowledge and, I hope, to return.

Stéphane MARTIN
President of the Musée du quai Branly

Summary

THIRTY BOXES OF VARIOUS SIZES EMERGE ALL ALONG THE BUILDING FAÇADE, OVERLOOKING THE GARDEN ON THE NORTH SIDE. INSIDE THE MUSEUM, THEY HOUSE OBJECTS FROM THE ASIAN AND AFRICAN COLLECTIONS, WITH THE AIM OF CREATING MORE INTIMATE SPACES WITHIN THE PERMANENT COLLECTIONS AREA. UNDER THE FOOTBRIDGE OF THE PERMANENT COLLECTIONS AREA SITS THE GARDEN GALLERY, CONSTRUCTED TO HOLD TEMPORARY EXHIBITIONS. THE VERTICAL GARDEN, DESIGNED BY PATRICK BLANC, COVERS THE QUAI BRANLY BUILDING.

TO THE SOUTH, THE BUILDING ON THE RUE DE L'UNIVERSITÉ DISPLAYS AN ARCHITECTURE OF GLASS AND STONE. EIGHT AUSTRALIAN ABORIGINE ARTISTS HAVE WORKED ON THE FAÇADE AND CEILINGS TO CREATE ORIGINAL WORKS OF ART IN HARMONY WITH THE ARCHITECTURE.

THE MUSEUM LOOKS AS IF IT HAS BEEN PLACED ON THE GARDEN DESIGNED BY GILLES CLÉMENT. ITS GLASS FAÇADE IMPRINTED WITH PLANT MOTIFS **FILTERS IN THE NATURAL LIGHT, MAKING THE GALLERY SEEM LIKE THE INSIDE OF A GROTTO.**

THE TERRACE HAS A SPECTACULAR VIEW OVER THE SEINE, THE EIFFEL TOWER, **THE PALAIS DE CHAILLOT HILL, THE GRAND PALAIS, THE INVALIDES AND THE ENTIRE PARISIAN LANDSCAPE.**

FROM THE RECEPTION HALL, VISITORS
TAKE THE WINDING RAMP UP TO THE PERMANENT
COLLECTIONS AREA. AT EACH CURVE THEY'LL
DISCOVER NEW SPACES: **THE GARDEN GALLERY
AND THE GLASS TOWER, WHICH HOUSES
THE MUSICAL INSTRUMENTS RESERVE
AND CROSSES THE WHOLE OF THE MUSEUM.**

A VAST AREA WITHOUT PARTITIONS, THE PERMANENT COLLECTIONS AREA EXHIBITS OVER 3,500 WORKS OF ART FROM FOUR CONTINENTS: AFRICA, ASIA, OCEANIA AND THE AMERICAS, LINKED BY THE TRANSVERSALS CREATING PLACES OF EXCHANGE BETWEEN THE CIVILISATIONS. **LIGHTING SHOWS THE OBJECTS IN THEIR FORMAL PURITY. NEARBY, A VARIETY OF INFORMATION DEVICES – TEXTS, CARTELS AND MULTIMEDIA SCREENS – ENABLE VISITORS TO SITUATE EACH WORK OF ART IN ITS CONTEXT.**

The collections and the museographic itinerary

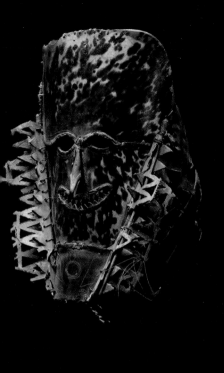

THE COLLECTIONS AREA

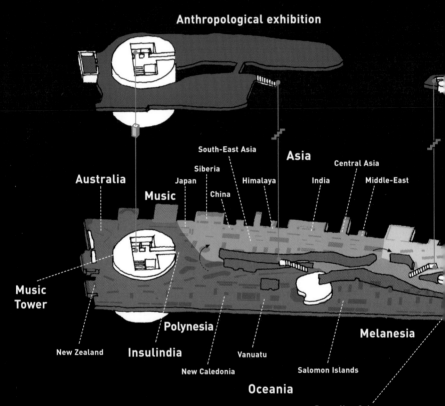

Anthropological exhibition

Asia

Australia

Music

South-East Asia

Siberia

Japan

China

Himalaya

India

Central Asia

Middle-East

Music
Tower

New Zealand

Insulindia

Polynesia

Vanuatu

New Caledonia

Salomon Islands

Melanesia

Oceania

Papua New Guinea
and West Papua

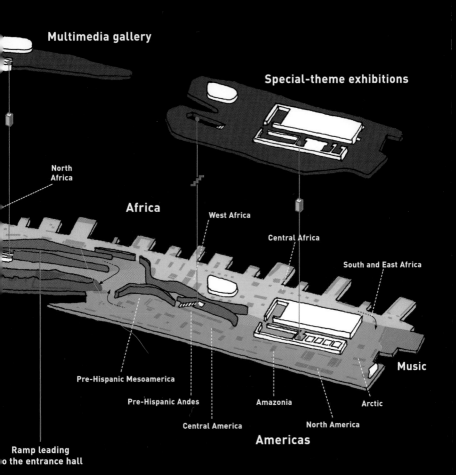

Multimedia gallery

Special-theme exhibitions

North
Africa

Africa

West Africa

Central Africa

South and East Africa

Music

Pre-Hispanic Mesoamerica

Pre-Hispanic Andes

Amazonia

Arctic

Central America

North America

Americas

Ramp leading
to the entrance hall

ONE OF THE FUNDAMENTAL AIMS OF THE MUSÉE DU QUAI BRANLY IS TO EXHIBIT A WIDE SELECTION OF REMARKABLE WORKS OF ART IN ITS PERMANENT COLLECTION. AFTER DECADES OF DISPERSION, DIFFICULTIES, AND OCCASIONAL PROBLEMS OF ESCHEAT, THE TIME HAD COME TO UNVEIL THE PRICELESS COLLECTIONS ACCUMULATED BY FRANCE OVER THE PAST FIVE CENTURIES, FOR WHICH THE MUSEUM NOW BEARS THE RESPONSIBILITY VIS-À-VIS ITS NATIONAL AND INTERNATIONAL VISITORS, AS WELL AS THE PEOPLES OF THEIR COUNTRIES OF ORIGIN.

Even before the architect of the new museum had been selected, a considerable amount of work was done on tracing origins, as well as on the digitisation and computerisation of the 300,000 items from the Musée de l'Homme and the Musée national des Arts d'Afrique et d'Océanie that had finally been brought together – a job undertaken by working groups made up of the curators of these collections and experts from the wider scientific community.

This collaborative work led to the uncovering of major long-existing resources that had hitherto remained unexplored, and identified gaps in the collection that can be traced to France's colonial history and areas of influence. In an attempt to fill these gaps, an ambitious acquisitions policy was therefore implemented from 1997 onwards, first for the Pavillon des Sessions galleries in the Louvre, and then for collections of the new museum.

The presentation of the collection had to match the spirit of Jean Nouvel's architectural design, an impressive interior landscape full of mystery and surprises, in which the finest of the many treasures were to be displayed. The preferred approach was a journey through the regions covered by the museum – Oceania, Asia, Africa and the Americas. This placed the art works in the context of their history and the customs they express, using cross-cutting sequences or themes to group together objects in ways that highlight the extraordinary range of forms and skills.

The objects are presented without artifice, on stands or supports that do not detract from the exhibit, in large glass display cases with hidden structures, or in spaces that are intentionally eye-catching – some specifically designed for items that merit the greatest respect because they contain human remains, and others in the thirty "boxes" on the facade, showing scenographies of particular cultures. In addition to the many splendid sculptures whose mysterious presence reigns throughout the museum, three domains demonstrate the extent to which art played a part in the everyday life of these societies: music, textiles, and precious metalwork.

Detailed information is provided for each item, in a carefully designed sequence: first, captions and descriptions beside each object, then maps, texts and still or moving pictures on the side of the display case, and finally interactive multimedia stations situated nearby. On the central mezzanine visitors can access more general data on the museum collections, as well as on anthropology, languages and music.

8,000 musical instruments are displayed in a glass tower that soars to the very top of the building. Standing at the very heart of the museum, it is a visual symbol of the artistic links between past and present. Multimedia stations provide audio and visual back-up. Two "music boxes" on the facade show audiovisual productions that place different types of music in their cultural contexts and original settings. Photography and visuals in general are used to place cultures in a historical or contemporary perspective, and also to show the museum's exceptionally rich collection of illustrations.

Two galleries are suspended on either side to house temporary exhibitions – either short-term or longer-term thematic exhibitions – providing the opportunity to systematically explore the collections using a variety of approaches that alternate angles of study. Held back-to-back, they provide a widely varied contemporary vision of research and art to experts from many different backgrounds, and are part of the museum's cultural action policy.

Germain VIATTE

Mask
Australia,
Queensland,
Torres Strait
19th century
Tortoiseshell,
vegetable fibres,
cassowary
feathers,
pigments
57 x 32 cm
Donation
Former
collections of
J. Hooper and
A. Fourquet
Inv. 70.2004.1.3

Oceania /

The route through the arts of Oceania and Insulindia takes visitors on a journey across the geographical and cultural regions of Melanesia, Polynesia, Australia and Insular South East Asia. The works exhibited here reflect the trading relationships between the various peoples of the Pacific and the strong connections of these peoples with their ancestors. They show an extraordinary diversity of artistic expression, ranging from the spectacular to the intimate.

The Oceanian collections presented at the Musée du quai Branly record the major stages in the history of French collections in the Pacific region since the early 19th century. Polynesian arts are represented by a rare group of artefacts brought back by French expeditions led by Jules Dumont d'Urville, Louis de Freycinet and Louis Duperrey. They also show the attraction that Oceanian art had for early French collectors such as Dominique-Vivant Denon, founder of the Musée Napoléon – the present-day Louvre. The Melanesian collections evidence the scientific missions undertaken by museums throughout the 20th century, from those of the Musée d'Ethnographie du Trocadéro to those conducted by the Musée national des Arts d'Afrique et d'Océanie. Finally, a series of contemporary paintings by Australian Aboriginal artists attests to the energy and creativity of societies in Oceania today.

50,000 BC
Earliest population of Australia and New Guinea by migration from Southeast Asia

3500 BC
Austronesians from South China settle throughout Melanesia

Circa 2000 BC-circa 1000 AD
Spread of Lapita culture from the Bismarck Archipelago to the Fiji Islands: production of decorated pottery

5th century BC-3rd century AD
Spread of the Dong Son civilisation from North Vietnam: the oldest decorated metal objectsartefacts found in the Indonesian Archipelago are Dongsonian in style

200 BC
Peoples from Fiji, Samoa and Tonga settle in the Marquesasise Islands: emergence of Polynesian culture

300-500
Polynesian settlement of the Hawaiian Islands and Easter Island

600-1000
Polynesian expansion in the Society Islands and the Cook Islands

Circa 1000
Population of New Zealand by migration from the Society Islands

1511
The Portuguese take Malacca

1519-1522
Ferdinand de Magellan crosses the Pacific Ocean in the name of Spain and discovers the Philippines

1546
The island of New Guinea is claimed by the Spanish

1602
The Dutch found the East India Company (VOC)

1768
The explorer-navigatorsailor Louis-Antoine de Bougainville takes possession of Tahiti in the name of the King of France, naming it "Nouvelle-Cythère"

1769-1771
The English navigatorsailor James Cook's first Pacific voyage: New Zealand, the Society Islands, the coast of New Guinea and the east coast of Australia

1772-1775
Captain Cook's second voyage: New Zealand, the Society Islands, Easter Island, the Marquesasise Islands, New Caledonia and Vanuatu

1776-1780
Captain Cook's third voyage: New Zealand, Tonga, the Society Islands, and Hawaii (Cook murdered by the Hawaiians)

27 April 1778
Creation of the Batavian Society of Arts and Sciences, dedicated to promoting medical, literary, historical, ethnographic and scientific research. After independence, the society became the National Museum of Indonesia

1785-1788
The Jean-Francois de Galaup, comte de La Pérouse's expedition. He disappeared in Vanikoro (Santa Cruz Islands)

1788
Australia is declared Terra Nullius (uninhabited land) by the British. Almost a million Aborigines lived on the continent at the time

1797
The London Missionary Society establishes itself on the Society Islands and on the Marquesaes. The Pomare, the Tahitian royal family, are converted

1811-1815
Java is governed
by Sir Thomas
Stamford
Raffles,
who rediscovers
and restores
Borobudur

1819
Raffles
establishes a free
port in the south
of the Malaysian
Peninsula,
so founding
Singapore

1828-1829
First voyage of
the Frenchman
Jules Dumont
d'Urville:
Australian
coastline,
New Zealand,
New Britain,
New Ireland,
Vanuatu,
New Caledonia,
Tonga, and Fiji

1828
The Dutch East
India Company
takes possession
of western
New Guinea

1840
Treaty of
Waitangi
between the

British and New
Zealand's Maori
chiefs: the Maori
recognise British
sovereignty but
remain masters
of their ancestral
lands

1842
The French
admiral Abel
Dupetit-Thouars
signs a
protectorate
treaty covering
Tahiti and
Moorea

1853
Annexation of
New Caledonia
by France

1855
Presentation
of Aborigine bark
paintings at
the Universal
Exhibition
in Paris

1884
England declares
a protectorate
in Papua
(southern part
of the island),
and Germany
declares a
protectorate in
New Guinea
(northern part
of the island)

1888
Chile takes
possession of
Easter Island

1891
The painter
Paul Gauguin
leaves for Tahiti.
He dies in the
Marquesasise
Islands in 1903

1898
Treaty of Paris:
end of the
Spanish
American War.
Spain withdraws
from its last
remaining
colonies,
including the
Philippines,
Porto Rico and
Guam, iln return
for 20 million
dollars

1906
British New
Guinea is put
under Australian
administrative
control. Franco-
British
condominium
in Vanuatu

1911
Indonesia –
apart from
northern Borneo
(British)
and Timor
(Portuguese) – is
in Dutch hands

1921
Australia takes
German New
Guinea under its
administrative
wing

1942-1945
Japanese
military forces
occupy
Indonesia, the
Philippines and
New Guinea

1945
Indonesian
independence
declared by
Ahmed Sukarno

1946
The Philippines
declare
independence

1959
Polynesia
becomes a
French Overseas
Territory (TOM);
Hawaii becomes
a territory of
theone of the
Uniteds States
of America

1962
Dutch New
Guinea becomes
an Indonesian
province

1967
The Australian
government
grants Australian
citizenship
to Aborigine
peoples

1969
West Papua
(Irian Jaya)
becomes the 26th
province
of the Republic
of Indonesia

1971
Birth of the
Papunya Tula
Aborigine
artistic
movement

1975
Independence
of Papua
New Guinea,
which becomes a
Commonwealth
member. East
Timor becomes
an Indonesian
province

1980
Vanuatu obtains
its independence
from France and
Great Britain

1989
Assassination
of the Kanak
independencetist
leader Jean-
Marie Tjibaou

1992
End of the "Terra
Nullius" concept
in Australia

1995
Inauguration
of the Vanuatu
Cultural Centre
in Port Vila

1997
Opening of the
new Museum
of Asiatic
Civilisations
in Singapore

1998
Inauguration
of the Jean-Marie
Tjibaou Cultural
Centre in
Noumea

2002
Declaration of
independence by
East Timor, after
adoption of a
constitution

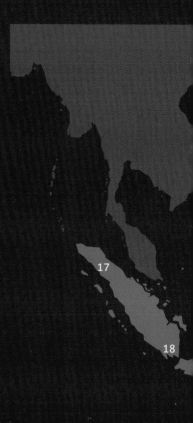

INDIAN

OCEAN

Map

Insular South-
East Asia, New
Guinea, North
Australia

1. Iatmul/Sawos
2. Abelam/Wasera
3. Asmat
4. Chambri
5. Kapriman

6. Kambot/
Tin Dama
7. Mundugumor/
Biwat
8. Tolai
9. Baining
10. Yolngu
11. Kuninjku
12. Bamu
13. Elema

14. Mimika
15. Mendi-Kewa
16. Sulka
17. Batak
18. Paminggir
19. Iban
20. Ngaju
21. Kenyah Kayan
22. Toraja
23. Manggarai

24. Nage
25. Atoni
26. Tetum
27. Ifugao
28. Kalinga
29. Isneg
30. Kankanay
31. Babogo
32. T'boli

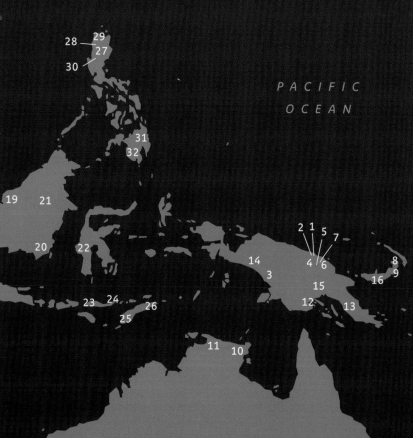

Ancestral beings in Melanesia

Melanesian ancestors, mythological heroes or real human beings from the distant past, gave men the order of the world. They continue to exist side-by-side with the living who, through art and ritual, demonstrate the eternal nature of these ties.

Magical hook for warfare
Iatmul
Papua New Guinea,
Middle Sepik,
Lake Chambri
Mid 20th century
Wood, pigments
66 x 32.5 cm
F. Girard mission, 1955
Inv. 71.1955.76.197

Roof sculpture
Iatmul/Sawos
Papua New Guinea,
Middle Sepik
Mid 20th century
Wood
193 x 26 cm
J. Guiart mission, 1965
Inv. 72.1965.14.45

_The ancestor house in New Guinea

The ancestor house is the symbolic meeting point between the living and their ancestors, and is represented by the primordial female entity so often perceived as the creator of the first living beings. The facade of the house symbolises her face and the house itself, her body. As a symbol of the world and a repository for sacred objects, the house holds together the unity of the group and ensures the continuation of life.

/ YUAT PAINTING

In the Sepik region, along the banks of the Yuat River, the Mundugumor people created large ceremonial paintings. This painting, over 8 metres high, was done on sago palm leafstalks stitched together with rattan. It stood inside the village between two supporting coconut palms during the ceremonial exchanges of yams (a tuber widely consumed throughout Melanesia). In 1932, it came into the possession of the anthropologists Margaret Mead and Reo Fortune, and was bought in 1935 by members of the French *La Korrigane* expedition. The central motif represents a very powerful spirit, a crocodile with the head of a sawfish in whose belly lies a red disc. The multiple interlacing and circles surrounding this motif evoke thorny leaves and seeds floating upon water. The superimposed human figures at the top of the painting refer to two mythical heroes. The interweaving and constantly changing motifs across the entire work are a common feature of Sepik art. It allows the painting to be interpreted on several levels, depending on the sex, age and stage of initiation of the viewer. M.M.

Ceremonial house post
Iatmul
Papua New Guinea,
Middle Sepik
Early 20th century
Kwarap wood
(*Intsia bijuga*)
417 x 44 cm
Donated by M. and E. de Ganay, R. and C. van den Broek, *La Korrigane* expedition, 1934-1936
Inv. 71.1961.103.317

Depending on the region, the terms "spirit house", "men's house" and "ancestor house" are all used to define this meeting house exclusively reserved for initiated members of a clan.

Organisation of the house

A village contains as many men's houses as it does clans. They are always set apart from family dwellings, in open clearings, and are of varied architecture. In the Sepik River region, they can measure up to 18 metres in height and 40 metres in length. Built on piles to keep them safe from flooding, they include two levels. The men from the clan meet daily on the lower floor, with each member's place fixed according to the clan's internal organisation. Some take their meals there and make preparations for hunting or fishing expeditions. It is also here that major public issues regarding the community are debated, rituals planned, and the horizontal slit drums decorated with the clan's mythical figures, are located. Sacred objects, such as flutes, masks, skulls and ancestor stones, are kept on the upper floor.

Malu board
Iatmul/Sawos
Papua New
Guinea,
Middle Sepik
Mid 20th century
Wood, pigments
165.5 x 38.5 cm
Inv. 72.1980.1.1

Mowok
***Lebolabon* slit**
drum
Kapriman
Papua New
Guinea,
Middle Sepik
Early 20th century
Numbus wood
(*Vitex cofassus*)

255 x 48 cm
Donated by M.
and E. de Ganay,
R. and C. van
den Broek,
La Korrigane
expedition,
1934-1936
Inv. 71.1961.103.328

<u>Omnipresence of ancestral beings</u>

Both inside and out, these houses contain a
wealth of imposing images representing mythical
or real ancestors. In the middle Sepik region, large
masks of painted carved wood or wickerwork are
attached to the outer walls, beneath the shade of
thatched awnings. They represent an ancestor
from the clan to which the house belongs and
provide a protective mantle. The clan's founding
myths are illustrated by the exterior sculptures
overlooking the house's raised rooftop. These
make visual associations between a human hero
and a totemic animal, images, which can also be
found on the wooden pillars of the structure.
Birds, snakes and crocodiles are among the
fundamental totemic animals of the Sepik region.
Scrolled and spiral motifs also adorn these
artefacts, evoking an aquatic world whose
shimmering twists and turns are associated with
the habitats of ancestral beings such as
the crocodile. Fibre bags hanging from hooks
contain food or clan artefacts. On the upper floor,
hooks are decorated with figures whose forms
and functions are symbolic: spirits linked to
magic practised in times of war or to promote
fertility, for example. These may be represented
in pairs of opposites (often a man and a woman)
mirroring the concept of complementarity
evident in the house itself: a symbolically female
place inhabited by men.

Hook
Papua New
Guinea, Middle
Sepik
Early 20th century
Wood, pigments,
vegetable fibres
118 x 64.5 cm
Donated by
R. Chauvelot
Inv. 71.1914.1.7

Facade mask
Chambri
Papua
New Guinea,
Middle Sepik
Mid 20th century
Wood, pigments
120.5 x 57 cm
Donated by M.
and E. de Ganay,
R. and C. van
den Broek,
La Korrigane
expedition,
1934-1936
Inv. 71.1961.103.316

Headrest
Kapriman
Papua New
Guinea,
Middle Sepik
Late 19th century
Wood, pigments
42 x 15.5 cm
Donated by M.
and E. de Ganay,
R. and C. van den
Broek,
La Korrigane
expedition,
1934-1936
Inv. 71.1961.103.301

Statuette
Biwat (?)
Papua New
Guinea, Lower
Sepik, Yuat River
Early 20th century
Wood
80 x 17 cm
Donated by M.
and E. de Ganay,
R. and C. van
den Broek,
La Korrigane
expedition,
1934-1936
Inv. 71.1969.51.41

_Relations with ancestral beings

Ancestral beings figure prominently in Papua
New Guinea statuary. The painted or sculpted
image is not intended as a portrait but as a
symbolic evocation. The head is accorded great
stylistic importance, while the body provides
the artist with a springboard for daring
innovations. Many figures are hybrid, half man
and half animal, as the idea of metamorphosis is
at the core of mythical beliefs and their artistic
expression. A man with a bird's beak or head plays
a major role in initiation rites, for example.
In the Sepik River region, a disproportionately
long beak indicates virility. Figures are often
depicted in a squatting position, elbows resting on
knees, evoking everyday attitudes, burial
practices or someone simply observing insects.
Images of ancestral beings are carved on the clan's
important objects, such as the carved posts,
walls and rooftops of the men's houses. Inside,
sculptures of ancestral beings may be placed
beside the skulls of the group's more illustrious
members. Other effigies are attached to the tops
of poles used in ceremonial dances, during
initiation rites for example.
Headrests establish a more personal link with
ancestors. They enable the user to make contact

Dance stick (?)
Papua New
Guinea,
Lower Sepik
Early 20ᵗʰ century
Wood, pigments,
vegetable fibres,
feathers, hair,
pig's teeth
90 x 10 cm
Collected by
La Korrigane
expedition,
1934-1936
Inv. 71.1962.1.20

Headrest
Papua New
Guinea,
Middle Sepik
Early 20ᵗʰ century
Wood, vegetable
fibres, cord
59.5 x 10 cm
Inv. 72.1969.3.2

with them while asleep and to benefit from
their power and other virtues, especially on the
eve of war or hunting expeditions. In earlier
times, these objects were carved with stone
blades and the designs engraved with a pig's
tooth. Every man owned his own headrest
adorned with a crocodile, bird, dog or cockerel,
each linked to a specific clan ancestor.

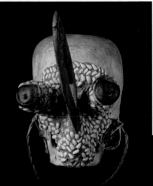

Trophy skull
Bamu
Papua New
Guinea,
Gulf of Papua,
Bamu River
Mid or late 19th
century
Bone, resin,
vegetable fibres,
seeds, wood,
mastic
37 x 17.5 cm
Former Webster
and Pitt Rivers
collections
Inv. 72.1967.2.2

Ancestor's skull
Asmat
Indonesia,
West Papua
20th century
Bone, seeds,
fibres, feathers,
wax
22 x 15 cm
Inv. 71.1966.60.2

/ FUNERAL PRACTICES

In Melanesia, the preservation of human skulls is a common practice, usually the skulls of ancestors whose memories must be kept alive, or those of enemies, to be displayed as trophies. The skull is transformed by modelling its owner's features with a vegetable, clay or resin paste. Symbolic ornaments such as seeds, shells, feathers and assorted designs were sometimes added. These relics are kept in private dwellings, perpetuating the ties between ancestors and descendants, or in the men's house, arranged in groups of specially designated structures, or sometimes displayed on the front of the building. The Asmat wore the skulls around their necks or used it as a headrest: The descendant could then draw upon the powers of the ancestor while asleep. As a result of Western influences (missionaries and government administrators), the use of skulls was gradually replaced by that of wooden masks.
M.M.

_Secrets of initiates

In Melanesia, initiation rites group together boys in the same age range. Youths are isolated in a house for several weeks, or even months. Initiation consists of "killing" them symbolically as children so that they may be reborn as adults. Their behaviour and diet are governed by strict rules. During their reclusion, the relatives in charge of their initiation teach them the correct techniques for making objects such as musical instruments. In the Sepik, bamboo flutes are among the most secret of musical instruments. Their unceasing song, echoing from the depths of the men's house, is the voice of ancestral beings reciting the heroic deeds of their warrior days. The instruments are decorated with feathers and effigies of ancestral beings, and remarkable

Flute mask
Tin Dama
Papua New
Guinea,
Keram Valley
19th century
Bone, shells,
cassowary
feathers, hair,
pig's teeth
47.5 x 12.7 cm
Former
collections of
W. Bondy,
F. Fénéon, and
Dr Girardin
Inv. 72.1983.1.1

Flute ornament
Biwat
Papua New
Guinea,
Yuat River

19th century
Wood, seeds, hair,
mother of pearl
45 x 11 cm
Former
A. Flechtheim
collection,
C. Côte bequest
Inv. 71.1960.112.6.1

Crocodile
Papua New
Guinea,
Porapora region
20th century
Basketwork,
shells
114 x 64 cm
Former collection
of the Society of
the Divine Word,
Marienberg
Inv. 72.1966.12.14

for the extraordinary variety of materials from
which they are made.
Novices also acquire knowledge of their genealogy
and of the meaning of the great mythical cycles.
In the Sepik, the existence of their clan's founding
artefacts is also revealed to them in the form
of engraved stones, supposedly pieces of the bark
of a tree from which the first members of the
clan sprang. These may be placed in wickerwork
and shell-money "reliquaries" in the shape
of a crocodile for example, and represent the
original clan ancestor. The backbone encloses
the fighting club of a chief or "Big Man" while
the multi-material pendants that hang from
its sides serve as a reminder of ceremonial events.
M.M.

MASKS

Melanesia has produced a vast number of masks, remarkable for the variety of their shape and for the range of materials in which they are made. Each one has a specific purpose and, in rituals, may incarnate a mythological being, a mediator between the living and the dead, a children's teacher, or serve as the symbol of a group or given social status.
In New Guinea, masks are not always designed to be worn. The Abelam attach small wickerwork masks to large ceremonial yams, so making a symbolic association between tuber and ancestral being.
The wooden or bark face of the mask is often only one element in a costume, along with a robe composed of fibres, leaves, feathers and shells, as is the case for the *mwai* masks of the Iatmul people, worn by young initiates.

1/ Yam mask
Abelam
Papua New Guinea,
Maprik region
Mid 20th century
Basketwork, pigments
56 x 39.4 cm
Inv. 71.1962.47.3

2/ Mask
Papua New Guinea,
Kairiru Island
Late 19th century
Wood, lime
29 x 13 cm
Donated by Prince R. Bonaparte
Inv. 71.1887.67.12

3/ *Tago* mask
Papua New Guinea,
Gulf of Huon,
Tami Island
Early 20th century
Beaten bark, wood, pigments, moss, cassowary feathers
68 x 42 cm
Inv. 72.1982.2.1

4/ *Mwai* mask
Iatmul
Papua New Guinea,
Middle Sepik
Early 20th century
Wood, shells, pigments
64 x 12 cm
Donated by M. and E. de Ganay, R. and C. van den Broek,
La Korrigane expedition, 1934-1936
Inv. 71.1961.103.307

5/ *Tomban* helmet-mask
Kapriman
Papua New Guinea,
Middle Sepik
Early 20th century
Basketwork,

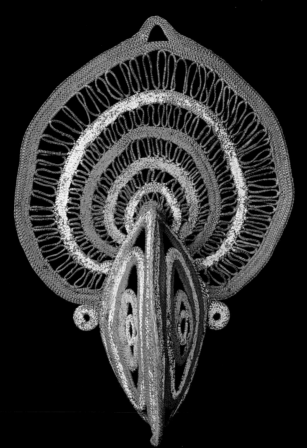

1

2

3

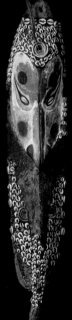

5

4

6

bamboo,
pigments
57.5 x 33.5 cm
Inv. 71.1961.103.306

6/Mask
Biwat

Papua New
Guinea,
Yuat River
20th century
Wood, pigments
34 x 21 cm
Inv. 70.2002.3.1

1

In earlier times, various forms of masks circulated
from one region or island to another, evidence of a wide-
ranging trade network. The structure, a bamboo frame
covered by a bark-cloth face with stitched-on "ears",
is similar in style to those of the masks of New Ireland,
just north of the Solomon Islands (Nissan and Bougainville).
The ceremonial but ephemeral aspect of some Melanesian
masks is particularly evident in New Britain. The beautiful
designs of Sulka people's large *hemlout* masks, made secretly
over periods lasting up to a year, are revealed to the public
only for a short time, as the masks are burned at the end
of the ceremony. *Vungvung*, the trumpet masks of the
Baining people, are used in nocturnal dances. Wearers'
voices reverberate through the long bamboo "trumpets"
to announce their arrival.
In northern Vanuatu, masks are linked with political power,
those fashioned from tree ferns being reserved for the
highest ranks. In New Caledonia, the mourners at funeral
rites for a dead chief wear masks of blackened wood topped
with a headdress made from their own shorn hair or from
bark cloth. M.M.

1 / *Vungvung*
mask
Baining Kairak
Papua New
Guinea,
New Britain,
Gazelle Peninsula
Late 19th-early
20th century
Beaten bark,
bamboo,
pigments
290 x 92 cm
Former
collections of the
Museum für
Völkerkunde,
Leipzig,
and the Musée
Barbier-Mueller,
Geneva
Inv. 70.2001.9.2

2 / Mask
Papua New
Guinea,
Solomon Islands,
Nissan Island
Early 20th century
Wood, rattan,
beaten bark, palm
leafstalks, resin,
pigments
55.5 x 40.2 cm
Former collection
of the Museum
für Völkerkunde,
Leipzig
Inv. 72.1995.2.1

3 / Mask
Papua New
Guinea,
New Ireland
20th century (?)
Vegetable fibres,
beaten bark,
feathers
66 x 73 cm
Inv. 72.1972.2.3

4 / *Nich-maget*
mask with
mouth ornament
Papua New
Guinea,
New Ireland
Late 19th century
Wood, beaten
bark, rattan,
turbo opercula,
vegetable pith,

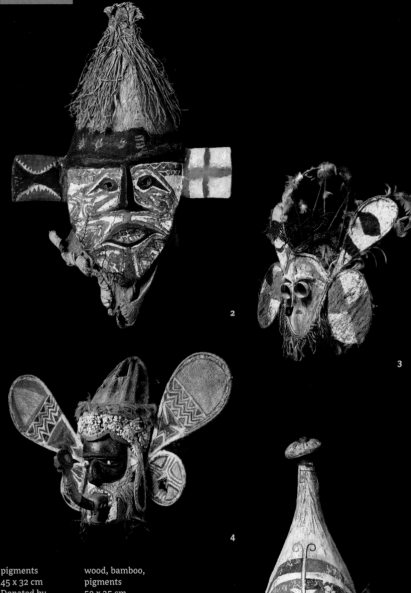

2

3

4

pigments
45 x 32 cm
Donated by
R. Chauvelot
Inv. 71.1914.1.2 Oc

5 / Mask
Papua New
Guinea,
Solomon Islands,
Bougainville
Island
Early 20ᵗʰ century
Beaten bark,

wood, bamboo,
pigments
50 x 35 cm
Inv. 70.2003.6.1

5

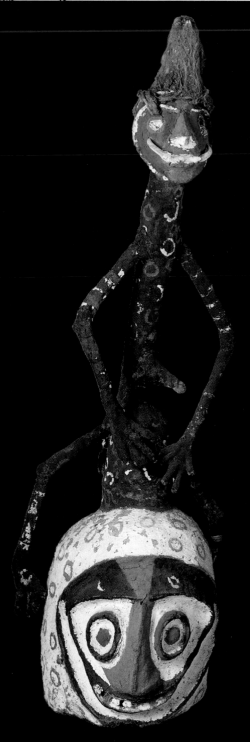

1 / Helmet mask
Small Nambas
Vanuatu,
southwestern
Malekula Island
20th century
Tree fern, spider's
web, vegetable
paste, pigments
118 x 37 cm
Donated by
M. and E. de
Ganay,
R. and C. van
den Broek,
La Korrigane
expedition,
1934-1936
Inv. 71.1961.103.17

2 / Mask
Vanuatu,
Ambae Island
Mid 19th century
Bark, wood,
vegetable fibres,
pigments
88 x 22 cm
Donated by
Dr Jollet
Inv. 71.1894.9.6

**3 / *Chubwan*
mask**
Vanuatu,
southern
Pentecost Island
or northern
Ambrym Island
19th century
Wood, coating
36.5 x 12.3 cm
Collected in 1891
by Lieutenant
P. Pénot,
Saône expedition
Inv. 72.1999.7.3

1

4 / Temes napal helmet mask (bald-headed spirit)
Small Nambas
Vanuatu, southern Malekula Island
Early 20th century
Tree fern, vegetable paste, pigments
41 x 31 cm
Former Austin collection, donated by the Commissariat of New Caledonia and Dependences
Inv. 72.1931.1.29

5 / Wimawi mourner's mask
Hwaap
New Caledonia, Koumac village
Late 19th century
Wood, liana bark, coconut palm fibres, pigments
95 x 45 cm
Inv. 72.1962.2.1

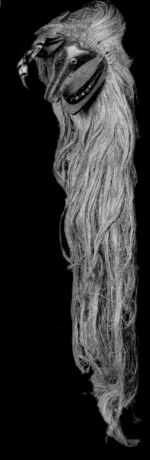

2

3

5

4

Headhunter's trumpet
Asmat
Indonesia,
West Papua
20th century
Engraved bamboo
76 x 7 cm
Inv. 71.1970.21.1

***Baba* helmet-mask**
Wosera
Papua New
Guinea,
Wosera district
Mid 20th century
Basketwork,
pigments, down
56 x 43 cm
Collected by
A. Forge
Inv. 72.1965.12.2

Ritual murder

Warlike confrontations are frequent in Melanesia and often involve the entire community, whereas other forms of violence are rare. At the same time, death, which is thought of as an unnatural event, results in major social unbalance that must be counteracted through rituals and acts of compensation.

_Ritual murder in New Guinea

Up until the mid 20th century, ritual murder was committed to compensate for the death of a group member and to appease the spirits of the dead. The death of a chief, or the inauguration of a house or dugout canoe, might require a human head. Some initiation rites for young boys include a murder phase, through which the novice shows proof of his courage. Among the Abelam peoples, the painted wickerwork *baba* mask serves to open this stage of the initiation ceremony as the boys, following their first assassination, take on their future role as warriors. This pig's head mask recalls the role of the ancestor in leading the spirit of the deceased into the world of the dead.

/ *BISJ* POLES

Among the Asmat people, death is often seen as resulting from the transgression of ancestral rules, and a murder must be carried out by close relatives of the deceased in order to set matters right. In such a case, *Bisj* poles are erected in a ceremony in which the living promise to avenge the dead and to set their spirits to rest.

Sheathed in bark and oozing sap, a tree is dragged to the village where it is greeted by cries from the women. Near the *jeuw*, the ceremonial house, the sculptor begins his openwork carving of the post.

The trees roots become the top of the *bisj*, the penis, or *tsjemen*, while the trunk is etched with the profiles of deceased dignitaries. Raised up side by side for the ceremony, in the past the *bisj* were kept until the next head-hunting, and were then deposited in sago palm marshes, where they rotted, transmitting their life force to the palm trees from which the living gained sustenance. (see p. 23) C.M.

Certain objects, such as delicately engraved cassowary bone daggers, sometimes adorned with seeds or feathers, show the prestige gained by warlike deeds.

The cassowary is a large black bird the size of an ostrich, feared in New Guinea for its aggressiveness, and often considered as an original ancestral being. In the Sepik region, lime containers and spatulas for betel chewing are also decorated with feather pompoms indicating the number of killings attributed to their owners. M.M.

Lime container and spatula
Papua New Guinea, Sepik
Mid 20th century
Engraved bamboo, wood, feathers, shells, bone, pigments
22.5 x 6.5 and 31 x 4 cm
J. Guiart mission, 1965
Inv. 72.1965.14.74 and 72.1965.14.179

Dagger
Chambri
Papua New Guinea, Middle Sepik
Mid 20th century
Engraved cassowary bone
32.5 x 3.7 cm
F. Girard mission, 1955
Inv. 71.1955.76.260

Daggers
Iatmul
Papua New Guinea, Middle Sepik
Early 20th century
Engraved cassowary bone
24 x 4.7 and 36.3 x 4.8 cm
Donated by M. and E. de Ganay, R. and C. van den Broek, *La Korrigane* expedition, 1934-1936
Inv. 71.1969.51.26 and 71.1969.51.28

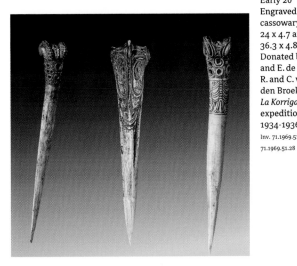

Prestige and trade in Melanesia

In Melanesia, prestige is a fundamental social concept, expressed above all in the creation, acquisition and trading of wealth. It lies at the heart of political, economic and social relations between groups.

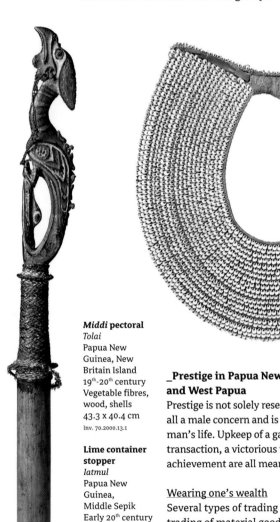

Middi pectoral
Tolai
Papua New Guinea, New Britain Island
19th-20th century
Vegetable fibres, wood, shells
43.3 x 40.4 cm
Inv. 70.2000.13.1

Lime container stopper
Iatmul
Papua New Guinea, Middle Sepik
Early 20th century (?)
Bamboo, pigments, vegetable fibres
69 x 9 cm
Inv. 72.1996.9.1

_Prestige in Papua New Guinea and West Papua

Prestige is not solely reserved for chiefs, but is above all a male concern and is acquired throughout a man's life. Upkeep of a garden, a successful transaction, a victorious fight, or an artistic achievement are all means of gaining prestige.

Wearing one's wealth

Several types of trading exist in Melanesia: trading of material goods such as raw materials (seashells, feathers, tortoise shells, etc.) or of objects, but also of such non-material goods as dance steps, songs and motifs. Shell money and feather ornamentation indicate the social status and prestige of their owners, and the composition

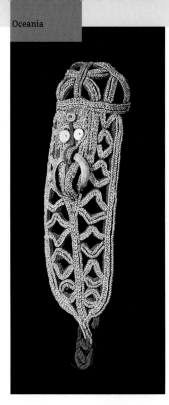

Ambusaap woman's headdress
Iatmul
Papua
New Guinea,
Middle Sepik
Mid 20th century
Vegetable fibres,
cowry shells, pig's
tusks
75 x 25.5 cm
J. Guiart mission,
1965
Inv. 72.1965.14.206

Spear-throwers
Papua New
Guinea,

Middle Sepik
Early and mid 20th
century
Bamboo, wood,
rattan
1/87.8 x 8.5 cm
F. Girard mission,
1955
Inv. 71.1955.76.187
2/88.7 x 10.3 cm
Inv. 71.1944.0.179 X
3/89.7 x 10 cm
Donated by M.
and E. de Ganay,
R. and C. van den
Broek, *La Korrigane*
expedition,
1934-1936
Inv. 71.1961.103.297

of the ornamentation provides information on trading networks between groups. *Ambusaap*, ceremonial headdresses from the Sepik River region, are worn by women at marriage ceremonies. Seashells (cowry and conus) attached to a flexible wickerwork frame confer great value to the ornament. Shells are traded between groups along the coast of northern New Guinea and those living further inland. During the 20th century, this practice increased with the migration of the populations from inland areas to European coastal plantations. *Middi*, the shell money of New Britain's Tolai people, is traditionally worn around the neck by chiefs on ceremonial occasions. Used in trade and funeral rites, in public contexts it symbolizes its owner's social prestige and his capacity to allocate wealth.

Men's prestige

In Papua New Guinea, the major transitional stages in a man's life are marked by the acquisition of objects that signal his newly acquired status and the secret knowledge that confers prestige and respect. During their initiation, adolescents are given ceremonial lime containers by their elders, which are used for chewing betel, a stimulant made from lime and betel palm nuts. The wooden stoppers of these containers are often carved with images of clan ancestral beings (cassowary, crocodile, etc.) upon whom the newly initiated youth depends. In their role as hunters and warriors of prestige, adult men employ wood and bamboo spear-throwers decorated with clan emblems indicating the owner's clan and social status.

1

2

3

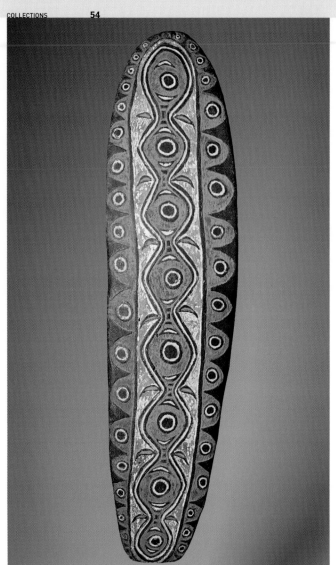

Shield
Papua New
Guinea, High
Sepik, April River
Mid 20th century
Wood, pigments
166 x 41.5 cm
J. Guiart mission,
1965
Inv. 72.1966.2.8

***Waguet* warrior's
shield**
Iatmul
Papua New
Guinea,
Middle Sepik
Early 20th century
Wood, pigments
152.7 x 46 cm
Donated by M.
and E. de Ganay,
R. and C. van den
Broek,
La Korrigane
expedition,
1934-1936
Inv. 71.1961.103.313

_Shields in Papua New Guinea

In Papua New Guinea, the role of the shield
highlights the existence of a true warrior culture.
It is not only an instrument of defence, but is
designed to provoke the enemy. As a group,
the vividly coloured advancing shields create
a visual impact that intimidates as much as it
serves to protect.
The Iatmul people living on the banks of the Sepik
River do not make shields. Examples collected
seem to have been booty from wars with

neighbouring groups, or traded objects. The faces painted on these shields might represent ancestral beings and be designed to terrify the enemy and protect the warriors who owned them. Shields of bark inlaid with mother of pearl and shells from Santa Isabel Island (central Solomon Islands) represent the power of the chiefs to whom they belong. Elaborately decorated and only produced in small numbers, they are ceremonial objects rather than instruments of war.

Aside from their usefulness in battle, some shields add to the prestige of high-ranking members of the group. In domestic use, they might serve as symbolic or actual doors to a garden or house. Although war was prevalent in Polynesia and in some parts of Melanesia (Vanuatu, New Caledonia, a number of islands in the Solomon Islands archipelago, and in certain regions of New Guinea) no shields have been found there.

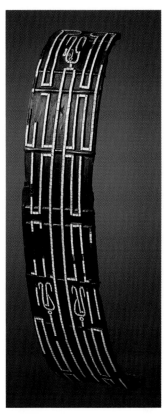

Shield
Solomon Islands,
Santa Isabel
Island
Early 19th century
Bark, mother of
pearl, parinarium
nut paste,
bamboo
87.5 x 23 cm
Former Hunter
collection
Inv. 70.2003.4.1

_Headhunting and bonito fishing in the Solomon Islands

Head-hunting – bringing back an enemy head as a trophy – was practised in the central and northern Solomon Islands until the end of the 19th century. Head-hunting expeditions were undertaken in specific circumstances such as the building and launching of a large dugout canoe, the inauguration of a communal house, the initiation of novices, or as part of funeral rites. It was seen as the symbolic equivalent of bonito fishing, both practices being connected with the regeneration of the group's life force.

Both kinds of expedition were undertaken in large single-hull dugout canoes, decorated with precious shells and mother-of-pearl inlays. A small human figurine, *musumusu*, was placed on the craft's prow, at the waterline. This effigy often held a carved bird or human head in its hands, a reference to headhunting and was meant to protect the craft from malevolent sea spirits. These sacred craft were kept in sheds with long vertical apertures in the walls to allow passage to their high prows and poops. The sheds were also used as men's meeting houses, where initiations, circumcision rites and fishing ceremonies were performed. Posts supporting the roof were often carved with the images of ancestral beings, facing into the building's interior and guarding the skulls and bones of great chiefs. These were kept in reliquaries shaped like miniature dugout canoes or fish depending on the social rank of the deceased. M.M.

Reliquary-fish
Solomon Islands,
Santa Ana Island
Early 20th century
Bone, wood,
pigments
211.5 x 35.3 cm
Donated by M.
and E. de Ganay,
R. and C. van den
Broek,
La Korrigane
expedition,
1934-1936
Inv. 71.1961.103.56

Statuette
Solomon Islands
Mid 19th century
Wood, mother of
pearl, pigments
39 x 13 cm
Inv. 71.1878.30.33

Funeral canoe
Solomon Islands,
Sa'a Island
(to the south of
Malaita Island)
Mid 19th century
Wood, mother of
pearl, feathers,
shells, fibres,
pigments
350 x 127 cm
Collected by the
reverend Father
R. H. Codrington
Inv. 72.1988.2.1

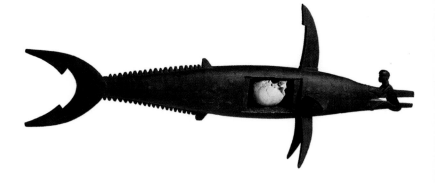

Canoe-shed posts
Solomon Islands,
Roviana Island
Early 20th century
Wood, mother of
pearl
228 x 40 cm
Collected by
Captain
Middenway circa
1920

Inv. 72.1984.2.1 and
72.1984.2.2

***Musumusu* canoe
prow effigy**
Solomon Islands,
Roviana Island
Probably 19th
century
Wood, mother of
pearl, pitch
20.2 x 9.3 cm
Former G. Ortiz
collection

Inv. 72.1978.2.1

Figures of power

Special political organizations have existed for a long time in Melanesia, in particular the emblematic model of the "Big Man" (chief with merited power): the Vanuatu grade hierarchies, for example, or New Caledonia's Kanak chiefdoms.

_Vanuatu hierarchies of grades

The Vanuatu system of grades is a remarkable example of the social and political hierarchical organisation of Melanesian society. Prevalent in the northern half of the archipelago, grading enables all men to increase their power in the world of the living and in the afterworld.

Grades are acquired by the purchase of prestige-enhancing objects and rituals in which the tusked pig plays a central role. The curve of the tusks is important: the more pronounced it is, the greater the pig's sacred worth. Several hundred pigs are ceremonially sacrificed to purchase a high grade and marking it, such as ornaments, sculptures and masks. The grade system is a dual one, made up of a public society and of secret societies, in which men progress in parallel fashion. The number of grades and related rituals vary from island to island. Hierarchies of grade societies for women also exist, but relatively little is known about them.

Bifacial flint magical stone
Vanuatu,
southern
Pentecost Island
Mid 20th century
Stone
18.7 x 9.3 cm
E. A. de la Rüe
mission, 1934
Inv. 71.1934.186.244

Magical stone
Vanuatu,
southern
Pentecost Island
Mid 20th century
Coralline stone,
pigments
12.2 x 5.8 cm
Inv. 72.1983.3.1

Magical stone
Vanuatu,
northern
Ambrym Island
Mid 20th century
Stone, pigments
14.7 x 4 cm
J. Guiart mission,
1963
Inv. 72.1964.2.47

Magical stone
Vanuatu,
northern
Ambrym Island
Mid 20th century
Volcanic tuff,
pigments
27.5 x 9.8 cm
Entrusted by IRD
Inv. 72.1962.1.29 D

Bifacial flint magical stone
Vanuatu, eastern
Malekula Island
Mid 20th century
Volcanic tuff
14.8 x 4.1 cm
M. Baton bequest
Inv. 72.1942.1.1

Grade sculpture
Vanuatu,
Malekula Island
Late 19th century
Tree fern,
pigments
261 x 42 cm
Donated by
J. Higginson
Inv. 71.1890.27.4

Nalot dish
Vanuatu,
Malo Island
19th-20th century
Wood
69 x 31 cm
Inv. 72.1963.11.2

Emblems of grade

In Ambrym and Malekula, grade monuments are set up in the dance square, a ceremonial area outside the village where grading rituals take place. Sculptures carved on the base of a tree fern trunk indicate the lowest grades. Linked to the world of the ancestral beings, they are coated with natural pigments traded between groups, making them all the more valuable. The highest grades are indicated by large standing stones. During these rituals, the men consume a range of culinary specialities prepared from cooked root vegetable paste (*laplap* and *nalot*) and served on wooden plates. Plates from Malo Island, decorated on each end with faces, are reserved for the highest grades, who are considered as living ancestral beings. The first part of the *nalot* is offered to the spirits whose effigies are carved on the plates. Serrations around the plates' rims are clear evidence of the importance accorded to the food.

Rambaramp
funerary effigy
Small Nambas
Vanuatu,
southern
Malekula Island
Bone, wood,
vegetable paste,
pigments,
spider's web,
pig's teeth,
feathers,
vegetable fibres
178 x 44 cm
Former Austin
collection
Inv. 72.1931.1.45

/ RAMBARAMP

**Found only in the south of
Malekula, the *rambaramp* is a
funerary effigy for men of
the highest grades. It makes a
brief public appearance during
the end-of-mourning ceremony,
before being taken to the
ceremonial house.**

**Through their rank, some men
achieve the status of ancestor
while still alive. When they die,
their skulls are used to fashion
the *rambaramp*. Their facial
features are modelled on the
skulls, using painted vegetable
fibre paste. The long bones
(tibia and femur) are kept
separately. The body of the
rambaramp, the same height as
that of the deceased, is
fashioned from tree fern, and its
limbs from rolls of banana-tree
leaves. These secretly
manufactured effigies
incorporate the symbolic objects
acquired by the deceased while
alive: pigs' teeth, pearl armband
and garter, knee and shoulder
maskettes, or pigments for face-
painting. Although the dummy
itself may be discarded, the
skull is always preserved,
secreted away within one of
the men's houses. M.M.**

Magic

The grade system not only enables men to
increase their political and economic power, it is
also closely linked to the knowledge of magic and
contact with ancestral beings. On Malekula Island,
secret hierarchies of grades make use of figures
known as *temes nevimbür* (*temes* means "spirit"),
which also accompany funerary effigies,
rambaramp, during the rituals that close the cycle
of life and death for men of high grade. These
figurines, a simple head and torso, are made of
coconut shells upon which faces are modelled in
vegetable paste, and are sometimes decorated
with spider's webs or pigs' teeth. They are
mounted on sticks and, above a vegetable screen
set up in a special enclosure, re-enact the deeds of
mythical heroes. Afterwards, they are kept in the

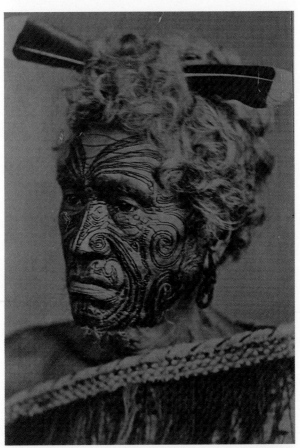

Anonymous, *Maori Chief with tattooed face*. New Zealand, 1860-1889.

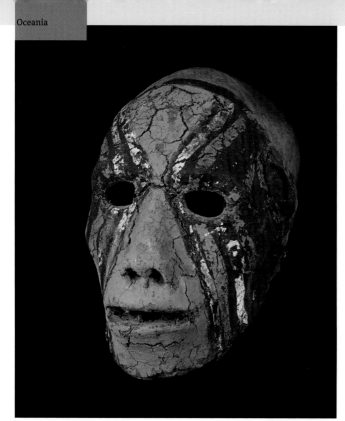

Overmodelled skull
Vanuatu, Malekula Island
Second half of the 20th century
Bone, vegetable paste, pigments
24.5 x 16.5 cm
Inv. 71.1969.130.15

***Temes* figure**
Small Nambas
Vanuatu, Malekula Island, Southwest Bay
Mid 20th century
Wood, pig's teeth, pigments, vegetable fibres, spider's web
43.5 x 26 cm
J. Guiart mission, 1963
Inv. 72.1964.2.22

men's house. The large number of pigs required as payment for grades occasionally calls for magical practices. In Ambrym, men use stones engraved with faces to help further partnerships with lenders of pigs. The use of such stones is highly codified, and is reserved for men of high grade, who rub them with special herbs, pigments or oils, and then place them facing the area where negotiations are to take place. Women and the uninitiated are forbidden to lay eyes upon them, and they are among the Vanuatu's most sacred and secret objects.

Finial arrow
New Caledonia,
northern Grande
Terre Island
Early 20ᵗʰ century
Wood
179 x 46.5 cm
R. Lescure
mission, 1931
Inv. 71.1931.50.6

_Chiefdom in New Caledonia

Traditional New Caledonian society is organised
into chiefdoms, whose hierarchy is evident in
village layout: the house of the Village Elder, as
the Kanak chief is called, overlooks the end of the
main avenue, and all other dwellings face towards
it along either side of the avenue. The chief's
house is a building symbolic of Kanak social
organisation: its foundations symbolize the elders
and the central support post, the Eldest.
A wooden roof finial stands atop the building,
its centre decorated with the face of an ancestral
being. This is sometimes surmounted by a spire
on which conch shell horns are strung, symbols
of the Elder's word. These conches, the most
important elements of the finial, are preserved
after the chief's death.
The name "Elder" is a reminder of the chief's
close ties to the ancestral beings. The entrance to

the chief's house is surrounded with carved
wooden door jambs reflecting his special
relationship with the land of the dead. Their
upper part represents a face, sometimes wearing
a headband similar to that of the chief; the lower
part is decorated with geometrical motifs, echoing
the woven matting with which the dead are
covered. For the Kanak, the houp tree, whose
wood is used to create these door jambs,
represents the refuge of the spirits of the dead.
Symbol of the unity of the village, the chief is also
his country's representative. His role and position
require him to own prestige-conferring objects,
such as the ceremonial axe. A jade (nephrite or
serpentine) disk at the end of the axe handle is
delicately cut along the edges to produce a
luminous, transparent effect when held up to
the sun. This precious material, from the south
and centre of the "Big Land", is distributed
among the islands of New Caledonia, through
the "wealth trading paths" (trading networks
for precious goods). The axe handle is covered
with decoratively woven *tapa* (bark cloth) or
European fabric, and the head is a coconut filled
with seashells. Such axes appear to have no
specific use, but are solely ceremonial and a part
of the chief's clan. M.M.

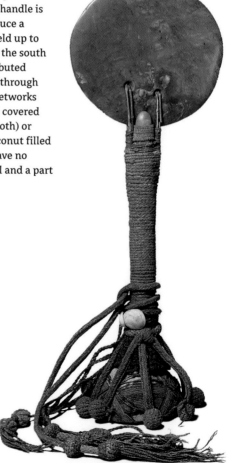

**Doorjamb
of a chief's house**
New Caledonia
Mid 20th century
Wood
155 x 69 cm
Donated by the
General Council
of New Caledonia
and the Municipal
Council of
Noumea
Inv. 71.1959.80.1

Ceremonial axe
New Caledonia
Wood, stone
(jadeite), flying
fox fur, shells
57.3 x 21.7 cm
Inv. 71.1946.0.51 X Oc

Men and Gods in Polynesia

For Polynesians, the origin of mankind is closely bound
to the world of the gods. To indicate this connection, images
of gods in human form and abstract sculptures – holders
of divine power – are set up in stone ceremonial places
known as *marae*.

_Receptacles of divine power

The Polynesian pantheon is organised around
a creator god who gave birth to humanity and
to other gods. On ceremonial occasions, the
divinities are incarnated in images fashioned
from symbolic materials. They contain the god's
breath and power, both beneficial to human life.

Sacred feathers and fibres

The sacred nature of these containers is
augmented by the materials from which they are
made. In Tahiti, the *to'o* consists of a wooden core
covered in coir upon which human features are
traced. Sacred red feathers are attached to fibre
cords or placed inside the effigy, and through it
the Tahitian primordial gods (mainly Oro, god
of war) are invoked. During the annual Pa'iatua
ceremony, the power (*mana*) of the *to'o* is
regenerated by replacing the sacred feathers
with new ones. Old feathers are redistributed to
minor divine effigies, which may then benefit
from *mana*.

Woven coconut fibres are often associated with
divine incarnations, such as *bure Kalu*, miniature
replicas of spirit houses found in the Fiji Islands.
Divine spirits are drawn into these fibre models
through the intermediary of an ivory statuette or
white tapa placed inside the *bure Kalu*.

***Patoko* offerings stand**
Gambier Islands,
Mangareva Island
Late 19th century
Wood
180 x 68 cm
Donated by
L. Capitan
Inv. 71.1929.14.921

Ceremonial spear
Papua
New Guinea,
Polynesian
outlier,
Takuu atoll
19th century (?)
Wood
248 x 8 cm
Inv. 70.2001.21.1

Wrappings bestowing power
Protective wrappings are of major importance in
ensuring divine presence within containers. Like
Tahitian *to'o*, the stick gods of the Cook Islands
come to life when covered with feathers, plant
ornamentation and thick beaten bark cloth (*tapa*).
These carved sticks make manifest the real or
mythical genealogies which link mankind to the
gods. Sticks from Mitiaro Island express these
ideas in visible form by a vertical series of spines,
each representing a generation. The small
spikes punctuating the *loatu* stick from Tauu
(a Melanesian atoll of Polynesian culture) may
be interpreted in similar fashion. In these islands,
images of gods take the form of spears.

_**Ceremonial objects**
Divine containers and effigies are displayed in
the sacred places, vast stone platforms known as
marae, *me'ae*, or *ahu*, depending on the island.
During ritual feasts, the images are honoured
by offerings of food or sacred objects, either in
supplication or in thanks for the benevolence of
the gods. In Mangareva (Gambier archipelago),
these offerings are often hung from display poles
such as the *patoko*. This wooden pole, crowned
by four carved arms, is the sole remaining
testimony of the practice, which was discouraged
by missionaries in the 19th century.

***Moai kava kava*
statuette**
Easter Island
Mid 19th century
Wood
29.3 x 7.5 cm
Inv. SG.53.290

_Images of the divine

Images of Polynesian gods are fashioned from durable materials and handed down from one generation to the next. Tiki was the "hero" who begat the first human beings. Endowed with supernatural powers, he is pictured as a male human figure with knees bent, hands flat against the chest, and a large head with big almond-shaped eyes. By extension, in Polynesia, the term *tiki* (*tihi* in Tahitian) is applied to all deified ancestral beings. In the Marquesas Islands, *tiki* take a wide variety of forms: wood, volcanic stone, and bone, measuring from 3 cm to 2.5 m. In the Tonga Islands, a number of ivory or wooden sculptures of female divinities exist, such as Hikule'o, who is invoked when a member of the royal family falls ill.

Some divinities that flow between the world of the living and that of the ancestral beings are pictured in a way that indicates their dual standing. The sunken features and protruding ribs of the *moai kava kava* on Easter Island evoke the spirits of the dead.

These effigies are only invested with power temporarily, usually on the occasion of major ceremonial events. M.M.

Tiki
Marquesas
Islands
Late 19th century
Basalt
14 x 7.7 cm
Inv. SG.84.221

Statuette
Tonga Islands
Late 18th century
Wood
14.1 x 7.7 cm
Former V. Denon
collection
Inv. SG.56.127

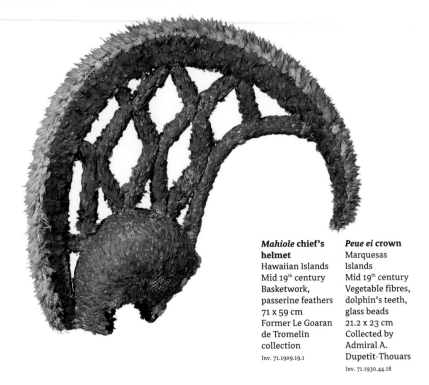

Mahiole **chief's helmet**
Hawaiian Islands
Mid 19th century
Basketwork, passerine feathers
71 x 59 cm
Former Le Goaran de Tromelin collection
Inv. 71.1909.19.1

Peue ei **crown**
Marquesas Islands
Mid 19th century
Vegetable fibres, dolphin's teeth, glass beads
21.2 x 23 cm
Collected by Admiral A. Dupetit-Thouars
Inv. 71.1930.44.18

Polynesian body arts

In Polynesia, the aesthetic sophistication of ornaments and adornments shows the great care lavished upon personal appearance, and of the body's role as a symbolic medium both in social and religious terms.

_Symbolic materials

The body's close relationship with the surrounding world is evident in Polynesian adornments, which are made from materials culled from the sea, and from the plant and animal kingdoms. Prestige adornments, such as tattoos or seashell diadems and necklaces, exist side by side with the more ephemeral varieties connected with ceremonial practices – woven leaves and flowers, perfumed oils, etc.
Such materials are valued because of their rarity (dolphin or sperm whale teeth, or certain types of feathers), indicating their owners' high social status at such special occasions as marriages, trading events and funerals.

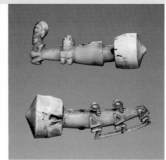

Pu taiana
**woman's ear
ornaments**
Marquesas Islands
Late 19th century
Ivory, shells
4.9 x 1.5,
4.8 x 1.6, 5 x 1.5
and 5.5 x 1.8 cm
Inv. 71.1887.31.42,
71.1949.41.3, 72.1970.7.1
and 72.1970.7.2

/ TATTOOING IN THE MARQUESAS ISLANDS

Signs of grade, geographical origin and identity, tattoos are also protection against malevolent powers. Tattooing is carried out in gradual stages to provide a protective "carapace" comparable to the plates of a tortoise's shell. The tortoise motif is highly prized as a source of strength.

Tuhuna, specialized craftsmen, work with a comb and small hammer, and a range of motifs carved into wooden boards or bamboo that serve as model designs. From the age of 15 upwards, boys are tattooed with decorative or grade motifs, while girls between the ages of eight and ten are tattooed behind the earlobes, around the lips, and on the hands. Warriors' eyes are encircled with spirals, as are the cheeks and hips of a chief. When they die, the corpses of such illustrious figures, tattooed from head to foot, are flayed so that the may enter naked into the beyond. Banned by the French authorities in 1898, tattooing is currently enjoying a major renaissance throughout Polynesia, as an affirmation of cultural identity. M.M.

_Head ornaments

Particular attention is paid to the head in Polynesia as it is often considered as the seat of vital force and of *mana*, a force as beneficial as it is dangerous.

Tiki engraved on ear ornaments and on the tortoiseshell plaques of Marquesas Island diadems protect the head symbolically. They refer back to the origins of mankind and the gods and enable their owners to stay in contact with the mythical histories of their clans. Hair taken from the dead is also used in body ornamentation, bringing the living into close touch with ancestral beings.

In Hawaii, feathers are a vehicle of divine power. Adorning helmets or capes, they confer high prestige upon chiefs and are signs of their divine ancestry. M.M.

**Engraved board
(tattooist's
board)**
Marquesas
Islands
Late 19th century
Wood
87 x 26 cm
Donated by Naval
Lieutenant Baule
Inv. 71.1894.77.1

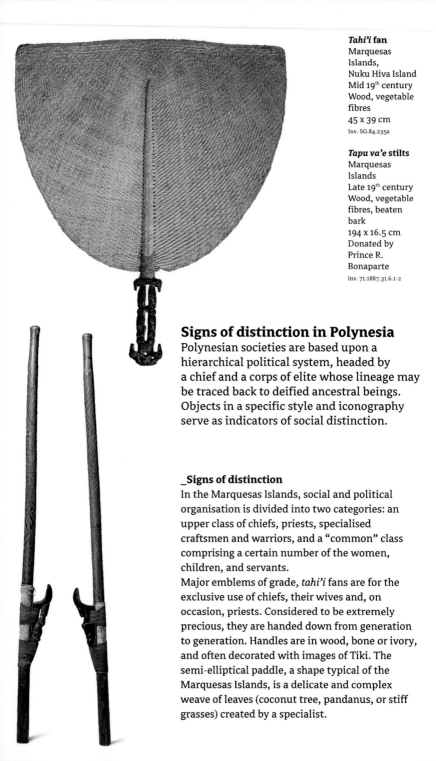

Tahi'i **fan**
Marquesas
Islands,
Nuku Hiva Island
Mid 19th century
Wood, vegetable
fibres
45 x 39 cm
Inv. SG.84.235a

Tapu va'e **stilts**
Marquesas
Islands
Late 19th century
Wood, vegetable
fibres, beaten
bark
194 x 16.5 cm
Donated by
Prince R.
Bonaparte
Inv. 71.1887.31.6.1-2

Signs of distinction in Polynesia

Polynesian societies are based upon a
hierarchical political system, headed by
a chief and a corps of elite whose lineage may
be traced back to deified ancestral beings.
Objects in a specific style and iconography
serve as indicators of social distinction.

_Signs of distinction

In the Marquesas Islands, social and political
organisation is divided into two categories: an
upper class of chiefs, priests, specialised
craftsmen and warriors, and a "common" class
comprising a certain number of the women,
children, and servants.
Major emblems of grade, *tahi'i* fans are for the
exclusive use of chiefs, their wives and, on
occasion, priests. Considered to be extremely
precious, they are handed down from generation
to generation. Handles are in wood, bone or ivory,
and often decorated with images of Tiki. The
semi-elliptical paddle, a shape typical of the
Marquesas Islands, is a delicate and complex
weave of leaves (coconut tree, pandanus, or stiff
grasses) created by a specialist.

U'u clubs are carved in blackened hard wood. The upper part is decorated with reliefs of interlinked human heads. Wielded by warriors in close combat, they are also carried by chiefs as an emblem of prestige. During their adolescence, future warriors train through simulated ritual combats on stilts, *tapuvae*, whose poles are carved with one or more Tiki.

_Design and Aesthetics

Common to many tropical cultures, headrests are an example of the importance attached in Oceania to an object's intrinsic beauty. Symbolically, they are associated with the head, a sacred part of the body and seat of status and power, which no one may touch without permission and which may not come into contact with the ground. From a practical point of view, the headrest keeps the head off the floor and protects the complex hairstyles worn for ceremonial occasions. In Polynesia, headrest forms are often related to the hierarchical status of their owners. They consist of one or several parts and, in the Fiji Islands in particular, the most prestigious – those reserved for the use of high-grade individuals – are inlaid with ivory.

As with headrests, plates and bowls are of elaborate design. Used for food, the size, shape and decoration of these containers correspond to the everyday or ceremonial purposes. At ritual feasts, large plates for collective eating are a matter of protocol and indicate social position, also evident in the order in which guests are served. In the Marquesas Islands, leftovers from ceremonial meals are preserved in covered, concave, oval wooden plates with simple Tiki head decorations at both ends.

'U'u club
Marquesas
Islands
Mid 19th century
Wood
153.6 x 17.2 cm
Collected by
Admiral A.
Dupetit-Thouars
Inv. 71.1930.44.64

Headrest
Tonga Islands
Mid 19th century
Wood
77.2 x 9 cm
Inv. SG.53.272

Chief's bowl
Marquesas
Islands
Late 19th century
Wood
49.5 x 20 cm
Donated by
Prince R.
Bonaparte
Inv. 71.1887.31.13

_Arts bestowing power in New Zealand

Important members of Maori society are considered as *tapu* – a term encapsulating the notions of forbidden and sacred – above all, when their blood is shed during tattooing. Any direct contact with them is dangerous. Facial tattooing can be extremely painful. The newly tattooed are fed with a *korere*, a special wood funnel, which in the northern province of New Zealand is highly decorated.

One of the body ornaments worn by powerful families is the jadeite pendant, *hei tiki* (the word *hei* means "hanging"). The half-human half-animal image of Tiki, its eyes circled with mother of pearl, or with red wax since European colonization, represents an ancestral being. Worn around the neck by men and women alike, it is passed down from one generation to the next, gaining in value along the way. Its value also stems from the rarity of the material in which it is made and the delicacy of the technique used to create it. Such precious family possessions are kept together in boxes with carved reliefs on the sides, enabling them to be hung from the house beams, and are decorated. These boxes are decorated with highly complex designs characterized by spirals, a mix of the symmetrical and the asymmetrical, the abstract and the figurative, that covers its entire surface. M.M.

Hei tiki pendant
Maori
New Zealand
Early 19th century
Jade, vegetable
fibres, bone, wax
15.5 x 9.8 cm
Former collection
of King Charles X
Inv. SG.84.225

Korere funnel
Maori
New Zealand
Early 19th century
Wood
14.8 x 8.2 cm
Collected by J. S.
Dumont d'Urville
Inv. SG.84.351

TAPA

Tapa, cloth made from beaten bark and decorated by women, is common throughout Oceania. It is used for a variety of purposes: everyday clothing, ceremonial dress, and shrouds for the dead. It is also an item of trade and prestige. In Polynesia, large amounts of tapa indicate wealth and status on ceremonial occasions. The cloth also establishes contact between men and their gods and ancestral beings. In Polynesia, it is often used to wrap sacred effigies, forming an essential part of their value. In Melanesia, tapa is above all associated with masculine rites, and is used in making ceremonial masks and headdresses. M.M.

Tapa (detail)
Society Islands,
Tahiti
Early 19th century
Beaten bark,
pigments
243 x 183 cm
Collected by
Dr R.-P. Lesson
Inv. 71.1894.24.1

ds
ᵗʰ century
ark,
s
cm
0.406 X

Tapa
Wallis Islands
Early 20ᵗʰ centu
Beaten bark,
pigments
238 x 74.5 cm
Donated by
M. Franc
Inv. 71.1933.66.1

Tapa
Fiji Islands
Late 19ᵗʰ century
Beaten bark,
pigments
190 x 37.5 cm
Donated by
M. Mason
Inv. 71.1887.13.2

Dreaming: Arts of Australia

Ever since the first nomadic peoples arrived nearly 50,000 years ago, art has occupied a central place in the life of Australian aborigines. It attests to and keeps alive the connection between mankind and the mythical beings born from "Dreaming".

Rover Thomas
Ord River, Bow River, Denham River
Western Australia, Kimberley, Turkey Creek-Warmun
1989
Acrylic on canvas
180 x 90.2 cm
Inv. 72.1999.4.1

_Dreaming

Dreaming is the aborigines' concept of the physical and spiritual order which governs the universe, and which dynamically unites past, present and future.

Dreaming refers back to mythical beginnings, when fantastical beings fashioned the flat surface of the Australian continent. These Dream entities – animals, plants, and natural phenomena – created places and things for all eternity, and instituted ceremonial rites and social rules. The aborigines believe that these mythical beings live in a separate reality, parallel to that of mankind, and interact with the living in their dreams. Ceremonial practices enable the transmission, reactivation and transformation of their deeds of creation.

Dreaming also springs from a spatial dynamic embodied in the roads that interconnect sacred places – routes originally travelled by the ancestral beings, which the living continue to follow, and of which they are the guardians.

/ ABORIGINE SCHOOLS OF PAINTING

In 1971, an art teacher by the name of Geoffrey Bardon persuaded old aborigine initiates to make a painting of their "honey ant" dreaming of the on the walls of the Papunya School, a centre for the assimilation of indigenous peoples. Public revelation of secret motifs and the transference of body painting on to canvas required certain changes, which would become emblematic of contemporary aborigine style: overall of colourful dots ans combinations of straight and curved lines and circles, representing mythological maps and routes taken by ancestral beings. Around Alice Springs and in the central desert, different communities are recognisable by a particular style (Yuendumu, Lajamanu, etc.). In Utopia, the women are active in printing on fabric. At the Balgo mission in Western Australia, artists of both sexes have been producing paintings since 1980, using thick paste mixes of brilliant colours.

Further north, the artistic community of Warmun-Turkey Creek, under the tutelage of Rover Thomas, covers canvases with flat tints of natural pigments, forming single motifs encircled with stippling. These groups reflect the personalities of individual artists who are able to travel to the communities in question, and it is difficult to assimilate them into schools. M.M.

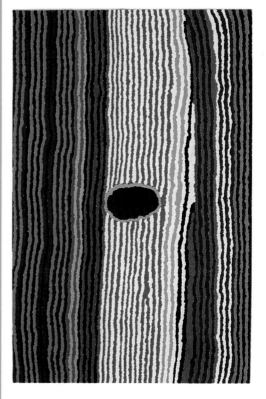

Helicopter
Tjungurrayi
**Paljukutjara soak
in the great
sandy desert**
Western
Australia, Balgo
1996
Acrylic on canvas
81 x 121 cm
Inv. 72.1997.7.3

Shield
Australia,
Queensland, Cape
York peninsula
Wood, pigments
89 x 34.2 cm
Donated by
M. Montefiori
Inv. 71.1883.3.10

George
Tjungurrayi
**Mythological
drawings
associated
with the Lake
Kurrakurranya
site, home of a
poisonous snake
to the north of
Lake Mackay**
Australia,
Northern Territory,
Central Desert,
Papunya
1997
Acrylic on canvas
183 x 152 cm
Inv. 72.1998.8.1

Shield
Western Australia,
Desert region
Mid 19th century
Wood, pigments
90.2 x 16.8 cm
Donated by
R. Bischoffsheim
Inv. 71.1880.39.32

Each Aborigine is attached to one or more Dreamings, connected to a specific place or to a journey across the territory. This link between Dreaming and territory is so strong that, in 1963, the inhabitants of Arnhem Land in northern Australia presented Dreaming painting to the examining government commission on property rights as evidence of their land ownership. Today, these paintings not only express the ties between an individual, his Dreaming, and the places featured therein, but also play an active part in settling identity claims.

_Range of artistic forms

The earliest aborigine art forms can still be seen in the engravings and paintings decorating rocky shelters across the Australian continent, and which date back at least 30,000 years.
Ephemeral arts (dance, song, body painting, ornaments, designs made on the ground, and painted and engraved objects), are common to all aborigine groups, and are carried out in secret during rituals commemorating Dreaming. The wooden weapons used by Aborigine hunter-gatherers are decorated with painted and carved motifs indicating their owner's status and serving to throw their adversaries off balance.
Some regions are home to more specific creations: paintings on eucalyptus bark produced in Arnhem Land are traditional depictions of myths recounted on ceremonial occasions. In the 1970s, in the central desert, acrylic paintings largely aimed at the Western market began to be produced alongside secret, ritual art forms.
These contemporary forms both perpetuate and reformulate age-old traditions. The title of George Tjungurrayi's painting clearly shows his attachment to the mythical places of the central desert: the canvas evokes a vast relief of plains and hills, and the composition is reminiscent of the carved wavy lines which decorate the wooden shields carried by Aborigines until European colonisation. M.M.

Mick Namerari
Tjapaltjarri
**Dream
of Tjunginpa
to Tjunginpa,
northwestern
Kintore**
Australia,
Northern
Territory, Central
Desert, Papunya
1996
Acrylic on canvas
153 x 122 cm
Inv. 72.1998.1.3

PAINTING

...gs on eucalyptus bark from Arnhem Land, an
...nal territory in Northern Australia, express and
...ate Dreaming. Originally painted on rock
...ngings, certain motifs are reproduced on bark using
...l pigments, and are used for ritual or educational
...ses. Today, aborigine artists' co-operatives are
...ing this particular art form across the world.
...styles are increasingly apparent in Arnhem Land:
...West, the motif stands out from a monochrome ochre
...ckground. Animals of mythical origin, Mimih spirits
...gures from Maam sorcery are depicted "x-ray style",
...nternal organs visible. These beings are covered in
...coloured hatching (*rarrk*) which produces a shimmering
...:, the visual incarnation of their power. Paintings from
...ast and centre of the territory represent mythical events
...ected to actual places.
...e bark paintings come from a major collection put together
...nhem Land in 1963 by the artist and ethnographer Karel
...a (1918-1993), whose pioneering work places aborigine
...ts very much in the foreground. M.M.

1/ Dawaran
Jabirus in a
Australia,
Central Arn...
Land, Milin...
Mid 20th cen...
70 x 40 cm
K. Kupka Mi...
1963
Inv. 72.1964.9.58

2/ Billy Yirav...
Seated Mim...
Man
Australia,
western Arn...
Land, Croke...
Island
Mid 20th cen...
71 x 41 cm
K. Kupka mi...
1963
Inv. 72.1964.10.1

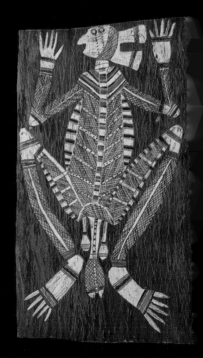

3

4

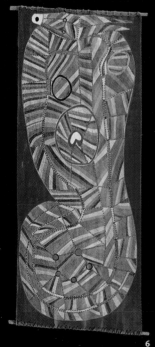

3/ Billy Yirawala
Female Kangaroo
Australia,
western Arnhem
Land, Croker
Island
Mid 20th century
73 x 70 cm
K. Kupka mission,
1963
Inv. 72.1964.9.148

4/ Billy Yirawala
**The mythical
snake-man
Luma-Luma
sleeping**
Australia,
western Arnhem
Land, Croker
Island
Mid 20th century
107 x 74 cm
K. Kupka mission,
1963
Inv. 72.1964.9.83

5

6

5/ Bininiywui
**Rivers and dwarf
palm trees
created by
Yurlunggur**
Australia, central
Arnhem Land,
Milingimbi
Mid 20th century
73.5 x 44 cm
K. Kupka mission,
1963
Inv. 72.1964.9.74

6/ John
Mawurndjul
**Horned rainbow
snake**
Australia,
western Arnhem
Land, Maningrida
1991
176 x 72 cm
Inv. 72.1997.6.2

7/ Billy Yirawala
Two Mimi men
Australia, western
Arnhem Land,
Croker Island
Mid 20th century
63 x 42 cm
K. Kupka mission,
1963
Inv. 72.1964.9.79

7

1

1/ David Malangi
**Funeral
Ceremony**
Australia, central
Arnhem Land,
Milingimbi
Mid 20th century
73.5 x 48 cm
K. Kupka mission,
1963
Inv. 72.1964.10.6

2/ Jimmy
Midjaw-Midjaw
Maam **man
attacking a
pregnant woman**
Australia,
western Arnhem
Land, Croker Island
Mid 20th century
52.5 x 41 cm
K. Kupka mission,
1963
Inv. 72.1964.9.106

3/ Mudupu
**Sunfish,
Moonfish**
Australia, central
Arnhem Land,
Milingimbi
Mid 20th century
75 x 34.5 cm
Karel Kupka
mission, 1963
Inv. 72.1964.10.7

4/ Paddy Compass
Namatbara
Maam **man
sleeping**
Australia, western
Arnhem Land,
Croker Island
Mid 20th century
75 x 56.5 cm
K. Kupka mission,
1963
Inv. 72.1964.9.122

5/ Jimmy
Midjaw-Midjaw
**Namarwon,
thunder spirit**
Australia,
western Arnhem
Land, Croker Island
Mid 20th century
77 x 50 cm
K. Kupka mission,
1963
Inv. 72.1964.9.110

2

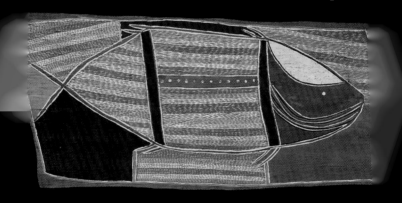

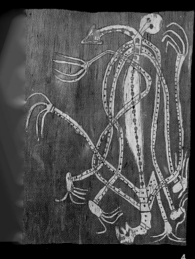

4

Insular South East Asia: land of the dead and of ancestors

A vast archipelago of around twenty thousand islands, Insular South East Asia separates the continent of Asia from New Guinea and Australia. Indonesia, eastern Malaysia (Sarawak and Sabah) and the Philippines are united by the origins of their language. They belong to the Malayo-Polynesian branch of the great Austronesian family that stretches from Eastern Island to Madagascar.

_Offerings and sacrifices

The complexity funerary rites performed by Insulindia archipelago societies demonstrate the importance they attach to these practices. Accompanying the deceased to his final resting place with the pomp befitting his rank, displaying his possessions and perfecting his alliances were all duties not to be neglected. Adherence to these rules enables the deceased to attain the world beyond and, in some instances, to attain the status of ancestral being or, more rarely, that of a deified ancestor.

Statues and altars served as a link with the world beyond and as an expression of ancestor worship. The world of the dead and that of the living were connected through offerings and sacrifices. In gratitude for the offering,

Ja yeda
horseman
Nage
West-central
Flores Island
20th century
Wood, porcelain
299 x 65 cm
Former collection
of the Musée
Barbier-Mueller,
Geneva
Inv. 70.2001.27.492.1 to 3

***Tavu* household
altar**
South Moluccas,
Tanimbar
Archipelago
19th century
Wood
236 x 146 cm
Former collection
of the Musée
Barbier-Mueller,
Geneva
Inv. 70.2001.27.444

the ancestors provide protection and benevolence.
The *tavu* altar is shaped like a human with
gracefully extended arms and at the same time
is decorated with an abstract spiral motifs. The
two fish above the openings represent the house's
founding ancestors. The *tavu* is part of the
architecture: its base is in the ground and its top
holds up the transversal beam of the roof on
which the ancestor's skull and vertebrae lie.
It reinforces the house's identity and reactivates
ancestral ties.
In Sumba, the *penji*, stones set up like prows
at the front of the tombs, are adorned with the
possessions of the deceased, reflecting the wealth
acquired during his lifetime.

**Clan founder
wearing an
engraved
marangga
on his chest**
Western Sumba
Island
19ᵗʰ century
Stone
146 x 35 cm
Former collection
of the Musée
Barbier-Mueller,
Geneva
Inv. 70.2001.27.584

***Penji* funeral
stele**
Southeastern
Sumba Island
19ᵗʰ-20ᵗʰ century
Stone
248 x 65 cm
Former collection
of the Musée
Barbier-Mueller,
Geneva
Inv. 70.2001.27.583

_Funerary sculpture in Sumatra

The megaliths and stone sculptures produced by the Toba and Pakpak peoples in Sumatra date back to ancient times. Commemorative or funerary effigies depicting seated people or couples astride imaginary animals are the work of anonymous artists. The effigy of Ronggur ni Ari *boru* Baratu, "Thunderclap-in Daytime", was commissioned by her husband from a sculptor belonging Toba peoples in the Barus region. Although the woman's features are not clearly individualised, the betel quid slightly swelling her cheek provides a touch of realism. She is seated, unclothed but wearing her jewellery, holding a ritual box in each hand. The work's sophistication reflects her family's prestige. C.M.

Ronggur ni Aru
boru **Barutu**
Toba
Sumatra, Barus region
19th century
Stone
112 x 76 cm

Former collection of the Musée Barbier-Mueller, Geneva
Inv. 70.2001.27.585

Tau tau ancestor effigy
Sa'dan Toraja
Sulawesi
19th-20th century
Wood, cotton, shells
169 x 50 cm
Former collection of the Musée Barbier-Mueller, Geneva
Inv. 70.2001.27.318.1-13

/ *TAU TAU*

For the Sa'dan Toraja people of Sulawesi, *tau tau* means "small person" or "like a person". Carved in jackfruit wood, the effigy is brought to life by a poem sung by the priest to *minaa*. Once consecrated, it draws in the shadow or soul of the deceased, *bombo*, becoming his double. Along with the deceased, it receives offerings of food, betel and palm wine. During the procession bearing the deceased to his final resting-place, the *tau tau* follows the cortege on a richly decorated palanquin. Then, set at the entrance to the tomb, it watches over the land of the living. Toraja funeral rituals are extremely complex. In order to help the "shadow" of a deceased of high grade to achieve ancestor status, the family must perform a series of rites of passage. Once the ceremonial cycle has been accomplished, the deceased attains the grade of "deified ancestor" and his wandering come to an end. But to achieve this goal, the living must adhere strictly to the rules, step by step and rite by rite. C.M.

Insular South East Asia: the influence of the chiefs, Nias Island

The many sculpted stones found on Nias Island are evidence of intensive ceremonial activity. They are closely linked to "merit feasts", also known as "prestige feasts" (*owasa*), the number and organisation of which are dictated by customary law.

Osa osa
ceremonial seats
Central Nias Island
19th-20th century
Stone
65 x 153 and
75 x 108 cm
Former collection
of the Musée
Barbier-Mueller,
Geneva
Inv. 70.2001.27.580
and 70.2001.27.586

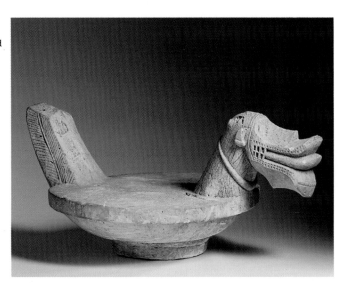

_Prestige Feasts

Held during rites of passage (marriages, funerals, inaugurations of houses, or successful raids), the purpose of a "prestige feast" is to consolidate grade or accede to higher social status, to gain prestige, and to obtain an honorary name. Most importantly, however, they enable entry into an exchange network, the basis of social relations in the hierarchically organised society. Feasts are an occasion for the sacrifice of large numbers of pigs. The slaughter calls for a meticulous sharing of meat. Each guest receives a chosen morsel, which necessitates giving one in return. Stone sculptures and seats of honour, *osa osa*,

are set up during "prestige feasts" on the initiative
of the nobility. The statues represent the
attributes of the chief at the peak of his power:
kalabubu necklace, emblem of the headhunters,
ear pendant, bracelet cut from a giant seashell.
Osa osa are seats of honour sculpted from stone for
men and women, and are found only in the centre
of the island. While some were placed in front
of noble houses, others were used as finishing
touches to *behu*, huge vertical stones attesting
to the greatness of a chief or village founder.
The heads decorating *osa osa* are often those of
lasara, a mythical animal, part stag, part boar
and part hornbill. A symbol of strength, wisdom
and beauty, the *lasara* is a recurrent motif on Nias
Island. It links the higher world to the lower,
protecting and strengthening the chief's power.

Lawölä **statue**
Central Nias
Island
Late 19th century
Limestone
122 x 35.5 cm
Former collection
of the Musée
Barbier-Mueller,
Geneva
Inv. 70.2001.27.549

Insular South East Asia: the treasure

The peoples of the Insular South East Asia archipelago islands attach great importance to the wearing and meaning of body adornments: they serve to indicate the social status of the wearer, strengthen alliances and as an intermediary with the world of ancestors.

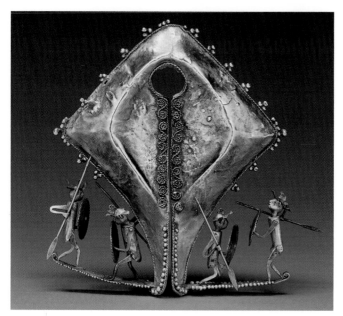

Crown
Southern Nias Island
19th-20th century
Gold
H. 16 cm
Donated by M. and J. P. Barbier-Mueller
Inv. 70.2001.27.645

***Lado* forehead ornament**
Nage
Central Flores Island
19th-20th century
Gold
50 x 26.6 cm
Donated by M. and J. P. Barbier-Mueller
Inv. 70.2001.27.709

Mamuli
Eastern Sumba Island
19th-20th century
Gold
12.7 x 11.7 cm
Donated by M. and J. P. Barbier-Mueller
Inv. 70.2001.27.753

_Display and exchange

In these societies, where the use of money was formerly unknown, jewels figured prominently in a complex exchange network that encompassed everything from marriage dowries to gifts given by figures of authority to the less wealthy in order to ensure their allegiance. Displays of wealth also accompanied major feasts, or rites of passage from one stage to the next of an individual's life. These exchanges were occasions to assess the wealth of the giver and the importance of the recipient, to bring the community together and establish new social ties.

_Competition

On the Nias Island in Indonesia, the nobles took part in wealth competitions in which the women wore crowns decorated with cosmic trees. Jewels were made, statues erected, and lavish "merit feasts" organised on these occasions. Gold jewellery – crowns and necklaces of beaten or hammered gold leaf – is designed to enhance the chief's glory, as gold is associated with power and prestige. The slave trade, long existent in these regions, most certainly influenced the development of jewellery and sculpted stone art as it provided chiefs and nobles with the gold required to make ornaments worthy of their rank.

_Prosperity

Coins imported by European travellers were introduced into the exchange system. Melted down, they were then transformed into body ornaments. Before being made of gold, *lado*, coronets from Flores Island, were fashioned from feathers. Worn by the nobility and handed down from father to son, they ensure lasting prosperity. *Lado* are worn at village ritual ceremonies, *pa sese*, which include animal sacrifices.

_Links with the world beyond

Certain types of jewellery ensure mediation between the world of the living and the supernatural world, protecting the wearer from illness or attack. Others enable access to the world of the dead.
Mamuli and *marangga* form part of the family treasure stored in the *Adat*, the house in which traditions are stored safe. Both indicate the power bestowed by lineage and attest to political and religious power. These sacred jewels are kept in darkness for fear that their power might harm those who see them, thereby disturbing the natural world order. *Mamuli* combine male and female opposing and complementary principles which, temporarily united, become the source of creation and power. C.M.

Marranga
pectoral
Western Sumba
Island
19th-20th century
Gold

30 x 21 cm
Donated by M.
and J. P. Barbier-
Mueller
Inv. 70.2001.27.754

Jhitku and Mitki
India,
Chhattisgarh,
Bastar
Early 20th century
Bronze
25 x 22 cm
Former
C. Niemoller
collection
Inv. 70.2000.1.40

Asia /

Stretching from the Mediterranean to the Pacific, separated from Africa by the Red Sea, Asia is the world's largest and most densely populated continent. The earliest known civilisations and all the major religions have their origins there. Asia is a plurality. Complex migratory patterns spread over several millennia have turned almost every country in the continent into an ethnic, linguistic and religious mosaic. The Asia collections, dating from the late 19th and the 20th century in particular, are a tribute to the memory of peoples too often forgotten. Complementing the collections in the Louvre and the Musée Guimet, which are essentially devoted to ancient history, they focus on contemporary societies, both nomadic and sedentary, village and city-dwelling, recording their daily lives, traditions and beliefs.

The visit begins in the east and travels westwards in geographical and cultural sequences, around a central bay which shows exhibits of textiles and costumes from a wide range of peoples. This arrangement highlights cultural and trade contacts between peoples, and the mutual influences this produced. In so doing, it underlines the transformations that have taken place over time, and contradicts the widely held belief that these peoples have remained frozen in their traditional cultures, cut off from history.

3300 BC
Earliest writing with the rise of cities in Mesopotamia

3000 BC
Earliest evidence of domestication of the horse found in the Ukrainian Steppes, the northern Caucasus, Russia, and Kazakhstan

2500 BC
Earliest cotton cloth discovered in the Indus Valley (present-day Pakistan)

1760 BC
Hammurabi's Code, a legislative text that influenced the Jewish Torah ("Law") and the Muslim Sharia

Circa 1300-1200 BC
Oracular inscriptions on cattle bones and tortoise shells. The earliest known forms of writing in China

Circa 1200 BC
The Phoenicians invent a writing system employing 22 consonant characters

Circa 1100 BC
The Hebrews, a race of nomadic shepherds, gradually settle in the Canaan highlands. They worship Yahweh, their national god, without excluding cults devoted to other deities

11th century BC
Earliest wool felt cloth found in the High Altai, Siberia

Circa 1000 BC
In Persia, Zarathustrian religion unifies the pantheon around Ahura Mazda, "The Wise Lord". Zoroastrianism becomes the State religion

under the Sassanid Dynasty (224-651)

8th-7th century BC
Height of the Dong Son culture in the province of Thanh Hoa (Vietnam)

6th century BC
Beginnings of Taoism in China with Laozi (whose actual existence is disputed)

597 BC
The Jews exiled to Babylon. Yahweh considered as god of the entire universe

551-478 BC
In China, Confucius emphasises the importance of ancestor worship

500 BC
Buddhism, which arose in India as a reaction to Hinduism, spreads into the

Himalayas and the Far East, and from Sri Lanka to Southeast Asia. It starts to disappear in India from the 13th century onwards

400 BC-400 AD
Compiling of the *Mahâbhârata* and the *Râmâyana*, founding Hindu epics

3rd-1st century BC
Bronze belt plates give evidence of the practice of buffalo sacrifice in the Dian culture, Yunnan province (China)

2nd century BC onwards
Rise of trade and cultural exchange routes between the Far East and the Mediterranean, with the Silk Road crossing Central Asia

Circa 9,500 BC
Earliest traces of agriculture in the Near East

8000 BC
Earliest domestication of animals in the Near East

5000 BC
Earliest silk fabrics in China. Earliest traces of rice farming near Shanghai (China)

Circa 4000 BC
Utilisation of lacquer in China

Mid 4th millennium BC
Domestication of the dromedary in southern Arabia

Mid 2ⁿᵈ century BC
Beginnings of paper production in China

180-87 BC
Chinese conquests in Gansu, Sichuan, Korea and North Vietnam in the reign of Han Wudi

70
Rome crushes the Jewish revolt, fall of Jerusalem and destruction of the Temple

380
Theodosius proclaims Christianity the State religion

6ᵗʰ-11ᵗʰ century
Formulation of the main storyline of the epic of the legendary Tibetan hero Gesar of Ling, which continues to be enriched and sung by storytellers in the regions of Tibet, Inner Mongolia and Qinghai

Early 7ᵗʰ century
Rise of Islam in the Arabian peninsula

Circa 800
Foundation of a paper factory in Baghdad: paper becomes the main medium for teaching and for spreading scientific knowledge

1096-1291
The Crusades help to bring about a major movement of trade and colonisation in the Levant

Early 11ᵗʰ century
Writing of *Genji monogatari* ("The Tale of Genji") by Murasaki Shikibu (Japan)

11ᵗʰ century
In China, invention of the printing press with movable characters and appearance of the earliest compasses with artificial magnets

Circa 1130
Earliest firearms (gunpowder, fireworks) in China

1275-1292
Marco Polo travels to China

1325-1353
The Maghrebian historian Ibn Battuta travels to China, via the Middle East. He crosses the Indian Ocean to Indonesia

Early 15ᵗʰ century
Zheng He's sea voyages take him to the Arabian peninsula and the coasts of Africa

1498
Vasco de Gama reaches Calcutta (India), where the Arabs are already engaged in trade

Late 15ᵗʰ century
Rise of Nô theatre in Japan

1535
Francis I and the Ottoman Sultan Soliman sign the

"capitulations" treaty promoting expansion of French trade with the Levant

Late 16ᵗʰ century
The first Jesuits arrive in China, introduction of European scientific knowledge

1607
First Kabuki theatre presentations in Edo (Tokyo)

1664
Foundation of the Society of Foreign Missions at the instigation of Alexander of Rhodes, who transcribed Vietnamese into Latin characters

17ᵗʰ century
Creation of the East India Companies. Imports endanger European textile production

18ᵗʰ century
Use of imported fabrics is

prohibited in Europe

1761-1764
Carsten Niebuhr, first European scientist to explore the Arabian peninsula

19ᵗʰ century
The Industrial Revolution leads to transfer to Europe of a large part of world textile production, so bringing ruin to Indian and Chinese craftspeople

1854
Opening up of Japan and the Japan-US Treaty of Peace and Amity after the arrival of Commodore Perry in 1853

1868
Start of the Meiji period in Japan

1876
Samurai are forbidden to carry swords (Japan)

1880-1900
John Errington
de La Croix (1880-
1886), Jacques de
Morgan (1884)
and Charles
Lapicque (1892-
1894) journey to
Malaysia on the
Sémiramis

1880-1881
Joseph Martin's
first expedition
to Siberia

1888
Mission in Korea
undertaken by
Charles Varat and
Victor Collin de
Plancy, a French
diplomat at the
court of Seoul

1892-1902
Organisation of
French Indochina
and annexing of
Laos following
exploratory
expeditions led
by Auguste Pavie

1892
The English
establish
protectorates on
the Arabian coast

1895
Baron Joseph
de Baye's
expedition
to Russia

1901
Rabindranath
Tagore founds
a school of
traditional
Indian arts in
Shantiniketan

1900
Establishment
of the École
française
d'Extrême-
Orient in Hanoi
(Vietnam).

1902
First Colonial
Exhibition in
Hanoi

**1906 and
1922**
Colonial
Exhibition in
Marseilles

1920
The Society of
Nations gives
Britain a
mandate over
Palestine, Jordan
and Iraq,
and France a
mandate over
the Lebanon
and Syria

1920-1930
Gandhi initiates
civil
disobedience
campaigns:
boycott of

imported
products and
promotion of
khadi, a fabric
woven in the
traditional
manner using a
spinning wheel,
an instrument
that became the
symbol of
anticolonialism
in India

1931
Colonial
exhibition in
Paris

1930-1931
The British
explorer Bertram
Thomas is the
first European to
cross the Arabian
Desert, the Rub'
al-Khali

1931-1932
The Citroën
"Croisière
Jaune" crosses
the Asian
continent from
Beirut to Peking

1945
Declaration
of Independence
by three
Indochinese
countries.
Creation of the
National Folk
Museum by the

American
military
government in
Seoul (South
Korea)

1949
Foundation of
the People's
Republic of China

1953
Foundation of
the Delhi Crafts
Museum (India),
devoted to tribal
ands rural crafts

1965
China institutes
the TAR (Tibet
Autonomous
Region)

1974
Opening of
the National
Ethnology
Museum in
Osaka (Japan)

1984
Foundation
of the Indian
National Trust
for Art and
Cultural Heritage
by Pupul Jayakar
and Indira
Gandhi

43
44

Map

1. Gie/Jeh
2. Muong
3. Miao (Guizhou)
4. Gejia
5. Hmong (Lao Cai)
6. Li
7. Phoutai
8. Êdê
9. Sedang
10. Tai Neua
11. Zhuang
12. Dong
13. Yao (Lao Cai, Lai Chau, Ha Giang)
14. Xa Pho
15. Phouan
16. Akha (Laos, Thailand, Myanmar)
17. Stieng
18. Bahnar
19. Lü
20. Jörai
21. Shan
22. Sré
23. Tai (Son La)
24. Kuy
25. Yi
26. Nivkh
27. Evens or Yukaghir
28. Evenks
29. Altaian
30. Ainu
31. Naga
32. Uzbek
33. Ladakhis
34. Mizos
35. Kondh
36. Punjabi
37. Assamais
38. Banjara
39. Gujerati
40. Turkomans
41. Aimaq
42. Hazara
43. Bedouins, tribe of the Sba'a Arabs
44. Bedouins of the Negev desert

Peoples and traditions of Siberia

Siberia is made up of approximately 20 ethnic groups speaking Ural-Altaic languages or, in rare cases, constituting separate linguistic entities. The extremely rich Siberian collections assembled since the end of the 19th century help us to better understand and appreciate the many different aspects of its cultures.

These societies evolved in the Arctic tundra of northern Siberia and in the dense Siberian forestland to the south. The populations that rely mainly on fishing have a semi-sedentary way of life, while those in the more southern regions, who live by hunting wild reindeer, or breeding reindeer or horses, are nomadic. Birch tree bark is the basic raw material for

communities throughout the Siberian taiga.
Durable, waterproof and easy to work, it is used
to make a wide range of everyday objects –
in particular, containers not used for cooking.
A variety of techniques and styles are identifiable,
depending on origin (Khante, Nivkh, etc.).
The museum has approximately one hundred
of these objects in its collections.

People in Siberia find a use for every part of the
reindeer. They eat the meat, carve its antlers into
countless sturdy objects, turn tendons into thread
for sewing, and use its hide and fur to cover huts
and make everyday or ritual clothing.

These aprons were fashioned from reindeer fur
by the Even tribes, while this Evenk shaman's
costume, collected by Joseph Martin at the end of
the 19th century, was made of chamois leather.
Fishing is practised throughout Siberia, often
as a secondary activity, but its produce in not
used as extensively. Nivkh fishermen stitch
together salmonid skins to make their clothes.
This beautiful ceremonial dress was worn by
the bride on the day she left her father's house
for her husband's. The upper back is made from
pieces of fish skin, cut and arranged like fish
scales. The various stylised motifs embroidered on
it are symbols designed to protect the wearer from

**Woman's
ceremonial dress**
Nivkh
Russia, far eastern
Siberia, Amour
River Basin
Late 19th-early
20th century
Fish skin
(salmonides)
H. 120 cm
Former
G. Montandon
collection
(collected
in 1919-1921)
Inv. 71.1934.15.105 D

Woman's apron
Evene or Ioukaghir
Russia,
northeastern
Siberia
19th-20th century
Reindeer fur,
beads
56 x 57 cm
Inv. 71.1966.46.145

**Bear, spirit
abode**
Nivkh
Russia,
far eastern
Siberia,
Sakhalin Island
19th century
Wood
4.3 x 12.8 cm
Donated by
P. Labbé
Inv. 71.1899.76.30

evil spirits. The centre of each scale and the cuffs are embroidered with bear's heads by the Nivkh embroideress whose skill was seen as magical.

_Evenk shaman's costume

This bulky shaman's costume, rich in symbolism, is considered to be the body that the shaman needs in order to mingle with the spirits during ritual ceremonies. The headdress, crowned with metal antlers, and the wild reindeer hide from which the costume is made evoke the image of deer, while the fringed sleeves look like birds' wings.

Symbolically, the shaman and his drum are the same: both are spirits. The drum may be seen as either the shaman's spirit-wife or as a wild

Shaman's costume
Evenk
Russia, eastern Siberia, Stanovoi Mountains
19th century
Chamois leather, metallic ornaments
H. 133 cm
Donated by J. Martin
Inv. 71.1887.42.1 to 71.1887.42.10

reindeer, and the drum stick as the essential link between the two. The red reindeer featured on this drum were meant to lead the shaman along the diurnal paths associated with the sun and the black reindeer, along the nocturnal paths that join up to the land of the dead. The drum stick with the elk's head probably served to lead the shaman along the former, while the one with the deer skull guided him along the latter. J.-L.L.

Ancestor spirit in a drum
Altai
Russia, southern Siberia, Altai
Late 19th-early 20th century
Wood, leather, skin
22 x 24.5 cm
Inv. 71.1966.46.129

Spirit abode hung on the wall of a dwelling.
The two ribbons are offerings.

Anthropomor-phic figurine, spirit abode
Evenk
Russia, eastern Siberia, Stanovoi Mountains
Late 19th century
Wood, beads, chamois leather
9 x 30 cm
Donated by J. Martin
Inv. 71.1887.42.13

/ SHAMANISM IN SIBERIA

Shamanism is central to Siberian societies, where Christianity and Buddhism have not taken hold. Shamanism enables its practitioners to communicate with the spirits of nature that provide game, as well as with the deceased or with disease-bearing spirits. Although Europeans have focused their attention mainly on the figure of the shaman himself, his assisting spirits, both anthropomorphic and zoomorphic, play an essential role in rites and rituals. They are often kept out of sight at the bottom of a covered sled, or in a closed chest in a corner of the yurt. Each has a specific function: the tiger is supposed to cure stomach-aches and help in hunting, while the pair of Nivkh anthropomorphic statuettes ("husband" and "wife") protect the souls of crying children. The loon is one of the most important of the shaman's assisting spirits because of its ability to unite the worlds of air and water. J.-L.L.

The Ainu

The Ainu, an ethnic group from the North-Western Pacific islands, reached their apogee around the 13th and 14th centuries when their population numbered between 100,000 and 200,000. Most of them have now been absorbed into Japanese culture.

The Ainu are thought to have been the first inhabitants of northern Japan; their territory also comprised the Sakhaline Islands, the Kouriles and southern Kamtchatka. The origin of this ethnic group of hunter-fishers is an enigma. Their language belongs to no known linguistic family, and their physical features and customs are quite different from those of neighbouring groups. Like some of these, however, they rear bear cubs, which are ritually put to death during the "Bear Feast".

They wear wide, overlapping garments. Men's clothing usually reaches to just below the knee, while women's are longer. Made from elm bark fibres, or occasionally from nettle, these colourful items of clothing are decorated with complex geometrical motifs that remain hard to interpret. J.-L.L.

Man's robe
Ainu
Russia, far eastern Siberia, Sakhalin
Late 19th century
Elm bark phloem, cotton, striped cloth, appliqué, embroidery
H. 122 cm
Donated by P. Labbé
Inv. 71.1899.76.94

Japanese stencil decoration

In Japan, dyed fabrics come in a wide range of forms, depending on the motifs, colours and methods used. Stencil dyeing is one of these techniques: it goes back to the 8th century and is still practised today.

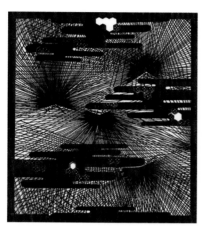

Stencil decoration uses plates made from sheets of paper that are superimposed and glued together with the sap of the persimmon tree (Japanese kaki), which makes them waterproof, and the patterns then cut out. A network of silk threads stretched between the plates keeps the design elements in place, and a thick pigment, or paste, is applied to the areas that have been cut out before the colours are applied. Sometimes the design consists of a single large motif, but more often it is a repeat pattern, used mainly for clothing. Garments are always made from panels of the same width, between 35 and 40 cm, assembled selvedge to selvedge, without seams at the shoulders. Stencil size is dictated by the panel's dimension, and the number of stencils by the number of colours planned. The repeat pattern requires that the seams be carefully calculated so that when the garment is assembled, it creates a harmonious overall effect of patterned and un-patterned areas in an asymmetrical single or multi-coloured design. The iconography combines geometrical and naturalistic shapes in a rich symbolism that is common to all Japanese decorative arts. F.C.

Stencils
Japan
19th century
Bark paper,
persimmon
(Japanese kaki)
sap, silk thread
55 x 42 cm
and 40 x 30 cm
Donated by
Maison Rodier
(collected by
P. Rodier in
the early 20th
century)
Inv. 71.1962.78.613
and 71.1962.78.565

Han China

China has many ethnic groups, or "nationalities", with the Han – named after one of the country's greatest dynasties – accounting for 93% of the total population.

_Emperor Yongzheng First Furrow rite

This silk painting, the third roll of an Imperial Academy painting, depicts the First Furrow Ceremony, which was held annually at the Temple of Agriculture, on the first day of the second springtime period.

After honouring the mythical emperor Shennong – inventor of agriculture and discoverer of the medicinal properties of various plants – in the Temple's main sanctuary, Emperor Yongzheng (1723-1735) would plough three furrows from east to west, using a plough yoked to a buffalo. Behind him followed a high-ranking courtier carrying a whip, along with the warden of Peking holding a container filled with seeds, which were sown by the Minister of Finance. Court dignitaries finished the work of cultivating the field and, in the Autumn, its harvest was stored in a special loft and reserved for offerings made to the temple god. The First Furrow rite, which opens the agricultural season, is still practised today by many Southeast Asian peoples.

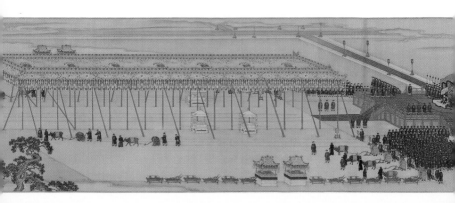

_Shadow theatre in Hebei province

This donkey-hide figure is characteristic of Hebei province, a major shadow theatre centre. It is part of the 18th century theatre complex owned by the famous puppet master, Luan Zhou. The puppeteer manipulates his characters between the screen and light source using three rods, one for the body and two for the arms. Puppets are made from translucent animal hide, which allows colours to filter through. The plays performed are not specific to shadow theatre, but make use of the same themes and stories as live theatre. As in classical opera, there are four main types of characters: men's roles (*sheng*), women's roles (*dan*), painted faces (*jing*), and clowns (*chou*). A small orchestra plays along with the action, providing rhythm (percussion instruments) and accompanying the singing (wind or string instruments). Originally, shadow theatre played an important part in funeral rites and at seasonal festivals. C.H.

Shadow puppet: cart
Han
China, Hebei province
18th century
Donkey hide
L. 49.5 cm
Former
J. Pimpaneau collection
Inv. 71.1990.108.84.1-2

Furrow Rite
Han
China, Qing dynasty, Yongzheng period (1723-1735)
Painted silk on paper
64 x 384 cm
Donated by Mme la générale Frey
Inv. 71.1939.37.1.1

From Dong Son to the present

From the 8th to 6th centuries B.C. up to the 1st and
2nd centuries A.D., the Southeast Asian Dongsonian
civilization (named after the Dong Son site in northern
Vietnam) was at the height of its glory. The bronze
drums found all the way from China to Insular South East
Asia first appeared at this time.

The drum exhibited in the museum was probably
discovered in Indonesia, and is one of the largest
ever to have been catalogued. Drums are the most
representative objects of the Dongsonian
civilization and are, by tradition, closely linked
to rituals. In China, they were inhabited by spirits
and played to invoke rainfall. Symbolising the
souls of ancestors, they belonged to dignitaries,
who used them in war. The custom of burying a
drum with its deceased owner exists among
the Han, as well as among minority groups in
the south.

**Anthropomor-
phic scarecrow**
Gie/Jeh (Die)
Vietnam,
Kon Tum,
basketwork,
pigments
119.5 x 114 cm
Donated by
F. Laforest
(collected in
1955-1956)
Inv. 71.1956.44.13
*The plane depicted
at the rear is a
reference to war
experience and
adds to its power.*

/ FUNERAL DRUM

Invaluable evidence of the contemporary use of Dongsonian drums, this instrument was given to Professor Rivet, founder of the Musée de l'Homme (Museum of Mankind), in 1933 by a member of a powerful Muong aristocratic family. The drum was buried in a secret place while the head of the family was still alive, then removed from the ground for his funeral, and reburied until his son's funeral. This particular drum belonged to the donator's brother, who died childless, thus bringing an end to its usefulness. In 1937, during her ethnographic expedition to Vietnam, Jeanne Cuisinier catalogued drums belonging to aristocratic Muong families. She reported that: "Drums are no longer to be found in the possession of all feudal lords. Some have been sold, others left behind and hidden when a family left the area, and still others buried along with the dead in whose funerals they were used. It cannot be said for certain whether tradition dictated that drums should always be buried with the dead, but the rarity of these objects and the absence of very old examples in families would lead one to believe so". The Vietnamese, like the Shan in Myanmar, continued to make drums up to the early 19th century. C.H.

Today, the Miao, the Zhuang and the Yi, in China, and the Lolo and the Tai, in Vietnam, use bronze drums at weddings, and during agricultural or new lunar year ceremonies. The Karen people of Myanmar also use them to summon rain. Among the Kantou in southern Laos, they are the property of the whole village and are brought out for major community rituals during which large numbers of buffalo are sacrificed. Some objects of power used by the populations of the central highlands of the Indochinese peninsula still bear a central star-shaped, bronze drum motif. Long identified with the sun or moon, it is now defined as a symbolic "vital centre". C.H.

Bronze funeral drum
Muong
Vietnam, Hoa Binh province
18th-19th century
H. 37.5 cm, diam. 60 cm
P. Rivet mission, 1931-1932
Inv. 71.1932.41.113

Bronze drum
Indonesia, Java
4th-1st century BC
H. 113 cm, diam. 148 cm
Former collection of the Musée Barbier-Mueller, Geneva
Inv. 70.2001.27.579

Peoples of Asia: tradition and modernity among the Miao/Hmong

The Chinese minority group known as the Miao comprises four linguistic entities. The main one is the Hmong, who were the largest group to emigrate to the Southeast Asian peninsula. The Musée du Quai Branly exhibits over 300 costumes and textiles that illustrate the rich variety in their style of clothing.

Clothing and jewellery play a major role in the social life of the Miao/Hmong as they are a mark of identity and social status. Each sub-group, each village, and sometimes each family, can be distinguished by subtle variations on traditional motifs, with remarkably successful combinations of batik, embroidery, appliqué and weaving. The making of clothing, from the growing of the hemp right up to the finished garment, is women's work. Little girls learn to sew and

Woman's skirt
Miao
China, Guizhou
province, Pinyong
20th century
Cotton, silk, indigo
Resist dyeing
(batik),
calandering,
appliqué
H. 61 cm
Inv. 70.2000.2.9

embroider at a very early age. By puberty, they already have the trousseau of costumes, baby slings and blankets needed during their first years of married life. To attract suitors they wear their finest creations and most valuable silver jewellery at festivals and on market days.

This enables young girls to show off their skills, prove their willingness to work, and demonstrate their family's wealth – making them attractive to young men and their parents.

Pleated skirts are worn by almost all groups. Made from one to three horizontally stitched panels, or sometimes as many as 30 when they are stitched vertically, skirts require fabric lengths of 20 metres or more. On the peninsula, skirts are simply starched and stitched in parallel to keep

Woman's costume
Miao (Qing Miao)
China, Guizhou province, Liuzhi
20th century
Cotton, silk, hemp, felt, hair, wool, wood
Brightly coloured resist dyeing (batik), embroidery, appliqué
Inv. 71.1993.68.1-4

Woman's costume
Gejia
China, Guizhou province, Huangping
20th century
Cotton, silk
Resist dyeing (batik), embroidery, appliqué
Inv. 71.1991.5.1.1-4

the pleats in place. On some regions of China, they are left to dry around a basket, tightly bound with cord, or are sometimes put inside a wide bamboo tube and steam heated. The finer the pleat, the more valuable the skirt.

Clothing and ornamentation also indicate age. Young girls from Zhenfeng in Guizhou wear a silver chain fastened to a hairpin but only before they marry. Gejia women put aside their red headdresses once they are married and wear their hair in a small chignon after their first child is born. Jewellery is a sign of wealth, but in the poorest regions, affluence may be shown by wearing a multitude of scarves bought at the market, or by red wool added to the chignon, as in the Nankai Mountains in Guizhou or in the north of Vietnam.

**Central part
of a baby-sling
(detail)**
Miao
China, Guizhou
province, Geyi
Late 19th century
Cotton, silk,
cloth, extra weft
decoration
130 x 74 cm
Former É. Boudot
collection
Inv. 71.1996.3.13

/ A LONG HISTORY

The culture of Miao groups is an ancient one. We find the Miao mentioned, under the generic term man, "southern barbarians", in Chinese records dating as far back as the time of the Warring States (475-221 B.C.). The term referred to non-Han groups of mountain people of all allegiances. These "Miao" did not form a distinct group until the last years of the Ming dynasty (1368-1664). Since the 18th century, the historical (i.e. identifiable) Miao, who populate a vast mountainous region but are mainly concentrated in Guizhou province, have undergone hard times, with frequent peasants' revolts invariably followed by bloody suppressions by imperial troops. These struggles were the main cause of their gradual dispersal throughout the southern Chinese provinces. Today they number around 9 million, while in the north of peninsular Southeast Asia, the furthermost region to which they migrated, there are currently about 1.2 million Miao, almost all of them Hmong. C.H. and J.M.

Exuberant clothing and hairstyles are the privilege of the young who, here as elsewhere, follow fashion. Techniques, like tastes, change and adapt to the market. Girls attending school spend less time than their elders making clothes, and have taken to using synthetic fabrics. Delicately woven designs are being replaced by embroidery. Motifs, which used to be geometric and abstract, are becoming figurative, inspired by Chinese, Vietnamese, Laotian and Thai cultures. Industrial fabrics are being substituted for weaving, and sewing machines replacing hand stitching.
In every area where the modern world is taking hold, especially in and around towns, costumes are now only worn for festivals – in particular at tourist events.

Women's costume
Hmong Len (Floral Hmong)
Vietnam, Lao Cai Province, Muong Khuong
Early 20th century
Cotton, hemp
Resist dyeing (batik), appliqué, embroidery
Collected for the Colonial Exhibition, Paris, 1931
Inv. 71.1931.42.41.1-5

A few traditions, however, refuse to die.
The Miao women of Danzhai in Guizhou, like
the Hmong of Sa Pa in Vietnam, who nowadays
wear trousers, make certain that when they die,
a hemp skirt – made specifically for their funeral
– is placed in their coffin. The traditional garment
will enable their ancestors to recognize them.
Today, many fine old pieces have ended up in
private and public collections. In some cases,
in particular among the Miao of Guizhou, the
items were sold by the women themselves, who
took in the profits. The "ethnic industry"
is very much in vogue, but unfortunately it also
attracts many unscrupulous dealers. C.H. and J.M.

Women's jackets
*Hmong Len
(Floral Hmong)*
Vietnam, Lao Cai
province, Muong
Khuong and
Bac Ha
1975, 1985, 1994
and 2000
Cotton and
polyester
Appliqué and
(hand, then
machine)
embroidery
C. Hemmet
mission
Inv. 71.1994.45.35.1,
71.1994.45.36.1,
71.1995.36.1
and 71.2000.9.2

ASIAN TEXTILES

Asian textiles and clothing are a documentary and iconographic treasure trove, and provide much information about man's relationship with the natural world, with his fellow human beings, as well as with the after life. A wide range of raw materials is used: some of these – such as cotton or silk – are known worldwide, while others – such as ramie or elm tree bark – are much less common and require special processing before use.

Decorative techniques include most of those practised throughout the world. In weaving, decorative elements are created through additional wefts and the *ikat* technique provides a wide palette. The same is true of dyeing and embroidery procedures, and those used to apply various design elements after weaving. Technical constraints, aesthetic choices and symbolic imagery all come together to define the decorative styles specific to each culture. F.C.

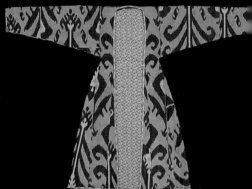

2

3

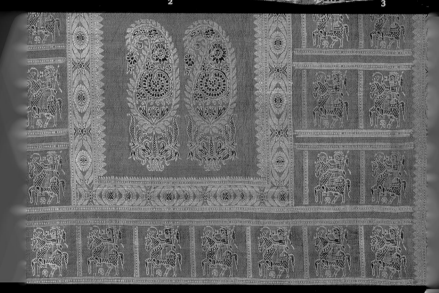

5 / Man's coat
Uzbek
Uzbekistan,
Bukhara
Late 19th century
Silk, gold thread,
silver thread
Flat-stitch
embroidered
velvet on
padding,
taffeta lining,
Warp ikat, corded
warp braid
H. 140 cm
Inv. 71.1989.24.29.3

5

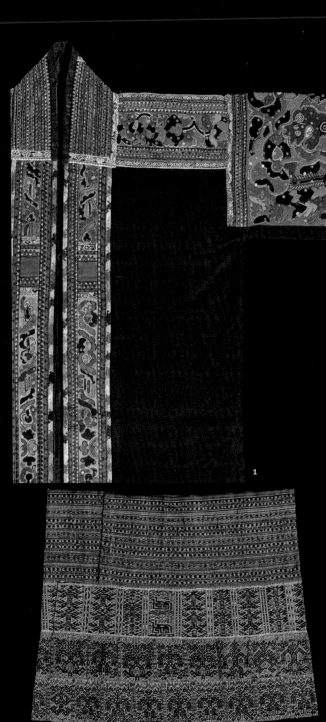

1/Woman's jacket
Miao
China, Guizhou province, Shidong
20th century
Cotton, silk thread, sequins
Twill weaving, indigo dye, relief embroidery, appliqué
H. 95 cm
Inv. 71.1991.5.5

2/Woman's skirt
Li
China, Hainan Island
19th century
Cotton
Four horizontally joined lengths of cloth, extra weft decoration, or extra weft depending on length
H. 29.5 cm
Inv. 70.2002.37.29

3/Wall hanging "with ships" (detail)
Cambodia
Early 20th century
Silk, twill, weft ikat (*hol*)
88 x 208 cm
Donated by the Agence de la France d'outre-mer (Colonial Exhibition, Paris, 1931)
Inv. 71.1962.22.115

4/Section of a woman's marriage bag (detail)
Miao
China, Guizhou province, Liping
Early 20th century
Cotton, silk, vegetable dyes, cloth, extra weft
26.5 x 22.5 cm
Inv. 70.2001.23.31

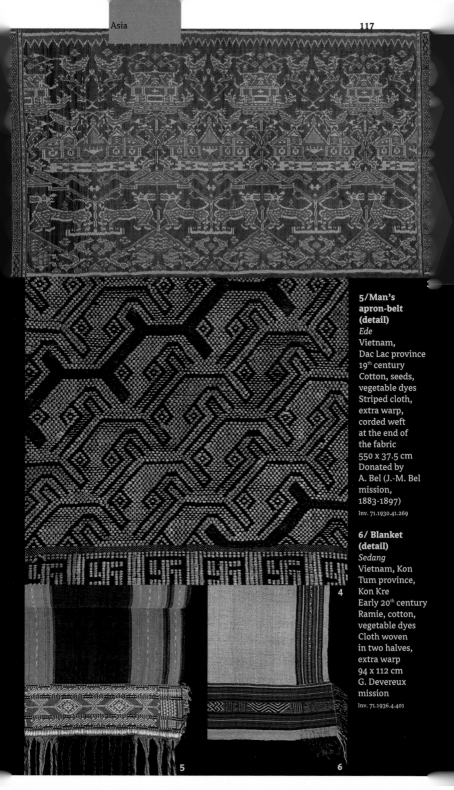

5/ Man's apron-belt (detail)
Ede
Vietnam, Dac Lac province
19th century
Cotton, seeds, vegetable dyes
Striped cloth, extra warp, corded weft at the end of the fabric
550 x 37.5 cm
Donated by A. Bel (J.-M. Bel mission, 1883-1897)
Inv. 71.1930.41.269

6/ Blanket (detail)
Sedang
Vietnam, Kon Tum province, Kon Kre
Early 20th century
Ramie, cotton, vegetable dyes
Cloth woven in two halves, extra warp
94 x 112 cm
G. Devereux mission
Inv. 71.1936.4.401

Peoples of Asia: age and status
Southern China and Southeast Asia encompass one
of the largest varieties of ethnic groups in the world,
with languages belonging to five major families.
Most of these peoples originally came from China,
where the majority still live today.

_Costumes as markers of identity
In China, the largest groups are those who speak
the Tai languages – 16 million Zhuang, 3 million
Dong, 1.2 million Dai, the Buyi, etc. In the first
millennium, many of them began to settle
in the high valleys of the north Vietnamese
mountains: the Tay and the Nung in the east,
then the Tai Khao (White Tai) and Tai Dam (Black
Tai) in the west and in Laos, the Shan in Myanmar.
Some groups descended to the plains of Laos
and Thailand and set up their own states.
All weaving and decorative techniques are
represented here. In most groups, Tai women

**Woman's
costume**
Tai Neua
Laos, Houa Phan
or Xieng Khouang
province
Early 20th century
Cotton, silk

Extraweft,
appliqué
M. Colani mission
(collected circa
1930)
Inv. 71.1933.37.154
and 71.1934.62.148

Woman's ceremonial jacket
Zhuang
South China
19ᵗʰ century
Silk, cotton, gilt paper, silver, embroidery, appliqué
H. 55 cm
Mme A. François bequest
Inv. 71.1974.92.432

Woman's jacket (detail)
Dong
China, Guizhou province, Liping
20ᵗʰ century
Cotton, silk
Calendering, embroidery, appliqué, extra weft
H. 99 cm
M.-C. Kuo-Quiquemelle mission
Inv. 71.1995.50.7.2

wear tubular skirts that combine Ikat, weaving and brocade work, the most elaborate of which were produced in Laos. Most women have stopped wearing the traditional jacket. Only the Tai Dam still wear a shirt, brightly coloured these days, and fastened by silver buttons shaped like butterflies, cicada or bees. The Tai Lu of Vietnam also continue to wear the traditional jacket in everyday life, its close-fitting cut highlighted by a row of silver coins.

There are over 2 million Yao, members of the Miao-Yao linguistic family, in China. They came to Vietnam as early as the 13ᵗʰ century, where they number 500,000 today, then to Laos and Thailand, where they constitute a population of around 40,000. Yao women are famed for their

remarkable embroidery, done from memory on the back of the fabric, without the help of patterns. True works of art, their costumes take nearly a year to complete.

Jewellery and clothing, varying in their magnificence, indicate both the wearer's social status and age group. Each village is a homogenous cultural family with its own particular style adopted by all of the villagers with hardly a dissonant note. Everywhere, however, young girls and married women wear specific costumes or hairstyles that immediately identify

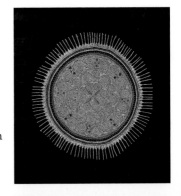

**Woman's
costume**
Yao
Vietnam,
Lao Cai province
Late 19th century
Cotton, silk,
wool, silver,
glass beads
Embroidery,
appliqué
Donated by
Mme Barbencot
(collected by
Colonel Barbencot
between 1900
and 1912)

Inv. 71.1932.74.1

their status. The Tai Dam wear a chignon once
they are married. On market days and at festivals,
young "Red Yao" women from both sides of
China's border with Vietnam wear voluminous
red turbans adorned with multitudes of pompoms
cascading down their backs. Their elders are
always much more soberly attired. The birth
of the first child, more important than marriage
itself, is announced by details on costume
or hairstyle. In the same region, Hani of the
Lopi group wear a thick braid wrapped around
their head when the first child is born; when
the second arrives, two more braids are added,
worn high on the forehead.

_The Akha bonnet
Costume is a major indicator of age group,
in particular among the Yao and, even more
so, the Tibeto-Burmese and starts at birth with

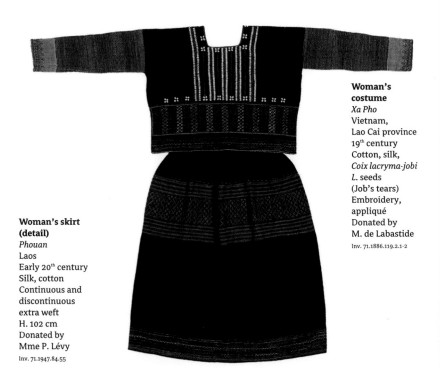

Woman's costume
Xa Pho
Vietnam,
Lao Cai province
19th century
Cotton, silk,
*Coix lacryma-jobi
L.* seeds
(Job's tears)
Embroidery,
appliqué
Donated by
M. de Labastide
Inv. 71.1886.119.2.1-2

**Woman's skirt
(detail)**
Phouan
Laos
Early 20th century
Silk, cotton
Continuous and
discontinuous
extra weft
H. 102 cm
Donated by
Mme P. Lévy
Inv. 71.1947.84.55

the progression in the style of bonnets worn by children. The Tibeto-Burmese group, which covers an enormous territory, is a vast and complex entity. It brings together peoples from the Himalayan regions, the Naga of Northeastern India and Myanmar (3 million), the Yi of China (around 8 million), and the Hani and the Akha of China's Yunnan province and surrounding areas (around 2 million). It also includes for the majority of Myanmar's population. In Vietnam, along its border with China, small Lahu, Hani (Lopi and Akha), and Yi communities form part of this linguistic group.

Among the Akha, boys and girls under the age of seven wear a skullcap of soft indigo cloth decorated with horizontal and vertical rows of buttons, white seeds, cowry shells or silver-plated cupules, and often adorned with pompoms and coins. At the age of seven, this is replaced for girls

by a skullcap decorated with alternate strips of
embroidery and braiding, and including half-
lozenge motifs evocative of dogs' teeth and
serving to protect the wearer. The mother gives a
third headdress to her daughter when the latter
reaches puberty, with strings of seeds (Job's-tears)
or miniature gourds attached to it indicating the
status of "marriageable daughter".

An Akha wife's headdress comprises a vegetal
support covered with indigo cotton cloth forming
an egg-shaped (Akha Loimi), conical (Akha Ulo),
cylindrical (Akha Opa) or trapezoidal (Akha
Phami). The outside is almost totally covered

**Married
woman's
headdress**
Akha Loimi
North Laos
20th century
Silver, bamboo,
cotton, coins,
metal, seeds,
wool, squirrel
fur, plastic
C. Hemmet
mission, 1989
Inv. 71.1989.42.1

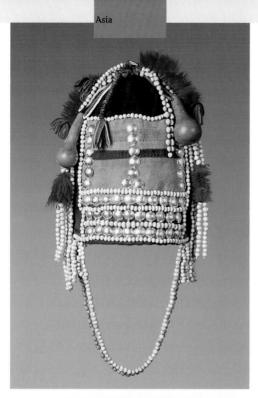

Girl's bonnet
Akha Loimi
Thailand, Chiang
Rai province,
Mae Sai
Late 20th century
Cotton, seeds,
gourds, metal,
squirrel fur,
appliqué
C. Hemmet
mission, 1989
*Gourds indicate
that she is
marriageable.*
Inv. 71.1989.41.1

**Baby boy's
bonnet**
Akha Loimi
North Thailand
Late 20th century
Cotton, seeds,
silver, squirrel
fur, embroidery,
appliqué
C. Hemmet
mission, 1992
Inv. 71.1992.15.7

**Young girl's
headdress**
Akha
Myanmar,
Shan State
Early 20th century
Cotton, silk, silver,
cowry shells, seeds,
metal, scarabs,
porcelain buttons
Donated by
Mme de
Chambure, 1944
Inv. 71.1944.12.1

with regularly spaced silver-plated hemispheres,
and decorated with silver coins (Indochinese
piastres or British Indian rupees), from which
hang rows of metal disks or half-disks.
Each change of headdress is accompanied
by a domestic ritual symbolically marking
the acquisition of a new status. The nuptial
ceremony, the culmination of these female rites,
requires a total change in dress. C.H. and P.B.

ORNAMENTATION AMONG MOUNTAIN PEOPLES

Women, and most men, wear a profusion of silver, copper, brass, seed or glass pearl jewellery. The Hmong and the Yao have a particular penchant for solid silver jewellery; the Hani like to attach it to their clothes or, like the Nung, make works of art of their buttons and fasteners. These adornments represent a family's wealth, add to its status and show that a man is taking care of his family. Traditionally, men from the Central Highlands of the peninsula adorned their chignons with combs decorated with pins and feathers. This was not only for the sake of elegance, but was also a form of decoration worn at festivals and in battle. C.H.

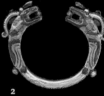

2

1/Woman's hair ornament
Yao Lan Tien
Vietnam, Ha Giang province
19th-20th century
Silver, bone, rattan, horsehair
Diam. 80 cm
Donated by C. and H. Péri (collected by H. Péri in 1933)
Inv. 71.1938.121.13

2/Bracelet
Yao
Vietnam, Lai Chau or Lao Cai province
19th-20th century
Silver, enamel
P. Rivet mission, 1931-1932
Inv. 71.1932.41.101.1

3/Torque
Dong
China, Guizhou
province
19th-20th century
Silver
30 x 33 cm,
2.178 kg
Former P. Fatin
collection
Inv. 70.2004.24.1

**4/Man's
Ghignon comb**
Stieng
Central Vietnam,
Highlands
Early 20th century
Wood, pewter
22 x 6.5 cm
Donated by
M. Pagés
Inv. 71.1933.11.2

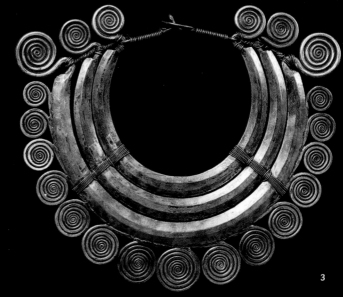

3

4

5/Man's hairpin
Bahnar
Vietnam, Kon
Tum province
Early 20th century
Aluminium, glass
beads, copper,
aluminium
and silver wire
H. 53 cm
P. Rivet mission,
1931-1932
Inv. 71.1932.41.193

6/Bracelet
Lu
Laos, Phongsaly
province
Silver
8.3 x 11.4 cm
Collected for
the Colonial
Exhibition, Paris,
1931
Inv. 71.1931.42.88.4

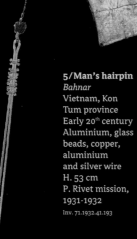

5

6

Harmony with nature

Southeast Asian cultures have often been defined as living in harmony with nature. They all belong to a civilization where the group lives in total harmony with the natural cycle. The museum's Southeast Asian collections are an invaluable source of information on village people of the early 20th century.

Flat basket
Sedang (or Jorai)
Vietnam, Kon
Tum province
19th century
Bamboo
basketwork,
vegetable binding
56.5 x 60 cm
Donated by
A. Bel
(J.-M. Bel mission,
1883-1897)
Inv. 71.1930.41.117

_Predominance of plant life

Agriculture provides a wide range of edible vegetables, as well as tobacco, cotton, hemp, plants used for dyes, and gourds to serve as containers. Forests supply the basic materials for everyday use. Wood, bamboo and rattan are used in both the construction of houses and the production of household objects.

Village dwellings are usually built on stilts and normally accommodate an extended family: grandparents, parents, unmarried children, the first married couple, and sometimes even the couples that follow – at least a dozen people in all. More rarely, smaller homes house nuclear families (a couple and their children).

Furniture is generally designed to store food, as well as clothing and precious objects. Everywhere, gathering, trapping, hunting and, above all, fishing are essential to providing food. The gathering of leaves, fruits and tubers is a regular activity, especially between harvests when rice supplies become short, and meat is obtained by trapping small animals and hunting,

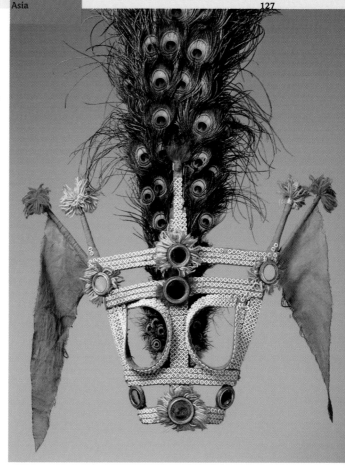

**Mask for bull
leading a caravan**
Shan
Myanmar,
Shan State
Early 20th century
Peacock feathers,
bamboo, fabric,
porcelain
buttons, wool
pompoms,
mirrors
H. 154 cm
Donated by Mme
de Chambure
Inv. 71.1939.40.26

Machete
Sre
Vietnam, Lam
Dong province
Bamboo, metal,
leather, pewter
decoration
99 x 13.6 cm
Donated by
J. Berthelin
Inv. 71.1953.3.1
*Given by the head
of the village
to Captain
Berthelin on
the occasion
of his wedding.*

with rifles or crossbows. But it is fishing, in rivers
or paddy fields, where fish traps are the
instrument of choice, which is the most common
activity for men, women and children alike.

_Mountain peoples
Mountainous regions are slash-and-burn
territories – areas for itinerant dry farming on
burned land. A stretch of forestland is burnt at
the end of the dry season. To sow it, men with
digging sticks make seed holes in which the
women place the seeds. Harvesting takes place
at the end of the rainy season. Protection
of growing crops is ensured by performing
numerous rites, as well as by an assortment
of scarecrows, sometimes equipped with moving
noisemakers set in motion by wind or water.
The machete, a tool specific to the populations

Oil lamp
Muong
Vietnam, Thanh
Hoa province
Early 20th century
Wood, bamboo,
terracotta
32.5 x 33.5 cm
M. Colani mission
Inv. 71.1930.75.34.1-2

of the central highlands of the Indochinese
peninsula, is used for work, for war, and also in
ceremonies. It can rapidly hack a path through
thick undergrowth, open up a clearing
in the forest, cut wood for the kitchen or, if
necessary, defend its owner. Made from bent-
to-shape bamboo, it is carried balanced on
the shoulder with the blade pointing upwards.
The most finely worked machetes are used
as ornaments for ceremonies and as offerings
on important occasions.

The back basket, which is always made by men,
is a carrying instrument specific to the mountain
regions. The most common type has straps.
Among the Khmou and some of the Tai, the basket
is equipped with a forehead band, while among
the Akha, it has both a forehead band and back
support so that the weight is evenly distributed
between the head and shoulders. Some small
baskets are carried at the waist. They usually hold
personal items or are used as containers for seeds
during sowing, or for rice grain during the time
of the harvest when the grain is picked by hand
from the stalk.

Jewel box
Sedang
Vietnam, Kon Tum province
Early 20th century
Multicoloured basketwork, bamboo strips with carved decoration
H. 9.5 cm, diam. 28.5 cm
P. Rivet mission, 1931-1932
Inv. 71.1932.41.209

Ceremonial sword
Vietnam, Son La province
19th-20th century
Metal, ivory hilt, repoussé silver decoration
L. 64.6 cm
Collected for the Colonial Exhibition, Paris, 1931
Inv. 71.1931.42.301

/ TAI SWORDS

The Tai-speaking peoples originated in southern China, where they number around 30 million, and then spread across the whole of continental Southeast Asia. They can be found in Vietnam (3 million in the northern mountains), in Myanmar (the Shan), and in Northeastern India (the Ahom). Always organized into chiefdoms, with noble families, they established confederations that were sometimes very powerful. The Thais and the Lao set up their own states in the vast plains they occupied. Decorated knives and swords, handed down from elder to elder, indicate the rank of their owner. Many have worked ivory handles, and the finest are covered with silver or even gold, Tai goldsmiths being held in high esteem. Worn on ceremonial occasions, they also represent the symbolic "presence" of the noble family at the altar during a variety of rites. C.H.

_Peoples of the plains and valleys

The Khmer developed a remarkable civilization, which is still evident in the objects used in daily village life. Woodcarving with traditional designs adorns everyday utensils. The serpent-shaped sickle, representing *nâga*, the ophidian spirit so popular in Cambodia, is a true work of art. To harvest his crop, the farmer thrusts the sickle's "wing" (blade?) into the paddy-field, draws it back to grab the fully formed sheaf with his left hand, then thrusts it in again to cut the stalks. This sickle remained in use in the Phnom Penh region until the end of the 20th century.

Weaving sley in the form of a dragon
Kuy
Cambodia, Kampong Thom province, Cheom Ksan
Late 19th century
Wood
52.8 x 18.3 cm
Donated by G. Naudin
Inv. 71.1934.1.30

Sickle in the form of a *nâga* snake
Khmer
Wood, metal
51 cm
Collected for the Colonial Exhibition, Paris, 1931
Inv. 71.1931.80.17

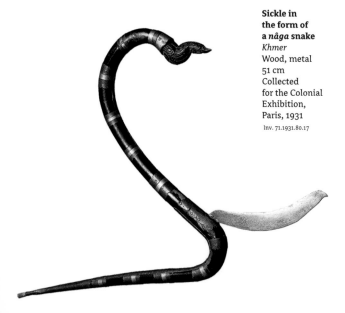

Ritual manuscript
Yi (Nossu)
China
19th-20th century
Ink on paper
48 x 33 cm
Inv. 70.2004.7.15

In mountainous regions, inhabitants of lower altitude areas are organized very differently from those who live higher up. Valley peoples, the Tai in particular, grow their rice in paddy fields terraced up the mountain slopes, which requires the building of numerous irrigation networks and an extensive use of the bucket waterwheel. C.H.

/ WRITING AND ORAL TRADITIONS

Most mountain people have no written language. Among those who do, the Yao write their language in Chinese ideograms, as do the Tai in the east (the Zhuang in China and the Tay in Vietnam), while all other groups use an Indian alphabet. A few Tibeto-Burmese, including the Yi, have ritual manuscripts whose partly pictographical writing is known only by shamans (and religious or medical specialists).

The enormously rich body of oral traditions among the populations with no written language is not easily accessible. Customs and tales of justice rendered in verse form, of courtship, myths, legends, sagas, epics: the art of the spoken word and poetry fill every moment of communal life. This oral literature contains the memory of traditions going back over hundreds of years, although a good part of it is now threatened with extinction. C.H.

Theravâda Buddhism and indigenous rites
The great cultural influences of India and China, which also introduced writing and religion, spread throughout the plains of Southeast Asia, but had little effect on mountain region cultures.

_Buddhism in daily life
"Indianised" Southeast Asia has experienced Buddhism in a variety of forms since the beginning of the first millennium A.D. Around the 14th century, societies in the region adopted Theravâda from Ceylon, along with the Pali canon, which still defines it today. The doctrine spread throughout the plains, where it has become the dominant element in a series of complex religious systems. Buddhism is practised as a way to gain merit, be reincarnated and eventually liberated from the Hindu karmic cycle. Rituals marking stages in a person's life are more or less Brahman in nature, and everyday life is full of spirits to which appropriate cults must be dedicated.

_Thai Buddhist amulets
Amulets, which are very popular in Thailand, come in many different forms, from images of Buddha and numerous other divine beings and spirits to symbolic or spontaneously created figures.
Phallic talismans, *palat khik*, always linked to fertility, were in use well before the advent of Brahmanism and the *Shivalinga* cult (worship

Tomb sculpture
Bahnar
Vietnam, Kon Tum province
Late 19th-early 20th century
Wood
H. 145 cm
Donated by F. Laforest
Inv. 71.1956.44.1

Anonymous, *Hmong woman.* North Vietnam, circa 1920.

**Dasajâtaka,
the final ten
incarnations
of the Buddha
(detail)**
Khmer
Cambodia
17th or 18th century
Painting on
canvas
192 x 86.4 cm
Donated by
the Municipal
Library of
Versailles
Inv. 71.1934.33.423

of the god Shiva in the form of a phallic stone).
They are often associated with an animal: the
tiger, symbol of strength and invulnerability,
the lizard, which keeps love alive and brings
victory, or the monkey, which ensures agility
and clever repartee.
These objects are usually made by monks,
luang phô, who are known for their supernatural
powers.

_Autochthonous cults

A wide range of religious systems exists among
the mountain people who have remained
untouched by Buddhism. However, the belief in
a multiplicity of "souls" and in the numerous
spirits that inhabit the earth and the sky, as well
as everyday objects, is omnipresent. Animal
sacrifice is always the cumulative point of rituals,
and the buffalo the most valued victim.
Burial rites are of utmost importance and explain
the care taken over the preparation of the tomb.
Tomb sculptures by the Jorai and Bahnar of
Vietnam are among the most remarkable
examples of this art form. The sculptures are
carved during the "leaving the tomb" ceremony,
when the final tomb is built, decorated, then
abandoned. The human and animal figures
adorning the tombs are servants of the deceased
in the after world. This type of statue, with hands
crossed on knees, is the *bram*, a masked man who,
even today, plays a role in funerary rites. C.H.

**Phallic amulet,
seated figure,**
Thai
Thailand
Late 20th century
Wood
H. 6.9 cm
C. Hemmet
mission
Inv. 71.1988.13.11

Himalayan Buddhism and village traditions

The Himalayan world, where India and China meet up, is populated by many ethnic groups, each with its own language and customs. It encompasses a range of ecological environments in which Buddhism, Hinduism, Islam and indigenous beliefs co-exist, and often intermingle.

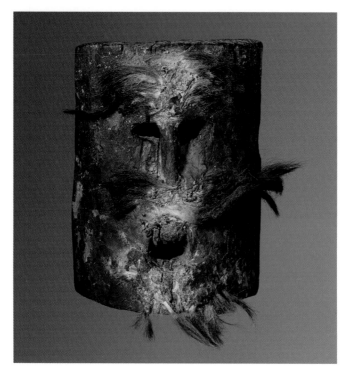

Anthropo-morphic mask
Nepal
19th century
Wood, goat's hair, clay, resin
22 x 16 cm
Former M. Petit collection
Inv. 70.2003.1.10
Mask possibly representing a forest spirit.

Protecting deity of Buddhist law, syncretic form of Mahâkâla and Pal-ldan-lha-mo
Ritual Buddhist painting (*thang-ka*)
China, Tibetan Marches
Late 17th century
Tempera on unfinished canvas
105 x 136.6 cm
Donated by J. Bacot
Inv. 71.1934.27.1

Little was known about the old Himalayan kingdoms until the mid 20th century, as they remained protected by the rigorous mountain topology. Difficulty of access made the region a place of mystery, stirring the imagination and curiosity of Western explorers, from the time of the religious missions of the 17th century and the scientific expeditions of the early 20th century, through to the ethnographical surveys of modern times.

The first objects obtained for the museum's collections reveal the appeal of Vajrayana Buddhism (an esoteric offshoot of Great Wheel Buddhism, with beliefs and rituals similar to those of Hinduism). They are ornamentation worn by officiating Tantric priests, portable paintings (*thang-ka*), manuscripts, ritual musical instruments made from bone, and dance masks, which were collected in Tibet and in Tibetan Marches (Sino-Tibetan "frontier") in the early years of the 20th century by famed travellers such as Jacques Bacot and Alexandra David-Neel. Alongside these Tibetan objects, so heavily impregnated with Chinese influences, Indo-Nepalese influences are apparent, particularly in Buddhist statuary. A remarkable work attests to the richness of Nepalese artistic production:

Pe-rag woman's headdress for festive occasions,
Ladakhi
India, Ladakh
19th-20th century
Wool, turquoise, carnelians, coral, silver
122 x 90 cm
Inv. 71.1986.38.1-5

Shâkyamuni Buddha
Post-Gupta Nepalese art
Nepal
11th century
Copper, mercury gilt
H. 52.5 cm
Former collection of Mme la générale Frey
Inv. 71.1939.19.1

a subtly sculpted Buddha, at once gentle and sensuous, reflecting the elegant aesthetics of the 8th and 9th centuries.
Ethnological collections assembled in the 1960s have added to the number of small "catalogues raisonnés" offering insight into the cultures of a number of Himalayan peoples, in particular, man's relationship with his environment, and well-documented descriptions of everyday objects. Traditional festival finery adorned with good luck stones, protective and village cult objects, and a group of Nepalese masks all evoke aspects of local traditions dating back to pre-Buddhist times. These still little known masks were probably linked to ritual or festive village customs. Minimalist in style, they merge Hindu and Buddhist iconographical elements with features characteristic of animistic traditions. D.C.

Naga clothing and ornamentation

Today, the Naga number almost 3 million inhabitants.
They are grouped into 60 or so 'tribes' or sub-groups who
were once rivals and very much closed in on themselves,
and who all practised the tradition of headhunting.
The museum's collections, rich in items from the beginning
of the century from English and German collections,
illustrate the importance of this ancient tradition.

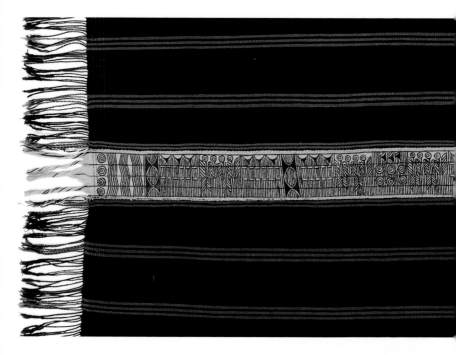

A major ethnic group in the eastern Himalayas,
the Naga inhabit the range of hills separating India
from Myanmar, to which they have given
their name (Naga Hills). Their culture is closely
tied to the practice of headhunting, an institution
linked to the idea of fertility and which
the British gradually brought to an end during
the colonial era.
Naga costumes and ornaments mark the identity
of both individuals and groups, and are used to
differentiate sub-groups, tribal sections, clans or
groups of villages. Whatever the entity, textiles

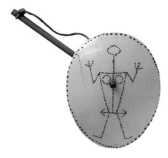

are always in three dominant colours: red, white and black. The main male garment is a cotton shawl, usually composed of three panels separately woven then stitched together, upon which straight lines and geometrical motifs are woven or embroidered. The central panel plays a special role as a background for motifs exalting the society's prowess in war or symbolising fertility: human heads, spears, felling-swords, tigers, and *mithan* (type of buffalo).

Men's ceremonial ornamentation is particularly elaborate. Within village communities, it indicates the wearer's social status and its use is strictly governed by tradition. The finest shawls, metal pendants and torques were once reserved for warriors who had brought back either a human trophy taken from the enemy, or a tiger, to their

Warrior's shawl (detail)
Naga Lhota
India, Nagaland
19ᵗʰ-20ᵗʰ century
Cotton, resin
131 x 167 cm
Former collection of the Pitt-Rivers Museum, Oxford
Inv. 71.1946.69.29

Man's necklace
Mizo
India, Mizoram
20ᵗʰ century
Animal claws (probably tiger), fabric, red glass beads, shells
68 cm
Former C. Niemoller collection
Inv. 70.2001.8.18

Warrior's arm ornament
Naga Angami
India, Nagaland
19ᵗʰ-20ᵗʰ century
Brass, goat's hair, *Coix lacryma-jobi L.* seeds. (Job's tears), yellow orchid stems, felt, rattan, hair
13 x 47.5 cm
Former collection of the Pitt-Rivers Museum, Oxford
Inv. 71.1946.69.3

Earring
Naga
India, Nagaland
20ᵗʰ century
Engraved Conch, bamboo, fibres, glass beads
H. 19 cm
Donated by M. and J. P. Barbier-Mueller
Inv. 70.2001.27.54

village. These adornments could also indicate a person who had made a major sacrifice at a "merit festival", a collective ceremony during which a feast is organised for the whole community and the organiser makes codified offerings. They culminate in the sacrifice of a *mithan* and the erection of a commemorative megalith. By organising a feast, a man can symbolically convert the distribution of food into social prestige, and earn dress and ornamentation privileges that often extend to his wife.
P.B.

Myth and ritual in India

The Musée de quai Branly's Indian collections evoke
the profusion of myths and rituals encountered in present-
day India. Shaped at the crossroads of many different
traditions – Hindu and other, scholarly and popular – these
myths and rituals serve as a springboard for artistic creation.

_Multiple traditions

The invention and development of myths and
rites, along with objects associated with them,
stem from the internal dynamics of Hinduism.
The rich scholarly Sanskrit traditions were
important, but so was the role played by various
popular traditions. For example, the repertoire of
the Andhra Pradesh shadow theatre comes from
the great Hindu epics (*Râmâyana* and *Mahâbhârata*),
originally written in Sanskrit but reinterpreted
in vernacular versions and by the storytellers
who recite them (an essentially oral tradition).
The collections lead one to look at indigenous
cultures and pan-Indian culture as two aspects

**Manasa, the
snake goddess**
India, Assam,
Goalpara
Mid 20th century
Wood, clay
coating, paper,
sapwood,
coloured
vegetable pith,
paint
60 x 89 cm
Donated by
G. Bertrand
Inv. 71.1956.45.98

Lankeshwar
Chitrakar
**Painting
of Yama**
India, Bihar,
Santal Pargana
20th century
Paper, cotton,
wood, pigments
140 x 30 cm
Donated by
J.-B. Faivre
Inv. 71.1981.59.119

*Tholubommalata
shadow figure,
"Sita under
his tree"*
India, Andhra
Pradesh
Early 20th century
Cut-out, stitched
and painted
deerskin or
goatskin
71 x 97 cm
Inv. 71.1967.25.47

of contemporary India that are constantly
interacting. The stories illustrated and told by
Bengali Hindus, using painted rolls, come mainly
from Hindu mythology although they are
addressed to the Santal, a non-Hindu people from
Northeastern India, especially at formal occasions
such as funerals.

On another level, specialists in classical Hindu
mythology were long uncertain about the correct
identification of Manasa the snake goddess.
She was the daughter of the Hindu god Shiva,
as well as the one who, according to pre-Hindu
tradition, strove to be worshipped in his place.
Her cult, which is central to contemporary
Bengali Hinduism, is also reminiscent of the
Bengali folktales and the snake cult common
to the entire subcontinent.

_Ritual and everyday life

The collections also show another aspect of Indian
culture, which does not dissociate ritual from
everyday life. Performances such as the recitation
of painted rolls and the *tholubommalata* shadow
theatre, based upon artistic production (from
manufacture of artefacts to their sung, acted or
narrated exhibition), are occasions for spectacular
entertainment and events inseparable from ritual
contexts. Theatrical presentations incorporate
the villagers' world, bringing in characters from
folklore foreign to Sanskrit epics. M.C.

BRONZE CASTERS

The village peoples of central India traditionally cast statuettes in bronze using the lost wax technique. These figurines, human beings, animals, gods and fantastical creatures, are usually offerings of gratitude to be placed on village or household altars. They sometimes take the place of clan gods or legendary beings to whom a cult is dedicated and who ensure the protection and prosperity of the owner and the village. These bronze statuettes, cast by master craftsmen, do not follow any specific iconographic precepts, but are the expression of individual creative skills. D.C.

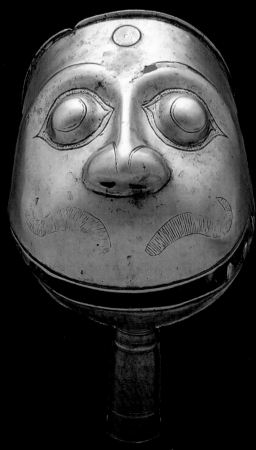

1

1/Ritual mask, Bhairava
India, Karnataka
18th-19th century
Bronze
17.2 x 31.4 cm
Former
C. Niemoller
collection
Inv. 70.2000.1.2

2/Ritual swing
India,
Chhattisgarh,
Bastar
20th century
Bronze
25.3 x 30.7 cm
Former
C. Niemoller
collection
Inv. 70.2000.1.56.1-5

3/Horseman
India, border
region between
Gujarat and
Madhya Pradesh
18th-19th century
Bronze
21.4 x 34.8 cm
Former
C. Niemoller
collection
Inv. 70.2000.1.12

4/Mother breast-feeding her child
Kondh
India, Orissa
19th century
Bronze
15.2 x 30.5 cm
Former
C. Niemoller
collection
Inv. 70.2000.1.60

5/The goddess Durga
India,
Chhattisgarh,
Bastar
Early 19th century
Bronze
12.1 x 13.6 cm
Former
C. Niemoller
collection
Inv. 70.2000.1.44

2

**6/Twofaced
rider on a
bicephalous
elephant**
Kondh
India, Orissa
18th-20th century
Bronze
11.5 x 14 cm
Former
C. Niemoller
collection
Inv. 70.2000.1.76

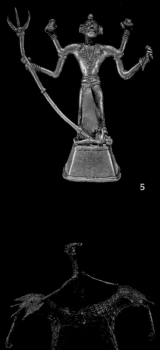

5

3   4   6

Peoples of Asia: draped and tailored clothing

In South Asia, clothing styles include a very wide variety of forms, materials and designs. Draped clothing, starting with the Indian sari, contrast with intricate cut garments.

Contemporary garments have inherited a number of clothing traditions that have coexisted or succeeded one another over the centuries.

In India, although Hindu ideology favours fabric lengths worn as they are, direct from the weaver's loom, many examples of cut and stitched garments also exist. Regional and climatic differences, social category and circumstances lead to varying choices in material, form, colour and design, as well as in the way the clothes are worn.

There are a number of styles of women's dress. The best-known garment is the sari, worn in much of India, and draped in many different ways. This long piece of cotton or silk cloth of varying quality is woven to size using a range of decorative techniques, depending on regional specialisations. In Northwestern India and Pakistan, the types of garment worn show the influence of the Mogul Empire: veil, tunic and trousers in the Punjab; veil, blouse and ample skirt in Rajasthan and Gujarat. Decoration is

Woman's veil (detail)
Pakistan, Punjab
20th century
Cotton, silk floss
(*pat*)
Three lengths of
cloth, drop-stitch
embroidery
257 x 120 cm
Inv. 70.2003.8.4

Woman's skirt (detail)
India, Assam
20th century
Muga silk, cotton,
cloth, extra weft
81 x 103 cm
Inv. 71.1974.148.4

Sari (detail)
India, Gujarat,
Patan
Late 19th-early
20th century
Silk, gold thread
Taffeta, double
ikat decoration
446 x 118 cm
Donated by
J. Millot
Inv. 71.1963.1.14

Blouse
Banjara
India, Madhya
Pradesh
20th century
Cotton, metal
alloy, mirrors
Cloth,
embroidery,
appliqué
46 x 48 cm
Donated by
Mme E. Balfour
Inv. 71.1996.63.2

carried out by various dyeing processes and by embroidery in styles determined by type of thread used, stitching and motifs. In the northeast, in Assam, dress consists of a scarf and a tubular skirt, woven in fine raw silk with designs brocaded in cotton for ceremonial events. These local fashions, still common in villages, are seen less and less in cities.

Men's dress also combines draped and cut and stitched garments with regional variations. White is the predominant colour, except for the checked cotton fabrics draped into skirts and worn by Muslims, mostly in southern regions. In towns, forms of dress are becoming increasingly standardised. F.C.

Peoples of Asia: nomadic and sedentary cultures

Central Asia, a pastoral area with shifting borders, is home to a wide range of populations. They can be divided into two main groups: the Indo-Iranian stock breeders, who follow their herds on foot and live in black goatskin tents, and Turko-Mongolian stock breeders who travel on horseback and inhabit felt-covered yurts.

Horse's saddle
Uzbek
Uzbekistan,
Boukhara
19th-20th century
Wood, birch bark,
bone, leather,
iron
45 x 35 cm
Donated by
Citroën, Croisière
Jaune, 1931-1932
Inv. 71.1935.115.65.1-5

People who live by wide-ranging, mobile stockbreeding, commonly referred to as nomads, have always been major consumers of luxury goods, either brought to their camps by caravans, or acquired at city markets in the foothills. In some cases, in Turkoman for example, it was a matter of transforming "animal capital", exposed to bad weather and sometimes impossible to increase because of lack of pastureland, into precious metal. Russian, Persian and Chinese coins had no prestige value in the eyes of the nomads, and were consequently melted down and transformed into solid silver jewellery inlaid with carnelian. These ornaments, worn by girls and women to protect them from bad luck, were also social and cultural identity markers recognized by all.

Jewellery was for women what belts and horses' harnesses were for men. As traditional male garments were pocket-less, men attached necessities such as flint lighters to their belts or carried them tucked into their clothing, as they did with their snuffboxes. Men's gatherings, on pastureland, at markets or in

Back pendant
Turkmen
Afghanistan
18th-19th century
Gold-plated
silver, carnelians
26.7 x 16.5 cm
B. Dupaigne
mission
Inv. 71.1972.12.195

Yurt carpet
Aymaq
Afghanistan
Circa 1950
Woollen felt
137 x 376 cm
B. Dupaigne
mission
Inv. 71.1975.22.167

/ FELT

One may think of the heart of Asia as the home of a "felt civilization". Felt, a material making full use of the stiff, coarse wool from local ovine species, is waterproof and thermostatic, and can be put to an amazing number of uses. It covers both the inside and outside of nomad dwellings, provides head-to-toe clothing, and is made into bags and pouches for carrying utensils and protecting valuable items when travelling.

Made by women according to the dictates of their imagination, felt carpets may be black and white or multi-coloured, with the types of motifs decorating them determined, in part, by the milling process that compacts the tufts of different coloured wool. These carpets usually have a border of geometrical motifs (triangles, symbols of female fertility, in the case of Aymaq carpets) and a central area with stylised ram's horns as the most classic form of decoration. S.J.

taverns, were accompanied by a succession
of quids of tobacco and bowls of tea.
Major trading centres, where nomadic
and sedentary cultures crossed paths, were ideal
for showing off one's finery, and wealthy
townspeople commissioned richly decorated
saddles from local craftsmen, which they
used without horse blankets. Among nomads,
the seat was not decorated, but covered with
a thick felt or fur blanket.
Nomads sold their animals or, as was perhaps
the case with the Turkomen, their jewellery
when years were lean. Transformation of animal
products was carried out by the women
to meet domestic needs, and it was also a
woman's job to provide decoration for her
household and adornments for her family.
Felt carpets to cover the floor, woven bands
to encircle the yurt, and embroidery and appliqué
work to embellish clothing – domestic crafts
to be sure, but practised with imagination
and taste. S.J.

Naswar tobacco pouch
Turkmen
Afghanistan,
Aqcha
20th century
Gourd, silver, red
cotton pompons,
white beads
H. 19.5 cm
B. Dupaigne
mission
Inv. 71.1973.91.17.1-2

Woman's dress
Hazara
Afghanistan,
Herat
19th-20th century
Silk, cotton, gold
thread, mirrors,
glass beads
Taffeta and
cotton cloth,
embroidery,
appliqué
H. 147 cm
Donated by
M. Roubelat
Inv. 71.1983.73.1

Peoples of Asia: societies and traditions in the Near East

Assembled at the start of the 20th century, the Near Eastern collections contain a wide variety of objects mirroring the societies that produced them – above all, rich traditional costumes, reminders of the region's nomads and city-dwellers, and of the communities and ethnic groups that coexisted there.

_The Bedouin of the Syrian steppes

To the north of the Arabian Desert lie the vast Syrian steppes, home to the Bedouin, so-named from the Arabic word *badw* meaning "people of the desert". Their life is an endless journey and their survival dependent on pastureland, and therefore on rainfall. During their traditional roaming in search of pastures, women and young children travel in palanquins, sheltered from dust and sun. Today, very few nomads live in tents all year round. Most of them have homes in the steppes or in towns, where they spend part of the cold season. The dromedary, the "ship of the desert", is gradually giving way to motorised transport, allowing the region's inhabitants to access new territories with greater speed.

Ketab **woman's camel palanquin for travelling**
Bedouin,
Sba'a tribe
Syria, Palmyrene Steppes
Early 20th century
125 x 380 x 75 cm
Inv. 71.1933.84.31.1 to 71.1933.84.31.11

_Costume, symbol of identity

Succeeding civilisations in the Near East have left their marks on habits of dress and ornamentation. Men and women's dress has developed over the course of the centuries, influenced not only by fashions in vogue, but also by political events. Very early on, costumes became a symbol indicating the wearer's inclusion in a particular category of the population. Each social group wore specific dress that provided information on the wearer's regional origin, religion and social class: nomad or city dweller, Arab or Kurd, Christian, Jew, or Muslim... Traditional clothing is seen less and less these days, supplanted by European styles of dress.

Headdress
Turkey, Istanbul
Cotton, Ottoman coins, glass
Diam. 18.5 cm
Donated by the Turkish Government
Inv. 71.1973.77.644

***Khanjar* dagger and sheath**
Turko-Persian
19th century
Steel, walrus ivory, silver, velvet
L. 51 cm
Inv. 74.1962.0.983.1-2

***Malak* festival dress**
Palestinian Territories, Bethlehem
Early 20th century
Silk, cotton or linen, cotton, gold thread
L. 139 cm
Inv. 71.1989.25.64.1

/ FACE VEILS

Bedouin women indicate their tribe by their dress and face veil. Among the southern Palestinian Bedouin, a married woman's wealth is worn on her veil: she sews the coins and jewellery of her dowry on to the forehead band and ribbons that partly obscure her features. Twenty years ago, only elderly Bedouin women wore these types of adornments, which are gradually disappearing today. Although no one knows exactly where or when face veils first made their appearance, it is certain that draped veils were an integral part of Eastern female costume a thousand years before Christ. The earliest laws obliging married women to cover their heads outside the house are attributed to the Assyrian king, Teglath-Phalasar I (1115-1077 BC). This Near Eastern custom, first practised in Greece and in Rome, was adopted successively by Judaism, although without legal enforcement, by Christianity, for women at prayer, and by Islam, which made it into a sacred duty. H.C.

_Adornments for women and for men

Jewellery is essentially the prerogative of women, and is worn at marriage ceremonies, various ritual feasts, and upon the birth of a child. The attraction of jewellery certainly has something to do with its beauty, but it also due to the security it offers: jewels given by the husband as dowry remain the wife's personal property even if he divorces her.

If jewellery serves as a woman's insurance for the future, the knife is symbol of a man's honour and his courage in battle. One traditional weapon is still popular in southern and eastern Arabia: the dagger, *djambiya* or *khanjar*, which every man wears at his waist, if not on a daily basis, at least on celebratory and formal occasions. H.C.

Burqa **face veil**
Negev Desert Bedouins
Palestinian Territories, Gaza
Circa 1930
Textile, coins, silver, glass, cornelian, agate, cowry shells
L. 36 cm
Donated by A. de Rothschild
Inv. 71.1973.51.1

Cults, beliefs and symbols in the Near East

The civilizations that developed and interacted in the Near East have made the region a mosaic of ethnic groups and religions. The objects contained in the collections, which are of more recent origin, reflect this diversity and illustrate the cults and beliefs of different communities: Jewish, Christian, Muslim, and others.

**Tattooing stamp
(Christian)**
Jerusalem
17th-18th century
(?)
Olive wood
115 x 6 cm
Donated by
A. de Rothschild
Inv. 71.1970.23.1

**Ex-voto
(Shiite)**
Iraq, Khadimain
Silver
H. 6.6 cm
D. Champault
mission
Inv. 71.1967.100.99

Magical practices, some forms of which are forbidden by religious authorities – those contrary to monotheistic belief, for example – find followers in all classes of society, but most frequently among the lower classes and in rural areas. They can be traced back to age-old local customs and beliefs.

Various methods are used to protect against evil spells and to cure sickness, the most common of which are the wearing of amulets inscribed with verses from the Bible or Koran and the names of the Eternal or of Allah. Tattooing, now on the

decline, is practised by some rural, mountain and Bedouin peoples as protection against disease. To ward off the evil eye, a widespread superstition in the Mediterranean basin, some Jews and Muslims use the hand, a non-religious symbol identified with the figure five, a supposed purveyor of good luck. To show thankfulness for a successful cure, Christians and Shiite Muslims leave special offerings in churches or at the tombs of saints, as people have done since Antiquity. H.C.

Amulet in the form of a *Khamsa* hand (Judaism)
Jerusalem
20th century
Engraved nickel silver
7.7 x 4.8 cm
Donated by D. Champault
Inv. 71.1983.92.8

/ MAGICAL LETTERS AND PROTECTION

The inside of the bowl is covered with engraved verses from the Koran and magical letters and numerals. Stylised human figures and animals, inlaid with silver, stand out from circular medallions. This type of object used to be very fashionable in the Arab world because of the curative properties attributed to it. It was believed that any liquid poured into it – water, milk or oil – was charged with magical and therapeutic powers upon contact with the beneficial and religious formulae inscribed inside. The text engraved on the bowl's outer surface reveals its many curative properties: it is supposed to combat all manner of poisons – snake, scorpion or rabid dog – and cure stomach-ache and skin diseases, as well as offer protection against witchcraft and the evil eye. The science of astrology was called upon, as it was for other forms of talisman, to make the bowls even more effective. They have now fallen out of use. H.C.

Tasat al-afiya **talismanic cup (Islam)**
Yemen, Djebel Ba'dan
Metal alloy
13.5 x 4 cm
Donated by J. Le Corre
Inv. 71.1974.179.3

**Androgynous
figure**
Djennenke style
Pre-Dogon
Mali, Bandiagara
cliff, village of
Damagari (?)
10th-11th century
Wood
H. 191 cm
AXA donation
Inv. 70.2004.12.1

Africa /

The Musée du Quai Branly's Africa collections are presented geographically, in a journey of discovery aiming to acquaint visitors with the continent's art from the Maghreb to its southern and eastern regions. The itinerary begins with works from North Africa, highlighting their aesthetic value and illuminating the contexts in which they were used. Each object refers back to history – not only the history of art and its creations, and the history of Africa, but also that of the collectors themselves, such as the Harter bequest and the 1931 Dakar-Djibouti mission, which contributed many of the works and first-hand accounts that now form a key part of the West Africa collections. During he latter half of the 19th century, exploration missions to Central Africa led to the constitution of collections of art, which figures prominently through presentation of a number of its masterpieces. The many different art forms produced by Southern African cultures are evoked through recently made acquisitions. Malagasy funerary art and talismans are evidence of a multifaced cultural origin, with its beginnings in continental Africa and Insular South East Asia, passing by way of India. The journey comes to its end with a unique collection of Christian works from Ethiopia. In parallel to the regional sections, groups of African objects, exhibited either by type – such as textiles and musical instruments – or by theme – sculpted representations of the body, for example – illustrate the unity as well as the diversity of African artistic production, making the journey a fascinating experience.

Turn of 3rd century to 1100 BC
Pharaonic Egypt

9th century BC-1st century AD
In Nigeria, ironwork and exploitation, and development of the Nok culture

814 BC
Founding of Carthage (Tunisia) by the Phoenicians

146 BC
Taking of Carthage by the Romans

30 BC
Conquest of Egypt by the Romans

1st-4th century
Apogee of the Kingdom of Axum (Ethiopia)

2nd-16th century
Sao culture (Chad, North Cameroon, North-East Nigeria)

4th century
Christianisation of the Kingdom of Axum

430 AD
The Vandals seize Carthage. End of Roman domination in North Africa

5th century
Christianisation of Nubia (Egypt and Sudan)

622
Hegira, dawning of the age of Islam

674
Founding of Kairouan (Tunisia)

7th century
Islamisation of North Africa

7th century-1240
Empire of Ghana (Senegal, South Mauritania, Mali, Guinea, East

Niger), that ends with the destruction of its capital

9th-19th century
Empire of Kanem Bornu (Chad, North Nigeria, North Cameroon, Libya)

Since the 9th century
Ife (Nigeria), mythical and religious centre of Yoruba culture

970
Founding of Cairo by the Fatimids dynasty

10th-16th century
Songhay Empire (Senegal, Guinea, South Mauritania, Mali, Niger, North Nigeria)

1056-1147
Hegemony of the Almoravides from Senegal as far as southern Spain

1070
Founding of Marrakech (Morocco) by the Almoravides dynasty (Sanhaja Berbers)

12th century
Development of the Swahili towns along the coasts of the Indian Ocean. Construction of Great Zimbabwe

12th-15th century
Production of terracotta and bronze images in the Ife Kingdom

12th-13th century
Hegemony of the Almohades (Masmoudâ Berbers) throughout the Maghreb and southern Spain

1244-1420
The Merinid Dynasty reigns over the west part of North Africa as far as southern Spain

13th-16th century
Mali Empire (Senegal, southern Mauritania, Mali, Guinea)

13th-18th century
Kingdom of Kongo (Democratic Republic of Congo, Republic of Congo, South Gabon, Cabinda and North Angola)

Since the 13th century
Benin Kingdom (Nigeria)

Since the 14th century
Kingdom of Oyo (Nigeria)

Since the 15th century
Kingdom of Ijebu (Nigeria)

1482
Founding of Saint-Georges-de-la-Mine (El Mina, Ghana) by the Portuguese

1484
Diego Cao discovers the mouth of the Congo River

1497-1498
Vasco de Gama sails round the Cape of Good Hope (South Africa)

15th-late 19th century
Mossi kingdoms (Burkina Faso), kingdom of Owo (Nigeria)

15th-19th century
Expansion of the great kingdoms of Betsileo, Betsimiraka, Sakalava and Merina (Madagascar)

16th century
Christianisation of the Kingdom of Kongo. Constitution of the Lunda Kingdom in the Congo Basin

16th-17th century
Timbuktu (Mali) becomes a great intellectual centre

16th-late 18th century
North Africa, with the exception of Morocco, is ruled by the Ottomans

17th century
Expansion of Buganda (Uganda). Emergence of the Bamana kingdom in Segu (Mali)

1600
Founding by Ganyé Hessou of the Danhome Kingdom, in which Abomey becomes the capital in 1625 (Benin)

1601
Founding of the Bamum kingdom by Nshare Yen (Cameroon)

1625
Founding of the Kuba kingdom by Shyaam a Mbul a Ngoong (Democratic Republic of Congo)

1651
The Dutch found the Cape Colony (South Africa)

1680
Emergence of the Ashanti Kingdom (Ghana)

19th century
Spread of evangelisation missions throughout the continent

Turn of 19th century
Usman dan Fodio embarks upon a holy war (North-West Nigeria). Expansion of the Peul Empire of Macina (Mali)

1815
Treaty of Vienna establishing the illegality of the international principles of the slave trade. France abolishes slavery for good in 1848

1816-1828
Chaka, at the head of a military organisation, helps the Zulus to stand up to the Boers and the English (South Africa)

1821
Slaves freed in the United States return to Africa: the independent territory given to them becomes Liberia in 1847

1830
El Hadj Omar, founder of the Toucouleur Empire, opposes French penetration in Senegal. Conquest of Algeria by the French

1880
Iloo I and Pierre Savorgnan de Brazza, accompanied by the Senegalese Malamine, sign an agreement placing the Téké Kingdom under French protection (Gabon, Republic of Congo)

1880-1898
Samory Touré, Chief of the Mandinka Empire (West Africa), confronts European invasion

1882-1952
British control of Egypt until proclamation of the republic in 1953

February 1885
End of the Berlin conference: France, Germany, Great Britain, Spain, Portugal and Belgium share the African continent

1892-1931
Reign of Njoya in Bamum regions (Cameroon). He invents a system of writing in 1907

1895
Creation of French West Africa (Afrique occidentale française, AOF), a territory run by the French government, covering Mauritania, Senegal, French Sudan, the Upper Volta, Guinea, Niger, the Ivory Coast and Dahomey

1910
Creation of French Equatoriale Africa (Afrique équatoriale française, AEF), uniting Chad, Ubangi-Shari, Gabon, Middle Congo then, after 1919, Cameroon

1912-1951
Italian domination of Libya

1914-1918
Battalions of Senegalese infantrymen are involving in the fighting in France

1931
The Dogon sage Ogotemêli meets Marcel Griaule. His revelations on the Dogon way of thinking are published by Griaule in 1948 under the title *Dieu d'eau* (God of water)

1954
The war of independence breaks out in Algeria

1955
Afro-Asian conference in Bandoeng (Indonesia)

1956
Premier Festival des arts nègres (First Negro Art Festival) in Dakar (Senegal). Tunisia and Morocco gain independence, under French protection since 1883 and 1912

1960
Countries that made up French Africa gain independence. Léopold Sédar Senghor is elected President of Senegal

1962
Algeria gains independence

January-June 1977
Second World Black Festival of Arts and Culture (FESTAC) in Lagos (Nigeria)

1986
Wolé Soyinka wins the Nobel Prize for Literature

1991
Abolition of the apartheid in South Africa

1992
Première Biennale d'art contemporain (First Biennial Festival of Modern Art) in Dakar (Senegal)

1994
Premières Rencontres de la photographie africaine (First Encounters of African Photography) in Bamako (Mali). Genocide in Rwanda. Nelson Mandela is elected President of South Africa

1995
First Biennial Festival of Modern Art in Johannesburg (South Africa)

Map

Peoples

North Africa
1. Aït Seghrouchen / Aït bou Ichaouen
2. Ida Ou Zeddout / Ida Ou Nadif
3. Kel Ahaggar
4. Maure Beidane

Sub-Saharan Africa
5. Aduma
6. Agni
7. Ashanti
8. Baga
9. Balante
10. Bamana
11. Bamileke
12. Baoule
13. Bara
14. Bete
15. Dan
16. Diola
17. Dogon/Tellem
18. Edo (Bini)
19. Ejagham
20. Fang
21. Fingo
22. Fon
23. Gouro
24. Idoma
25. Igbo
26. Ijo
27. Jimma
28. Koma
29. Kongo
30. Konso
31. Kota
32. Krou
33. Kuba
34. Lobi
35. Luba
36. Lumbo
37. Malinke
38. Mambila
39. Mangbetu
40. Mbuti
41. Mende
42. Mossi
43. Nafana
44. Nalu
45. Ndebele
46. Ngbaka
47. Nkanu
48. Punu
49. Sakalava
50. Sapi
51. Senufo
52. Sherbro
53. Swazi
54. Tsonga
55. Yaka
56. Yoruba
57. We
58. Woyo
59. Zulu

Towns

60. Abomey
61. Algiers
62. Benin city
63. Djenné
64. El Djem
65. Fès
66. Gondar
67. Kairouan
68. Marrakech
69. Nabeul
70. Siwa Oasis
71. Ouargla
72. Tetouan

Regions

73. Anti Atlas
74. High Atlas
75. Middle Atlas
76. Aurès
77. Fezzan
78. Hoggar
79. Kabylia
80. Rif
81. Tassili n'Ajjer

Archaeological sites

82. Nok
83. Sao

ATLANTIC
OCEAN

North Africa

North Africa is made up of Mauritania, the Maghreb (Morocco, Algeria, Tunisia), Libya and Egypt and extends over most of the Sahara. Exposed to Eastern and European influences, its civilisations have preserved their ancient Berber cultural traditions and maintained ties with the people of the Sahel.

Fragment of a *minbar* preacher's pulpit
Morocco,
Koutoubia
Mosque,
Marrakech
Circa 1120
(Almoravid
period)
Wood
7.4 x 16.8 cm
Donated by
R. Parvillée
Inv. 74.1969.5.1

Work attributed
to Al-Jazuli
**Illumination
from the prayer
book *The Guide
of Blessings***
Algeria, Algiers
1066 H-1655/1656
AD
Paper, gilt, ink
17 x 12 cm
Donated by
F. Demay
Inv. 74.1962.0.1488.1-2

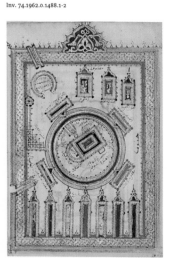

_Writing and book art

Since Antiquity, North Africa has developed alphabetic writing: first Phoenician, with the founding of Carthage, then Hebraic, a derivative of Phoenician. Libyan-Berber writing has been used from the Mediterranean to the Sahel for twenty-five centuries. It consists in inscriptions and human and animal figures engraved in stone. The Tuareg *tifinagh* is the current form of Libyan-Berber writing. As a medium of divine revelation, the Arabic alphabet has sacred connotations: its calligraphy symbolises the harmony of the world through the transcription of the word of God. Three styles can be distinguished: *Kufi,* stiff and angular, adapted to architectural design, *cursive,* flexible and fluid, joining up the letters in continuous movement, and *Maghribi,* round and fine, and a combination of the previous two. Books are extremely sophisticated works of art. The binding, made from the finest leather, and the calligraphy and illuminations create the beauty of the Book, the Koran; but also of tales, as well as medical, astronomical or mathematical

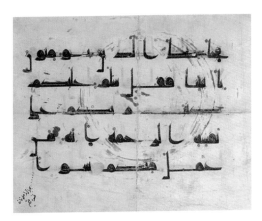

treatises. The cover may depict a geometric design
in a golden setting with floral arabesque margins.
For a long time, parchment was favoured over
paper to make copies of the Koran or collections
of the *Hadiths* (words of the Prophet transmitted
by his companions) and it was only after the 14th
century that the use of paper became widespread.

**Page of the
Koran, extract
from Sura 6
"Livestock"**
Tunisia, Kairouan
10th century
(Aghlabid period)
Parchment, ink,
Kufic characters
32 x 26.2 cm
Inv. 74.1981.2.11

Torah shield, *Tâs*
Algeria, Algiers
18th century
Wood, silver
27.4 x 16.3 cm
Former P. Eudel
collection
Inv. 74.1968.5.176

/ CULTURES AND RELIGIONS

North Africa, which extends from the Mediterranean to the Sahel,
was inhabited in prehistoric times by the paleo-Berbers, a population
of shepherds and hunters who created an immensely rich rupestrian
art. In the Nile valley, the Pharaonic dynasties, whose civilisation was
based on irrigation farming, reigned for over three millennia until the
Roman conquest. In the 7th century, the Arab invasion shaped a new
world as people began turning from Byzantine Christianity to Islam.
The influence of North Africa reached its peak under the Almoravids
who annexed Andalusia. A brilliant urban culture and refined
Hispanic-Moorish art blossomed. The influence of the Spanish Jews,
and the Ottomans in turn, could be discerned in the more urbanized
areas, where wealth and temporal and religious powers were
concentrated. The civilisations outside the towns continued to
preserve their deeply rooted animist culture. Islam successfully
integrated pagan rituals, such as fertility rites, into the Muslim
festivals associated with the agricultural world. The festival of
Achura, an ancient farming ceremony that took place a month before
the festival of the Aïd el Kabir, ensured the fertility of the land and of
women by uniting the living with their ancestors. M.-F.V.

**Bridal gown
for the first day
of the *ashera
nahuak essued*
ceremony**
Berber (Siwis)
Egypt, Siwa Oasis
Pre 1960
Cotton, silk,
mother of pearl
190 x 122 cm
Inv. 70.2001.1.16

Tenchifa
**decorative band,
draped around
mirrors for
ceremonial
occasions,
marriage in
particular,
to ward off the
Evil Eye**

Morocco,
Tetouan
18th century
Silk, natural
pigments
448.2 x 44.5 cm
Inv. 74.1961.10.36

_Urban art (female/male art)

Decorative art *par excellence*, urban art is applied
to architectural decor and everyday objects.
Floral motifs, arabesques and interlacings merge
with calligraphy. Human and animal figures are
rare because of the religious prescriptions
prohibiting the representation of living creatures.
Dress materials and furnishings are enhanced
in beauty by the silk embroidery in shimmering
colours made by women in high society.
In Algiers, embroidery flourished during the
Ottoman occupation, while in Morocco, each
town created a distinctive style with its own
technique, motifs and colours. Earthenware
production was a man's activity and carried out in
workshops. The clay was baked twice after being
turned on the wheel. The design was drawn in
freehand and covered with coloured enamel after
the first bake. Jewellery indicated the position of a
woman in society and the wealth of her family,
and also gave her prophylactic and therapeutic
powers. Her wedding provided her with the
opportunity to wear her most valuable jewellery,
which would remain her property. The gold or
gold-plated silver jewellery adorned with precious
stones and beads, filigreed, hammered, carved
and with openwork design, was almost always
made by Jewish jewellers.

Necklace in the
form of a bird,
symbol of
married joy
worn by Jews
Morocco, Fes
1012 H-1603 AD
Gold, emeralds,
amethysts,
natural pearls,
enamel
40 x 8.2 x 2.9 cm
Donated by Mme
Gradis-Koecklin
Inv. 74.1969.6.1.1-2

Tunsi jar
Tunisia, Nabeul
19th century
Terracotta,
stanniferous
enamel
39 x 20 cm
Donated by
the General
Government
of Algeria
Inv. 71.1899.30.133

/ WEDDINGS

Marriage is the most remarkable rite of passage passed on from Berber tradition and reinterpreted by Islam. Ancient magical practices are still very much a part of the seven-day ceremony. Before her wedding, a young girl learns the secrets of sexuality from an elderly lady and prepares for her future role as wife. A network of magical protection is set up: propitiatory rites (visits to the marabout), protection rites (talismans, prophylactic words) and ritual gestures that chase away the forces of evil and beckon protection and blessing. The ceremony then begins with two days of purification for the fiancee at the hammam. On the day of the Presentation, the bride is dressed like an idol in sumptuous tunics that fill the guests with admiration and her family with pride. This is also the day when the marriage is consummated. In the days that follow, the bride wears other clothes that are part of her trousseau, until the 7th day, "the day of the belt" that marks the status of the bride as a married woman and future mother and her integration into her new family. M.-F.V.

Earrings
Ida or Nadif
Morocco, central
Anti-Atlas
Early 20th century
Silver, niello,
enamel, glass
26.5 x 21.5 cm
Donated by
Colonel Bernard
Inv. 74.1962.0.65.1-2

Water jug
Beni Ouriaghel
Morocco, Rif,
El Hoceima
19th century
Terracotta,
natural pigments
17.3 x 15.7 cm
Melle Anthoine
bequest
Inv. 74.1965.3.68

_Rural art (women and men's art)

Rural art shows a continuation of Berber
traditions after the arrival of Islam. It is a simple
style, used in the decoration of everyday objects,
and consists mainly in geometric motifs, with
occasional anthropomorphic or zoomorphic
elements, that form a harmonious whole. These
motifs, which can be seen on all locally made
objects and in women's tattoos, are part of a
traditional symbolic repertory with prophylactic
and therapeutic properties. The design of carpets,
usually comprising these geometric figures, does
not conform to strict rules of composition, but
reflect the weaver's own inspiration. This freedom
of creation is nevertheless practised within a
traditional framework: colours and motifs are
specific to the tribe. Women work wool to provide
for their family's needs and to make clothes,
hangings and carpets. Embroidering the woollen
fabrics with silk, gold or silver threads is also a
woman's art. The brightly coloured designs are
inspired by the surrounding world and the
symbolic repertory. Women also made pottery for
use in the home, with simple elegant forms that
are always functional. Clay is fashioned by hand
and the white, ochre or brown pigmented decor

***Zerbiya* knotted carpet**
Aït Serhrouchen,
Aït bou Ichaouen
sub-tribe
Morocco,
Moulouya Valley
20th century
Wool, goat hair,
vegetable and
chemical dyes
400 x 187 cm
Inv. 70.2001.16.1

***Ajar* headscarf**
Berber
Tunisia, El-Djem
Late 19th century
Wool, gold and
silver thread, silk,
sequins, cotton
140 x 118.5 x 2 cm
Inv. 74.1966.7.19

is applied with the fingers or a simple brush. Pottery is baked on the bare ground before being coated in plant resin to make it watertight and give it a sheen.

Woodwork was a man's job and involved the construction of buildings and furniture-making. Architectural features and furniture were carved or painted with geometric, floral and epigraphic motifs.

The silver jewellery worn by women showed the tribe to which they belonged. It was moulded or cut, stamped, engraved or carved, decorated with niello, enamels, coloured glass, amber and coral and sometimes with cloves. It was supposed to ensure fertility and protect against illness and bad thoughts. The power to keep away the evil eye is ensured by the appropriate choice of material, shape and design.

_Nomadic art

In prehistoric times, the Sahara was where the forefathers of the North African Berbers met those of the Negro populations who lived south of the desert. The trade routes across the Sahara, established in the 3rd century B.C., were used throughout history by caravans bringing salt and products from the north, and gold, ivory, indigo and slaves from the south. Saharan trade was practised mainly by the Tuaregs, fiercely independent nomadic shepherds who held on to their Berber traditions and the *tifinagh* alphabet. Although Muslim, they kept their ancient beliefs, preserving the cross *ankh* (sign of life) of Ancient Egypt and adopting animist practices from Sub-Saharan Africa. Today, the Tuaregs still live in Algeria and Libya, as well as Niger, Lybia and Nigeria. Tuareg women work leather that is tinted in a

Arar shield
Tuareg,
Kel Ahaggar
Algerian Sahara,
Hoggar
19th century
Oryx hide, leather,
copper, steel,
wool, cotton,
natural pigments
108 x 94 cm
Donated by the
Musée de l'Armée
Inv. 71.1932.35.206

range of colours, especially green from Kano (Nigeria). The geometric design is created by applying layers of leather, silk or cotton embroidery, or by chiselling, stamping or painting. Among their most typical creations are men's wallets, large travel bags or *tassoufra*, men's bags or *eljibera*, women's bags or *tehaïhait*, and saddle and tent cushions.

Weapons, used also as male finery and ceremonial objects, are made by blacksmiths. Steel blades often bear magical engraved motifs or inscriptions. *Arar* shields, *takouba* swords and *telek* hand daggers were the prerogative of the nobility. Tuareg (and Moorish) jewellery shows similarities with jewellery from Sub-Saharan Africa in their mounting techniques (hammering and assembling by riveting in particular) and choice of materials: cowry shells, shells, ivory or bone, leather, *millefiori* glass beads.

Tehaïthait
woman's
saddlebag
Tuareg,
Kel Ahaggar
Algerian Sahara,
Hoggar
Late 19th-early
20th century
Leather, silk,
vegetable dyes
187 x 114 cm
Donated by
G. Soustelle
Inv. 71.1967.40.1

Asarou
scarf key
Moors and Tuareg
Mauritania,
Algerian Sahara,
Hoggar
Late 19th century
Copper, brass,
silver
19.5 x 6 cm
Donated by
M. and Mme
J-C. Humbert
Inv. 70.2001.28.28

Tent cushion
Tuareg,
Kel Ahaggar
Algerian Sahara,
Hoggar
Pre 1931
Leather,
vegetable dyes
58 x 55 cm
Inv. 74.1962.0.1425

Boliw
zoomorphic
composite altar
Bamana
Mali, *kono*
sanctuary,
Dyabougou
village
Early 20th
century
Clay, beeswax,
animal blood,
wood
44 x 59 cm
Dakar-Djibouti
mission
Inv. 71.1931.74.1091

Female figure
Mali, Djenne
region
13th-15th century
Terracotta with
red ochre slip
37.5 x 31 cm
Inv. 73.1991.0.39 AP

West Africa / Sudanese area

In this dry region of the Sahel and the
savannah, wooden statues and masks, carved
by blacksmiths, are associated in particular
with the ancestor world and water gods.

_Ancient Mali

Arabic scripts and oral tradition mention
the empires of Ghana, Mali, the Songhay and
the Macina, and the towns of the internal delta
of Niger, Timbuktoo and Djenne, south of the
Sahara. Archaeologists have dated the first
settlements of Jenne Jenno, next to present-day
Djenne, to the 3rd century B.C. This area, capitalising
on the caravans passing through between North
Africa and the Gulf coast of Guinea, reached
its peak in the 11th century. Djenne art is
characterised by the production of 12th-15th
century terracotta anthropomorphic figures.

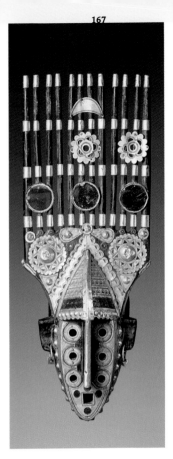

_Initiation into Mande culture

The Malinke and Bamana people share a common culture whose place of origin is in the Mande region, in the south of Mali. In addition to mandatory initiation for everyone, some men also join male initiatory societies to increase their knowledge and social power. Some of these societies, the N'tomo, for the uncircumcised only, the Ciwara (literally "wild farming animal"), and the men's society, the Kore, involved masked dancers performing in public.

Masks and magical objects of the Komo and Kono, however, can be seen only by the initiated. A thick patina, made by the dried blood of sacrificial animals and "medication", covers the sacred objects known as *boliw*. Full of vital energy, called *nyama*, these objects are used in mediation rites between villagers: reconciliations, judgments, alliance pacts, pledges, passages to the rank of ancestor. Thanks to the *boliw* that are kept in sanctuaries, the leaders of the initiated exert religious and political power over the community.

N'tomo
initiation
society mask
Malinke
Guinea
20th century
Wood,
aluminium,
brass, mirror
73 x 28 cm
Inv. 73.1998.3.1 A

MEGALITHS IN AFRICA

Southern Senegal, on the border with Gambia, is rich in megalithic evidence of the protohistory of this region of Africa. Megalithic circles, burial mounds with a frontal structure and cairns illustrate a long tradition that lasted at least two millennia (1000 B.C./1000 A.D.). Mentioned by Europeans in their travel writings starting in the late 16th century, surveys of these spectacular megaliths carried out in the 19th century revealed tombs and offerings, weapons, copper jewellery and ceramics. Some of the most complex layouts were of megalithic stones in the form of a lyre with a central tenon joint, facing a circle of raised stones.

In other regions of West Africa, especially in Mali (Tondidaru) and south Nigeria (Cross River), anthropomorphic raised stones can often be found, and are apparently linked to the ancestor worship.
(see p. 22) H.J.

Dege anthropomorphic statuette
Tellem
Mali, southern Bandiagara Cliffs
10th-12th century
Wood, sacrificial materials
27 x 6 cm
Donated Lieutenant L. Desplagnes mission, 1906
Inv. 71.1906.3.7

Hogon ceremonial stool
Dogon
Mali
20th century
Wood
39.5 x 34 cm
Inv. 71.1961.91.1

_The "Dogon region"

In 1931, with the Dakar-Djibouti mission, Marcel Griaule established the roots of French ethnology in the "Dogon region" along the Bandiagara cliffs. The Dogon were formed by populations moving from different areas between the 14th and 15th centuries. The Dogon would have lived alongside and then evicted their predecessors, the Tellem, who were the first to use caves as cemeteries and sanctuaries (10th-11th centuries). Androgynous statues with a thick sacrificial patina can be found there. They often have their arms raised, probably in a sign of prayer. The 11th century pre-Dogon hermaphrodite statue is poised in this gesture of tellem supplication. Chequered scarifications on the face show similarities with the Djenne style.

The Dogon pantheon gives a special role to the hermaphrodite water god *Nommo* and his twin the pale fox, followed by a generation in which there were four pairs of twins who would be the forefathers of humanity. They are represented abundantly in sculpture, such as this stool belonging to the religious chief, the Hogon. The theme of fertility is often illustrated by female figures engraved or carved on keyholes, doors, shutters, boxes and pillars of the *toguna* shelter where men gathered for meetings.

_Dogon funerary ceremonies

Masks are often carved at a distance from the village by initiated members of the men's mask society, *Awa*. They are worn for funerals, or to mark the end of the mourning period, *Dama*. The *Sigui*, which takes place every sixty years, celebrates the revelation of the word to man, and the appearance of death. The *Dama* brings together the whole community and a wide array of masks is worn to mark the departure of the soul of the deceased.

Each of these masks represents a myth or story accompanied by a dance and position in the procession. The *Satimbe* masks represent the only woman admitted to the initiatory society Awa, the Yasigine. The overall sculpture includes the statue, with jointed arms, and the mask. The various human and animal figures on the masks, whose number and form vary over time, reflect the Dogon commitment to show the integrality of the world in their funerary rites. Today, Dogon masks are also displayed for the benefit of tourists...

_Lobi divination and sculptures

In Burkina Faso, in the Lobi society, which has no form of centralised power, social organisation and authority are governed by spiritual powers called *thila* (sing. *thil*). They reveal themselves to men through an animal, a recurring dream, an illness, a bout of madness or the discovery of an iron object in the bush. It is the diviner (*thildaar*) who identifies the *thil* and interprets what it means and what it wants during a ritual divination. Often, through the diviner's voice, the *thil* asks to be embodied by an anthropomorphic statuette. Kept in a dark room of a house called the *thildou*, these sculptures reveal the power of the *thila* and their goodwill towards their owner – provided that the latter remembers to honour them. The beauty of the Lobi sculptures lies in the variety of shapes and positions of the figures, and show the talent of the sculptors (*tinthildaar*) who created them – such as Tyohèpté Palé. Works from his altar are displayed in the museum.

Karanga bladed "antelope" mask
Mossi
Burkina Faso, Yatenga region
Early 20th century
Wood, pigments
209 x 20 cm
Donated by
H. Rubinstein
Inv. 71.1966.34.2

***Satimbe* mask**
Dogon
Mali, Bandiagara Cliffs, Sanga village
Early 20th century
Kapok wood, pigments, vegetable fibres
138 x 33.5 cm
Dakar-Djibouti mission (collected on 7 November 1931)
Inv. 71.1931.74.1948

_Masked dances in Burkina Faso

The Mossi, Bwa and Bobo masks depict human or animal figures with carved or painted geometric designs. Often multi-coloured, the significance of their cosmogonic symbolism is understood only by the initiated. These crest or facial helmet masks, often surmounted by a blade, are still worn in public today at funerary or farming ceremonies. They invoke the soul of ancestors or the spirit of animals, emissaries of the gods. G.B.-B.

CARVINGS OF FIGURES

A statue is not a representation but rather an embodiment of an ancestor or spirit.
The sculptor, the demiurge, gives it form and life by drawing from the group's collective memory. The portrayal of these "statue-beings" is not restricted by realism, but is based upon the values and codes of each group. Parts of the body with symbolic importance – the head, navel, hands, for example – are enlarged, altering normal human proportions. Their symmetry is rarely perfect, as two identical parts (such as two objects or two beings, i.e. twins) is considered unnatural and has negative connotations. These sculptures are often accompanied by other ritual objects or are part of a group of statues. G.S.

1/ Work
attributed to the
sculptor Kwayep
Mother and Child
Cameroon
Circa 1912
Wood, pigments
H. Labouret
mission, 1932
Inv. 71.1934.171.607

**2/ Statuette of a
spirit,** *asie usu*
Baoule
Ivory Coast
19th century
Wood
32 x 8 cm
Donation
Former
collections
of A. Breton,
P. Eluard,
R. Rasmussen
and H. Goldet
Inv. 70.2003.3.2

**3/ Five-headed
being,** *guinin*
Bombu toro style
Dogon
Mali, southern
Bandiagara Cliffs
17th-18th century
Wood
35.5 x 9.5 cm
Donation
Former
collections
of R. Rasmussen
and H. Goldet
Inv. 70.2003.3.1

1

2

3

4/ *Jo* Female statue
Bamana
Mali, Bougouni or Sikasso region
Early 20th century
Wood, cotton, beads, string
64 x 15 cm
Donated by
G. H. Rivière
Inv. 71.1935.16.1

5/ *Ekwotame* female figure
Idoma
Nigeria, Benoue region
19th-20th century
Wood, pigments, fabric, metal, mother-of-pearl buttons
Former collection Barbier-Mueller
Inv. 73.1996.1.46

6/ Anthropo-morphic figure
Sherbro
Sierra Leone
16th-17th century
Steatite
21.5 x 9 cm
Donated by M. Lecesne
Inv. 71.1902.28.2

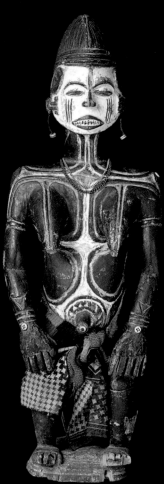

4

5

6

West Africa / Coast of Guinea

Looking outward towards the ocean, the coastal civilisations have traded with the most intrepid sailors since ancient times. Peoples speaking the Mande language predominate in the western savannahs and forests. Trade networks run through West Africa, facilitating contacts and commerce.

_African art and Europe

The first contacts between Europe and Africa were established in the second half of the 15th century when the Portuguese sailed around the Cape of Good Hope and opened up the Eastern route to India. The stop-offs and trading posts that they set up along the coastline fostered cultural and trade exchanges. In Sierra Leone, during the first quarter of the 16th century, ivory makers produced refined and valuable objects inspired by European models (ivory horns, salt cellars, spoons) commissioned by the Portuguese. The princely courts in Europe filled their tables with these objects of mixed design, acquired from contacts with the Sapi, Yoruba, Edo and Kongo tribes. During the latter half of the 19th century, exploration, followed by the colonial conquest of the African continent, led to the creation of ethnographical museums in Europe.

At the turn of the 20th century, artists based in Paris discovered the power of African sculpture: Braque and Picasso opened the way to Cubism and collected these "primitive" objects from which they drew their inspiration. The encounter of modern art with African art was to mark the 20th century. H.J.

Olyphant
Sherbro
Sierra Leone
Late 15th-late
16th century
Ivory
48.5 x 9 cm
Entrusted by
the Bibliothèque
nationale de
France, cabinet
des Médailles,
Paris
Inv. 71.1933.6.1 D

Statuette
Sapi
Guinea
16th-17th century
Steatite
24 x 9 cm
Inv. 70.2001.2.1

**Anthropo-
morphic mask**
Kru
Ivory Coast,
Sassandra region
Late 19th century
Wood, pigments,
feathers,
vegetable fibres,
cotton, shells
68 x 20 cm
Donated by
the Ivory Coast
Committee,
Universal
Exhibition of 1900
Inv. 71.1900.44.103

_Artists

It is extremely rare that a work can be attributed to a particular artist, although the distinctive style of some objects makes it possible to identify their author.

Miniature protective masks, anthropomorphic spoons or commemorative statuettes are closely linked to their owner, so much so that they can be compared to idealised portraits.

These objects are made for individual use and reflect the personal style of the artist more than the masks or sculptures for group use.

In the Dan region for example, on the border of Liberia and the Ivory Coast, the sculptor Zlan (who died circa 1960) was renowned for the beauty of his work. Born in Belewale, in the We region, Zlan worked for numerous people among the We, Dan or Maou populations and, throughout his lifetime, trained several young sculptors. A.G.

Miniature mask
We
Ivory Coast
Early 20th century
Wood, claws, traces of horse-hair, metal
14 x 8 cm
Collected circa 1930 by the aviator Captain Robert
Inv. 73.1983.1.2 A

Anthropomor-phic spoon
Dan
Ivory Coast
Late 19th-early 20th century
Wood, beads
71 x 19 cm
Donation
Former collection H. Goldet
Inv. 70.2003.3.8

Sculpture by Zlan (Sra)
Mother and Child
Dan
Ivory Coast
20th century
Wood, aluminium, vegetable fibres, pigments
63.5 x 20,3 cm
Inv. 73.1963.0.163

/ FOUR CENTURIES, ONE MASK

These *ejumba* masks of the Diola tribe in Senegal are an outstanding example of longevity and permanence. The first examples appear in a 17th century engraving and they are still used today in *bukut* initiation rites. These masks show how animist rituals have survived the conversion of the region to Islam by integrating Koranic symbols: written verses, amulets, etc. The consistency of style, spanning four centuries, illustrates how little we know about the history of sculpture and African culture: although we can identify when some masks or statues were made, it is impossible to trace all the developments and changes that have taken place in African sculpture over the past centuries. G.S.

Zoomorphic helmet masks
Diola or Balante
Senegal,
Casamance

1 / Pre 1892
Basketwork,
bull's horns,
shells, abrin seeds
123 x 30 cm
Donated by
Mr Lebrun
Inv. 71.1892.23.1

2 / Pre 1756
Bark basketwork,
bull's horns,
shells, abrin seeds
46 x 38.5 cm
Donated by the
Municipal
Library, Versailles
From the Marquis
de Serent's
cabinet of
curiosities
Inv. 71.1934.33.38

3 / 20th century
Basketwork,
wood, raffia,
abrin seeds
90 x 47 cm
Inv. 73.1963.0.33

Crested mask representing the snake, *a-mantsho na-tshol*
Nalu or Baga
Guinea
19th century
Wood, pigments
222 x 36 cm
Former A. and J. Kerchache collection
Inv. 70.2003.27.1

***Bedu* mask**
Nafana
Ivory Coast
19th-early 20th century
Wood, pigments
144 x 74.5 cm
Inv. 73.1995.5.1

_Masks: contexts of use

Masks are worn during festivals and rituals in traditional social, political or religious contexts. They have a wide range of uses, such as marking rites of passage. They belong to associations, known as secret societies who produce, handle and care for them. Membership in these associations requires initiation and payment of dues. Very often, masks convey a moral message: in the Mende region, when young girls return from an initiatory retreat after undergoing difficult tests marking the passage from childhood to adulthood, they wear *sowei* masks, evoking a female ideal that is both aesthetic and moral.

**Sande female
initiation
society mask**
Mende
Sierra Leone
20ᵗʰ century
Wood, mirror
41 x 21.5 cm
Inv. 73.1996.14.1

**Kpelie or kodal
two-faced mask**
Senufo
Ivory Coast
20ᵗʰ century
Wood
25 x 14.5 cm
Inv. 73.1972.3.1

**Poro initiation
society mask**
Senufo
Ivory Coast,
Korhogo
Early 20ᵗʰ century
Wood, vegetable
fibres
97.5 x 76 cm
Inv. 73.1965.1.4

**Anthropomor-
phic mask**
Gouro or Bete
Ivory Coast
Early 20ᵗʰ century
Wood, pigments,
monkey skin,
vegetable fibres,
metal
37 x 18 cm
Former T. Tzara
collection
Inv. 73.1988.2.1

Boys also endure physical tests and an
apprenticeship in secret knowledge. In Ivory
Coast, in the senufo *poro*, this rite is repeated
every seven years in the sacred wood. By renewing
man's relationship with the supernatural,
the masked dance expresses the fears and hopes
he has of forces that dominate him.
In a more secular context, the mask symbolises
the desire for social recognition and a higher
status. H.J.

AFRICAN MUSICAL INSTRUMENTS

Sculptures on African musical instruments usually feature
human and animal figures and, in particular, their heads,
the visible centre of creative thought, word and sound.
While the form of musical instruments is determined
mainly by the context in which musical repertoires are
performed and the materials available to make them,
it also reflects the ingenuity of the instrument-makers
who developed a multitude of playing mechanisms and
devices to enhance their art. M.L.

**1 / Timba single-
skin drum with
zoomorphic base**
Baga
Guinea
Early 20th century
Wood, skin,
pigments
132 x 61 cm
Inv. 73.1965.1.12

**2 / Kundi
arched harp**
Ngbaka
Democratic
Republic of Congo
19th-20th century
Wood, skin,
vegetable fibres,
metal, pigments
81 x 22 cm
Inv. 73.1990.7.1

**3 / Wasamba
sistrum**
Bamana
Mali,
Sikasso region,
Kelea village
Early 20th century
Wood, calabash
56.5 x 38.3 cm
Dakar-Djibouti
mission
Inv. 71.1931.74.1545

**4 / Zoomorphic
bell**
Yoruba
Nigeria,
Ijebu region
18th century
Copper alloy
14 x 9 cm
Inv. 73.1997.4.11

**5 / Tawong
lateral horn
topped with a
female figure**
Mambila
Nigeria or
Cameroon
Early 20th century
Wood, feathers
79.2 x 9.7 cm
Donated by
C. Tardits
Inv. 71.1969.93.1

1

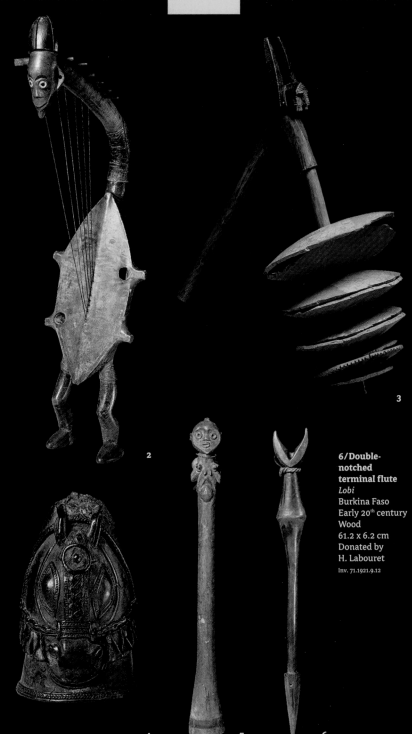

6/Double-notched terminal flute
Lobi
Burkina Faso
Early 20th century
Wood
61.2 x 6.2 cm
Donated by
H. Labouret
Inv. 71.1921.9.12

West Africa / The Akan world

The Akan people migrated from the North to the southern
gold-rich regions of Ghana, Togo and the Ivory Coast.
In the 17ᵗʰ and 18ᵗʰ centuries, they formed powerful states
and participated in the gold and slave trade with Europeans.
Matrilineal, they share the same symbols and beliefs.

_Baoule masks

According to oral tradition, the Baoule came
from present-day Ghana during the reign of
Queen Abla Pokou in the 18ᵗʰ century and are part
of the Akan people. They settled in the centre
of the Ivory Coast after travelling great distances
and adopted the sculptural tradition of mask art
from their Gouro and Yohoure neighbours.
Some masks are not meant to be seen by
the entire community. This is the case of the
goli-glin, the animal helmet-mask of Wan origin,
which is worn when someone dies and is meant
to absolve the family of the deceased from
any suspicions regarding the death, as death
is never considered natural.

Nowadays, masks are loosing part of their
sacred dimension and are being worn instead
for entertainment. Portrait-masks, discernible
by their fine, symmetrical traits, play an
essentially secular role in dance competitions
between villages. Crowned with twin faces,
they celebrate the perfect balance of twins.

Gou **mask**
Baoule
Ivory Coast
Early 20ᵗʰ century
Wood, pigments
43.5 x 14.5 cm
Inv. 73.1963.0.109

Goli-glin **mask**
Baoule
Ivory Coast
Early 20ᵗʰ century
Wood, pigments
26 x 50 cm
Donation
Former collections
of P. Guillaume
and H. Goldet
Inv. 70.2003.3.11

Richard Buchta, *Wife of an Arab sheik*. Sudan, circa 1875-1880.

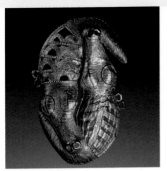

**Appliqué jewel
in the image
of two facing
crocodiles**
Baoule
Ivory Coast
Late 19ᵗʰ-early
20ᵗʰ century
Gold
7 x 10 cm
Inv. 73.1966.9.2

/ TERRACOTTA OBJECTS FROM KOMALAND

Terracotta objects from Komaland, North Ghana, were discovered in the 1980s in a vast burial site of over a hundred tombs dating back to the Iron Age. The graves in the burial grounds contain offerings and objects, notably terracotta human and animal figures. These images, which could be portraits of the deceased or evocations of ancestors or divinities, have a stylised realism often highlighting symbols of fertility. The deceased is placed on a platform with his head resting on earthenware and is adorned with numerous copper or brass necklaces, bracelets and ankle bracelets. The highly varied forms of the statuary attest to an agricultural society skilled in metal-working and probably part of long-distance trade networks extending across the Sahara to the Indian Ocean, in particular. H.J.

_Gold

The Akan people from the Ivory Coast's lagoon region and the south of Ghana attribute gold, which they have exploited for several centuries, with qualities that make it a precious and awe-inspiring metal. Gold nuggets are considered to be living creatures that take the form of a rainbows and express themselves by barking. Gold powder was used in the worship of water divinities and ancestors and as money in the pre-colonial era. It was weighed using the *dja*, scales, which included brass, spoons and tins to hold and preserve the powder. The gold is worked by goldsmiths who are among the most highly skilled craftsmen in West Africa. The jewellery worn or attached to objects of power (swords) becomes valuable family posessions over time and are displayed at ceremonies marking a change in social status. Gold leaf is applied to the carved wood of regalia, flyswatters, orators' batons and sometimes even statues. Akan kings and chiefs draped in silk loincloths adorn themselves with heavy gold bracelets, rings, necklaces and pendants for the benefit of their audiences.

Male statuette
Koma
Ghana,
Komaland digs
13ᵗʰ-16ᵗʰ century
Terracotta
28.5 x 15 cm
Donated by
A. de Monbrison
(Found
during digs by
J. Anquandah,
1984)
Inv. 73.1987.3.1

**Weights for
weighing gold,
hunting scene**
Ashanti or Baoule
Ghana or Ivory
Coast
Early 20ᵗʰ century
Brass
5.2 x 6.2 cm
Inv. 73.1963.0.441

_Souls of the living and the dead

The Akan believed that seven types of souls existed in one person. The *kra* (breath of life) is a divine soul that returns to the creator god Nyame upon a person's death. *Kuduo*, finely decorated lost wax cast brass containers whose form and decoration were influenced by Islamic fountains, are designed to hold the gold powder for the purification rites of the Ashanti's living souls. They are regularly filled with purifying water or sacrificial offerings during ceremonies to ensure well-being and prosperity.

They are also used during puberty rites or the twins' festival, which are especially important events in African societies, and are placed in the tomb with the deceased. They are closed with a chain and latch and decorated with non-figurative motifs. The lids, however, are enhanced by rounded figurative scenes, symbols illustrating proverbs or the complex imagery developed later on. H.J.

Mma **funerary statuette**
Image of an *Agni* **tambourine player**
Ivory Coast, Krinjabo
16th century (?)
Terracotta
34.5 x 17.5 cm
Former collections
Dr Lheureux,
F. Lem and I. Païlès
Inv. 73.1984.7.1

Kuduo **offerings jar**
Ashanti
Ghana
Copper alloy
19th century
27.5 x 24 cm
Donated by
J. de Menil
Inv. 71.1965.17.1

**King Gbehanzin
statue**
Danhome
Kingdom
Fon
Benin, Abomey
Between 1889 and
1893
Wood, pigments,
leather
168 x 102 cm
Donated by
General Dodds
Inv. 71.1893.45.3

King Glele statue
Danhome
Kingdom
Fon
Benin, Abomey
Between 1858
and 1889
Wood, pigments,
leather
179 x 77 cm
Donated by
General Dodds
Inv. 71.1893.45.2

_The Danhome kingdom

Founded in the 17th century, the Danhome kingdom
spread as far the Atlantic coast in the 18th century
and participated in the slave trade with the
Europeans. The kings lived in Abomey where they
each built their own palace. Court art blossomed
in the 18th century: ironwork, textile, wood sculpture
and bas-reliefs made from local or European
materials embellished the palace walls. Symbols
expressed the spirit of each king's reign and were
represented mainly through iconography. King
Glele's symbol, a lion, was depicted on insignia
such as the recade, a baton used to certify official
messages and worn over the shoulder, or on
statues. His son, Gbehanzin, was the dynasty's
last king before French colonisation. To express
his resistance, he chose the motto *the angry shark
comes to trouble the ocean waters* and is also
represented in the form of the shark. In 1892,
General Dodds returned to Europe with a
collection of palace objects as war booty.
These are now on display at the Musée
du quai Branly. G.B.-B.

Between West and Equatorial Africa: Nigeria

Bordering Lake Chad, and the Cameroon mountains to the east, Nigeria
was a centre of migration and a multicultural "melting-pot" during
the pre-colonial era. It can be subdivided into three areas: in the north,
the Haoussa, followers of Islam from the 15th century on; in the centre,
the Plateau region made up of a multitude of different ethnic groups;
and in the south, the Yoruba and Edo from the tropical forests which formed
three kingdoms: the Igbo (south-east), Ijo (Delta) and Ibibio (Cross River).

**Fragment
of male head**
Nok culture
Nigeria
1st millennium BC
Terracotta,
quartz, mica
15.5 x 12 cm
Former collection
Barbier-Mueller
Inv. 73.1996.1.1

**_The origins of West African sculpture:
Nok terracotta objects**

"Nok" terracotta objects were discovered by
accident on tin exploitation sites in the Plateau
region where mining activity began at the turn of
the 20th century. Named after the valley where
they were found, these terracotta objects are at
the origin of figurative sculpture in West Africa.
Modelled by hand and mounted using the
"colombin" or rolled clay technique, they feature
human figures with highly detailed adornments
and headdresses, as well as animals. Sometimes
whole (more than a metre high), but more often
in fragments, they reveal the great skill of the fire
masters and attest to a continuity of style
covering almost a thousand years and an

**Anthropomor-
phic figure**
Sao culture
Chad, Lake Fitri
region,
Tago site
9th-16th century
Terracotta
35 x 21 x 17 cm
J.-P. Lebeuf
mission,
1947-1948
Inv. 71.1949.3.843

/ ARCHAEOLOGY IN CHAD: THE SAO

Archaeologists have discovered bronze and terracotta objects vestiges of the Sao culture south of Lake Chad, in hundreds of sites located as far away as north-east Nigeria and north of Cameroon.

The oldest pieces have been dated to the 2nd century B.C., but most of the sculptures, featuring humans, animals or hybrid beings, were produced between the 10th and 13th century A.D.

The Sao buried their dead in large urns, along with the bronze and copper jewellery which was discovered on burial sites. Terracotta figurines were found in places of worship; although their religious role has been confirmed, several hypotheses have been put forward as to who or what they represent: ancestral beings, masked dancers or spirits of nature. From the 16th century onwards, the Sao no longer seemed to have exerted control over the region. A long period of conflict with the kingdom of Kanem Bornou ended with the disappearance of the Sao culture. A.G.

extremely vast area. The representation of the eye as an inverted triangle, in which the pupil is marked by a hole embodying the gaze, and the chamotte clay composition incorporating luminous grains of mica and quartz, are characteristic of the style. Along with ironware and quartz beads, the artistic and technical perfection of these terracotta objects, whose production and use are unknown, lead us to believe that they are part of a long artistic tradition that also includes wood sculpture. Dating back to the first millennium B.C., they are probably part of a larger production of objects from throughout North Nigeria.

_The first kingdoms: Ife and Benin

In 1910, the German ethnologist Leo Frobenius "rediscovered" the naturalist bronze and terracotta objects of the Classical period (12th-15th century) in Ife. Idealised portraits of the royal family and members of their entourage, these images evoke the traditions of the court of Ooni, the king of Ife. The copper alloy rings, in Ife as in the Bénin kingdom, depict specific and often macabre scenes associated with the enthronement rites of the king. There are images of Ooni, wearing a high silver crown made of glass beads, dressed in a short skirt and adorned with necklaces and numerous ankle bracelets, between two men who have been beheaded and whose bodies have been left to the vultures: these extraordinary rites signal the renewal of a divine and never-ending kingdom.

Ring evoking enthronement rites
Yoruba
South-west Nigeria, Ife Kingdom
17th-18th century
Copper alloy
18 x 17 cm
Former Barbier-Mueller collection
Inv. 73.1997.4.8

Work attributed to the Master of the Circled Cross
Figurative plaque
Nigeria, Kingdom of Benin
16th century
Copper alloy
39 x 29 cm
Inv. 70.2002.4.1

The arts of lost wax casting and copper alloy work were passed on to Benin from Ife. Copper trade with the Portuguese, in the form of shackles, from the late 15th century onwards fuelled the exceptional development of metal-working arts in the Benin kingdom. This artistic blossoming occurred in conjunction with the kingdom's territorial expansion. The decorative plaques that embellished the palace walls and pillars depicted *Oba*, the king of Benin, often in animal form, and his entourage, generally in a ceremonial context. On the palace altars dedicated to royal ancestors, commemorative brass heads are crowned by ivory tusks carved with the kings' genealogy.

Head of a royal ancestor
Edo
Nigeria, Kingdom of Benin
Late 18th century
Copper alloy

40.5 x 24.5 cm
Entrusted by the Musée des Antiquités nationales
Inv. 73.1969.3.1 D

_The Yoruba

Considered one of the major ethnic groups in Nigeria, the Yoruba formed numerous independent political entities in the past. However they all shared the same origins as children of Oduduwa, the king of origins, based on the the founding myth of Ife, the first kingdom of creation myths. At the summit of this diversified pantheon is a unique creator god, Olorun, represented on earth by the divine king and his council of chiefs. Secondary divinities known as the *Orisa* make up the divine family: Sango, the god of thunder, guarantees rain and fertility, his children, the *Ibeji,* bear the wealth, Ifa, the god of divination, knows the past, present and future and Esu, the ambiguous "meeting point" divinity, is the messenger of the gods. Yoruba styles vary according to the regions where the kingdom and local cult workshops developed: *Epa* initiation masks from the Ekiti region; Abeokuta style make-up palette; *Ose Sango* from

Bell for divination,
Iroke Ifa
Yoruba
Benin
19th century
Elephant ivory
42 x 4.1 cm
Inv. 71.1897.4.1

Work attributed to a studio in the Abeokuta region
Make-up palette
South-west Nigeria
19th century
Wood
13.2 x 36.4 cm
Inv. 73.1992.0.67

Works attributed
to a studio in the
Shaki region
Ibeji **statuettes
of twins**
South-west
Nigeria
Pre 1825
Wood, beads,
metal
27 x 7.5 cm
Donation
Former collections
Gbéhanzin,
C. Ratton,
G. de Miré, and
H. Goldet
Inv. 70.2003.3.7.1-2

**Ceremonial
staff,** *Ose sango*
Yoruba
South-west
Nigeria
19th century
Wood, pigments
44.2 x 14 cm
Former collection
Barbier-Mueller
Inv. 73.1997.4.130

Works attributed
to the sculptor
Osamuko
**Pair of veranda
posts**
South-west
Nigeria
Circa 1920-1930
Wood, pigments
150 x 31 cm and
180 x 31 cm
Former collection
Barbier-Mueller
Inv. 73.1997.4.63 and 64

Gelede **mask**
Yoruba
South-western
Nigeria
20th century
Wood
37 x 18.5 x 32 cm
Former collection
Barbier-Mueller
Inv. 73.1997.4.68

***Egungun* mask**
Yoruba
South-west
Nigeria
20ᵗʰ century
Textile, leather,
cowry shell, coral
163 x 52 cm
Inv. 73.1997.4.128

Ilaaro in the Egbado region; Egungun cloth masks
from Oyo representing ancestors returning from
the land of the dead; *Ibeji* twin worship figurines
from Saki; *Gelede* masks for "mother" worship in
the Egba region; a pair of *Edan* in brass, indicating
membership in the society of *ogboni* wisemen in
Ijebu; an ivory bell from Ifa, undoubtedly from
Owo, a kingdom half-way between Ife and Bénin.
Sometimes the artist can be identified: Osamuko,
a student of the master-sculptor Areogun
d'Osi-Olorin, created a set of veranda posts
depicting the Yoruba classic theme of a horseman
and maternity dated pre-1930.

_The Benue and Igbo regions

The Benue, an affluent of the Niger River dominated by the Jos plateau region, is a major communications point in east Nigeria. Mascarades, for which cattle heads are the preferred motif, are part of the farmers' calendar, celebrating harvests in particular. Settled on the border between Nigeria and Cameroon, the Mfunte, Keaka and Mambila carve ritual images used for therapeutic, divinatory or tribulatory practices. Their style prefigures the vigour and passion of Cameroonian sculpture.

The Igbo were organised in a multitude of village communities. They were active in trade (slaves, brass, textiles and other imported products) and a prosperous people. They created an impressive architecture with sun-dried earth: the *mbari* house, which honours the local divinities surrounding *Ala*, the earth goddess. The protecting divinities, the *Alusi*, represented by large multi-coloured images with outstretched and open hands in a sign of welcome, are present in each family unit during a special festival. Richly adorned and dressed, they receive offerings of cola nuts, white clay and libations.

Alusi **statue of a tutelary figure**
Igbo
South-west Nigeria
20th century
Wood, pigments
156.5 x 37 cm
Donated by J. and A. Kerchache
Inv. 70.2001.26.9

Anthropomorphic statue
Mambila
Nigeria, Donga Valley
Wood
19th-20th century
48 x 19.4 cm
Former collection Barbier-Mueller
Inv. 73.1996.1.88

Anthropomorphic crested headdress
Ejagham
Nigeria, Cross River region
20th century
Wood, antelope skin, basketwork, metal, bone
72.4 x 54 cm
Inv. 71.1948.8.2

_The Niger Delta and the Cross River

The Niger Delta region is characterized by the omnipresence of water and the special respect paid to water spirits. These spirits are embodied by masks of predatory animals (sharks, crocodiles), or of less harmful species, and are invited to visit the village during major annual festivals. The community welcomes these water spirits warily and at a certain distance, however their presence is necessary to guarantee protection and fertility. The Cross River region of tropical forest and oil palm is home to numerous groups that played a key role in the slave trade. Associations of hunters and warriors used naturalist wood masks covered with antelope hide. The ancient rivalry between the civilised world of the village and that of the bush where spirits reside lives on through a mascarade art expressing the traditional battle between order and the absence of harmony. Sombre, ugly masks evoking wandering spirits contrast with the handsome, pale-skinned masks of their more benevolent counterparts. H.J.

Crested headdress representing a sawfish
Ijo
Nigeria, Niger Delta region
20th century
Wood, pigments
33 x 43 cm
Former collection Barbier-Mueller
Inv. 73.1997.4.31

THE GREAT KINGDOMS OF CAMEROON - PIERRE HARTER'S LEGACY

West Cameroon is one of the "epicentres" of African tradition. Occupied since the 16th century by conquerors from Adamawa, these volcanic lands have gradually been taken over by numerous chiefdoms such as Foumban, Bandjoun and Kom. The chiefs, guarantors of the collective prosperity, reign with the help of secret societies. A land of magic and symbols, these kingdoms have been the source of a rich and varied ritual art. The monumental architecture of the "great houses" and the sculpture of royal thrones and masks are also part of the emblematic "treasures" of the *fo* Bamileke passed down from generation to generation.
The Pierre Harter legacy, donated in 1992 to the Musée des Arts d'Afrique et d'Océanie, includes 53 objects, twenty of which are masterpieces of African art. L.P.

1/ *Juju* mask
Bekom
Cameroon, north-west province, Kom
19th-20th century
Wood
34 x 28 cm
Inv. 73.1992.0.12

2/ *Atwonzen* representation of human skull
Bamileke
Cameroon, west province, chiefdom of Fonchatula
19th-20th century
Wood, glass beads, cowry shells, fabric
36.5 x 15.6 cm
Inv. 73.1992.0.49

1

**3/Queen
carrying a jar**
Bamileke
Cameroon,
west province,
chiefdom
of Bansoa
19ᵗʰ century
Wood, glass
beads, cloth,
cowry shells
115 x 46 cm
Inv. 73.1992.0.14

**4/Work
attributed to the
sculptor Kamteu
Calabash
offering figure**
Cameroon,
Dschang region,
chiefdom of Foto
Circa 1910
Wood, metal
127.5 x 52 cm
Inv. 73.1992.0.39

**5/Fragments
of *Nko* pillar**
Bali-Nyonga
Cameroon, north-
west province,
chiefdom of
Bali-Nyonga
Circa 1905
Wood
149 x 38 cm
Inv. 73.1992.0.33

**6/Royal mask
representing an
elephant**
Bamileke
Cameroon,
west province,
kingdom of
Bafu-Fondong
19ᵗʰ century
Wood
50 x 89.2 cm
Inv. 73.1992.0.50

3

4

5

6

Equatorial Africa

Equatorial Africa, which comprises Cameroon, Equatorial Guinea, Congo-Brazzaville and Gabon, is a region with an exceptional sculptural tradition. The spirit masks and sculpture associated with the worship of ancestors and discovered by Western artists at the turn of the 20th century are expressions of a secular culture in which the bond between the living and the dead was carefully maintained.

_The "images" of ancestors.
The Fang, Kota and Punu

Religious sculpture by the ethnic groups that inhabit the Atlantic equatorial forest, the Fang, Kota and Punu in particular, has given African art some of its most remarkable masterpieces. Called *Eyema-o-byeri* ("image of skull of the ancestor") by the Fang and *Mbulu-ngulu* ("reliquary guardian figure") by the Kota, these wooden ancestor effigies were placed on family reliquary boxes containing the skulls of deceased elders.

**Eyima byeri
reliquary
guardian**
Fang Betsi
Gabon, Woleu-
Ntem region
19th century
Wood, vegetable
fibres
42.6 x 15.3 cm
Donated by
Cartelle
Collected between
1905 and 1908
Inv. 71.1954.67.3

**Ngulu reliquary
guardian**
Kota Ondoumbo
Gabon, Haut-
Ogooue region
19th century
Wood, brass,
copper
63.6 x 29.5 cm
Donated by
J. Savorgnan
de Brazza and
A. Pecile
Inv. 71.1886.79.4

The Fang

The Fang settled in South Cameroon, North
Gabon and Equatorial Guinea in the 18th and
19th centuries. They split into numerous groups:
the Beti, Ngumba, Mabea in the north, the Ntumu
and Mvaï in the centre and centre-east, the Okak
in the west and the Betsi in the south. They
honour the relics of the deceased *(byeri)*, a clear
indication of the powerful bond that exists
between the living and the dead. The rites for
this family cult are designed to make everyday life
easier and to ensure the continuity of generations,
and have considerable political significance
as well: owning a large reliquary *(nsekh-o-byeri)*
is a sign of prestige and power. The skulls are
displayed periodically, especially to new initiates
learning their genealogy, while statues with
feather headdresses are "animated" like puppets
in a sort of ritualized scenography.
Given the size of the Fang region, it is not
surprising that diverse regional styles have
developed over time. The "stylistic geography"
of Fang sculpture includes elongated and
sometimes angular statues decorated with metal
incrustations (Ngumba and Ntumu in South

**Reliquary bundle
with a guardian
figure**
Punu or Lumbo
Southern Gabon
19th century
Wood, pigments,
skin, vegetable
fibres
32 x 18 cm
Inv. 71.1943.0.433 X AFN

/ THE BLACKSMITH

**The importance of metal-
working in Equatorial Africa
is illustrated by the diversity
of traditional iron, copper
or brass objects, as well as by
the predominant role of the
village blacksmith. Fire master
and great initiated member
of the main secret societies,
the blacksmith is a *Nganga*,
or doctor, judge and magician.
A blacksmith's work demands
technical expertise that can be
acquired only through extensive
training and an in-depth
knowledge of rites. This high
level of specialisation explains
the remarkable social and
symbolic value of metal objects:
throwing and fighting weapons,
chief emblems (bells), male
and female finery (necklaces,
torques, bracelets, ankle rings,
gaiters), dowry money, tools,
hunting utensils. The Kota
(Gabon, Congo) in particular
have used copper and brass
to adorn their ancestor
effigies, cherished as family
guardians. L.P.**

Cameroon and North Gabon) to the north; heads with rounded volumes and magnificent monoxylic braided headdresses (Betsi and Fang) in the centre-west; and larger effigies (Mvaï and Betsi) in the centre-east and further south to Ogooue. Some of these representations, both male and female, with their often oozing black patina, are elegant works whose enigmatic faces, long admired for their "savage" appearance, reflect, in fact, a very human spirituality.

***Mboumba bwete* reliquary basket with guardian figure** *Kota* Gabon, Haut-Ogooue region 19th century	Wood, brass, copper, basketwork, skin, bone, feathers 60 x 32 cm Donated by Ch. Vital-Roche Inv. 71.1897.39.1

The Kota

The Kota *Mbulu-ngulu* reliquary figures are very different in style. They are two-dimensional bas-relief sculptures made of wood with brass plaques or strips carved with decorative motifs fastened to them. Surprisingly abstract, Kota faces are more dream images than commemorative evocations. The "Kota" comprise a set of ethnic groups which are more or less related and have occupied the region of Eastern Gabon and the bordering North Congo for three centuries, including the Ndumu, Ndassa, Wumbu, Mahongwe, Obamba and Ambete. Here too, the diversity of the groups has led to a complex stylistic geography. In the North, the Mahongwe depict their ancestors with a refined outline and an arched face decorated with fine, perfectly joined horizontal strips. The Obamba and Ndassa in the South used more ample forms with a hollowed oval face or a face with an overhanging forehead, lined with rounded lateral shells and crowned by a majestic crescent-shaped headdress. The back of the wood scupture is entirely covered with brass plaques.

Head, *eyima byeri* reliquary guardian *Fang Betsi* Northern Gabon, Okano River and Abanga River interfluvial region

19th century Wood, brass 41.5 x 14 cm Donated by Mme P. Guillaume Former collection P. Guillaume Inv. 71.1941.13.10

**Anthropomor-
phic mask**
Fang
Gabon
19th-20th century
Wood, kaolin,
feathers
57 x 38 cm
Inv. 73.1968.7.1

Mvoudi mask
Aduma
Gabon, Haut-
Ogooue region
19th century
Wood, pigments
55 x 19 cm
Donated by
Schwebisch
and Tholon
Inv. 71.1884.37.4

The Punu

Ancestor worship to the west of Gabon is based
on the same underlying philosophy and is
accompanied by similar rites. However,
the painted wood effigies of the Punu are more
realistic and have a more refined finish.

_Spirit masks

While the styles of ancestor sculpture have not
changed substantially in ethnic communities,
mask styles are driven by a constant search for
innovation, reflecting a "hunger for the sacred"
and the intense desire to find the means for
accessing it.

The spirit world, which includes the souls of the
deceased and spirits of the "bush", is closely
linked to the world of the living. These entities,
feared but continually invoked, appear in the
dreams of the initiated: their representation
through painted wood, of varied realistic and
stylised forms, is a subtle way of provoking them
whilst keeping them at a distance. Each event
marking the life of villages involves a ritual
intervention from spirits and the wearing of
masks adapted to the particular function (some
propitiatory, others prophylactic or even judicial).
Equatorial African masks play a critical role in
keeping witchcraft at bay, for example.

Okuyi mask
Punu
Gabon
19th-20th century
Wood, pigments
37 x 27 cm
Inv. 73.1964.10.2

G-string
Mbuti
Democratic
Republic of Congo
19th century
Beaten bark,
pigments
91 x 75.3 cm
Inv. 73.1990.4.17

For the Fang, the great white masks of the _Ngil_
serve to regulate society; for the Punu, the
idealised "white" masks reinforce the impact
of secret societies; among the Tsogho and Aduma
from middle Ogooue, and the Kota, multi-
coloured and often expressionist masks are worn
for all initiations, the initiation of the _Bwiti_,
for example.

_Pygmy arts

The Pygmy can be found in South Cameroon (Baka), Gabon (Bongo, Kola) and the Democratic Republic of Congo (Mbuti of the Ituri), each group with its own distinct culture. Hunter-gatherers, they maintain a privileged relationship with their forest environment. They create pictorial arts on beaten bark and astonishing polyphonic vocal music. L.P.

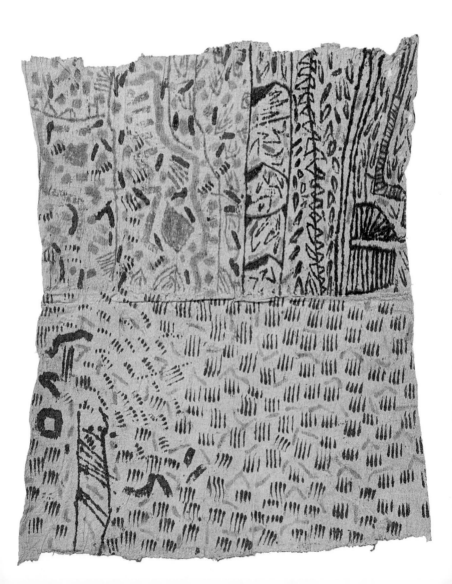

Central Africa

Central Africa comprises the areas around the equatorial forest near the Congo river and its affluents, and bordered by the savannah to the south. Prosperous kingdoms began to develop as early as the 9th century B.C. In 1483, the Portuguese arrived at the mouth of the Congo.

Work attributed to the Master of the Chiloango River
Magical male statue
Nkisi nkondi
Angola, angolan enclave of Cabinda
1880-1910
Wood, iron, pigments, cord, enamelled sheet metal, resin, clay, organic matter
108 x 49 cm
Donated by Lang, 1935
Inv. 73.1963.0.175

Crucifix with charm
Luba
Democratic Republic of Congo
19th century
Wood, organic elements
53.5 x 18 cm
Donated by M. and Mme C. Vérité
Inv. 70.2001.32.1

**Anthropomor-
phic mask**
Kongo
Congo, Loango
coast
Late 19th-early
20th century
Wood, pigments,
textile, monkey
hair, brass
34.5 x 18.5 cm
Former collection
A. Lefèvre
Inv. 73.1965.10.5

**Nkisi magical
figure
'Bumba ma zi'**
Woyo
Angola, angolan
enclave of
Cabinda
19th-20th century
Wood, cotton,
shells, horn,
metal, mirror,
snail shells,
seeds, fruit
38.7 x 27.2 cm
Donated by
R. P. C. Tastevin
Inv. 71.1934.28.13

/ THE DIVINER OR NGANGA

The *Nganga* is a diviner, healer
and judge. He is usually
consulted for an explanation or
a resolution of a problem. The
Nganga prepares the medecines
and activates the *Nkisi*. People
often become a *Nganga* after a
dream in which the *nkisi*
appear. A long secret initiation
rite then takes place in the
forest. The future *Nganga* learns
the formula of the magic
bilongo, the music that is an
integral part of the *Minkisi*, and
the numerous rules and
restrictions (food, space, etc.)
governing them. The divination
ceremonies are often as
spectacular as the *Minkisi*
themselves: the Nganga's face is
hidden beneath a thick layer of
red, white and black make-up or
behind a mask. He sometimes
wears a feather headdress and a
skirt made from strips of cotton,
hide, feathers, bells and small
bags filled with medecine. N.S.

_Magic statues: the Minkisi
in the Kongo region

The *Minkisi* (or *Nkisi*) in the Kongo region, at the
mouth of the Congo river, are among the most
famous power objects and are described in travel
accounts from the 17th century on. *Minkisi* contain
the powers of the invisible world of the dead.
They can take the form of a male figure studded
with nails and mirrors or of a medecine bag or a
crucifix to which *bilongo* medecines are attached.
They are composed of ingredients with names
which enable allusions or assonances to be made
in reference to actions. Their composition also
functions as a rebus that only a diviner is able to
decipher completely. *Minkisi* are used to identify
the causes of various evils, to provoke an illness,
as well as to find the remedy. Some *Minkisi* are
supposed to locate thieves while others can
be used as a pledge for a trading contract. The
properties and functions of *Minkisi* are boundless.

Work attributed
to the Master of
Boma Vonde
Canne, *mvwala*
Democratic
Republic of Congo
19th century
Wood
69 x 7 cm
Donation
Former collection
H. Goldet
Inv. 70.2003.3.9

***Mfunka*
fly-swatter
handle**
Kongo
Democratic
Republic of Congo
17th-19th century
Hippopotamus
ivory
13.7 x 4.1 cm
Inv. 73.1985.2.1

_The representation of women in Kongo art
While most diviners are men, a good number
of *Minkisi* are delicately carved female figures,
generally depicted breastfeeding a baby or
carrying it on her back. In sculptures representing
a couple, women serve to moderate the
destructive power of male *Minkisi*. Their expertise
is often tied to fertility and fecundity. One can
also find the mother and child image on the
handles of the elders' canes, or *mvwala*, and on
fly-swatter handles. By evoking the founding
ancestors of a lineage, the image of the mother
as a nurturer connects the world of the living
to that of the dead. The wearing the chief's hat,
mpu, as well as of bracelets, indicates wealth
and power and demonstrates the importance
of women in Kongo society.

_The symbols of authority/ instruments of power

To the East, in the Luba region, caryatid chairs and *kibango* sceptres are objects of prestige which chiefs use to affirm their power and rank. Before colonisation, they held a central place in investiture ceremonies. The chairs are containers for royal souls, while the *kibango* sceptres are often filled with magic ingredients for healing rites. Symbols of sacred authority and power objects, they also evoke the genealogical history of the lineage, each figure recalling an episode of royal history. Women also play a key role and represent the female founders of the various Luba royal lines. N.S.

Caryatid seat
Luba
Democratic
Republic of Congo
Wood
48.5 x 24.5 cm
Former collection
A. Lefèvre
Inv. 73.1965.10.6

***Kibango*
power sceptres**
Luba
Democratic
Republic of Congo
19th century
Wood
131.5 x 12.5 cm
Donation
Former collection
H. Goldet
Inv. 70.2003.3.10

_The Kuba group

The Biyeeng, Bangyeen, Bapyaang and Bushoong peoples make up the Kuba group from the centre of the Democratic Republic of Congo. They claim to be descendants of Woot, the first man created by the god Mbwoom.

Artists and craftsmen work for the king and his entourage. The power and the sacred character of the sovereign are expressed in a number of objects, particularly masks, which are worn by the king alone. This Bwoom mask is recognisable by its prominent forehead.

Bowl for drinking palm wine
Kuba
Democratic Republic of Congo
19th century
Wood
9 x 21 cm
Donated by A. Lefèvre
Inv. 71.1954.23.13

Ndeemba anthropomorphic mask
Yaka
Democratic Republic of Congo
20th century
Wood, woven raffia, pigments, vegetable fibres
62.2 x 40 cm
Inv. 73.1965.5.20

Panel from an initiation hut
Nkanu
Democratic Republic of Congo
19th century
Wood, pigments
77.5 x 35.7 cm
Donated by the Société des amis du musée d'ethnographie du Trocadéro
Inv. 71.1932.15.11

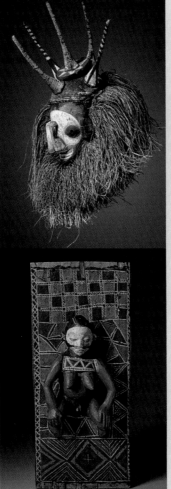

/ INITIATION

Initiation, which represents the death of a being and his rebirth as a new being, marks the stages of human life. The initiated wear masks to officiate in rituals during which adolescents pass into adulthood. The rituals take place in a sacred site far from the village and last several weeks. The young people's clothes are burnt symbolizing their separation from their family and their death. Distanced for the first time from those who cherish and protect them, they feel fear, but also rapture and ecstasy. They participate in imposing rituals: masked spirit parades, the crossing of gates and bridges, the passage through tunnels... As a last step, they must brave circumcision or excision. This period of initiation is devoted above all to learning the mysteries of the natural, social and supernatural life. The return to the village, marked by a celebration, highlights the start of a new life. G.S.

Richard Buchta, *Lango Chief*. Uganda, circa 1875-1880.

Anthropo-zoomorphic helmet mask
Kuba/Kete
Democratic Republic of Congo
19th century

Wood, pigments
39.1 x 43 cm
Donated by Arman
Former Arman collection
Inv. 73.1996.16.1

According to various accounts, it is the portrait the king's brother, a prince whose forehead was well developed. Elders compete with each other in their display of wealth, and luxury objects are common: head-shaped cups for drinking palm wine, boxes for storing *tukula*, and red wood flour used as make up. The geometric motifs decorating the boxes, the woven leaf walls of the royal palace and raffia weavings are all precisely named and codified.

Female figure
Mangbetu
Democratic Republic of Congo
20th century
Wood, cotton
46.3 x 14 cm
Inv. 73.1966.2.1

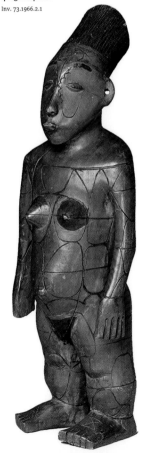

_The Mangbetu

In 1870, the German botanist Georg Schweinfurth became the first European to enter into direct contact with the Mangbetu, who lived to the north-east of what is now the Democratic Republic of Congo. He was fascinated by the lifestyle and art at King Mbunza's court and spread word of the Mangbetu in the West. One of the most striking elements of Mangbetu culture is the very pronounced elongation of the back part of the skull, produced by compressing the cranium of new-born babies with a headband. The headdresses accentuate this elongation, which is considered aesthetic, natural and a mark of identity. The form is also used as the motif of an array of objects: statuettes, earthenware, boxes, harps and knife handles.
Body painting is also very important for the Mangbetu. Motifs drawn on the body are reproduced on the walls of dwellings and textiles. A.G.

Southern and Austral Africa

Southern Africa is the homeland of ethnic groups of various origins. Populations of hunter-gatherers and shepherds occupied the territory before the farming Bantou. In the mid- 17th century, the East India Company set up a European colony at the Cape (South Africa). The area is made up of a mosaic of cultures whose artistic creativity was long neglected because of the rarity of masked traditions. Cattle is the predominant symbol in this part of Africa and perceived as a source of power guaranteeing the continuity of lineages.

Anthropomorphic figures
Tsonga
South Africa or Mozambique
19th century
Wood, leather, fabric, metal
54 x 14 cm and 61 x 11.5 cm
Donated by Baron Oppenheim
Inv. 71.1892.29.1 and.2

Anthropomorphic staff (detail)
Fingo
South Africa
Second half of the 19th century
Wood
100 x 3.1 cm
Donated by Dr É. Holub
Inv. 71.1881.59.26

_Entering the world of men

In the 19th century, political centralisation and the expansion of chiefdoms changed the face of South Africa. The emergence of the Zulu kingdom resulted in the transformation of initiation schools, where young boys normally underwent circumcision, into regiments organised in age groups. Wood sculpture, which mainly represented the image of the couple, was a predominant feature in the initiation rites. Staffs, one of the objects symbolising adult status, were carried by their owners wherever they went, announcing their presence, and were also used as dance accessories. The male image is often depicted on the staff handles, indicating power: coiffed by the ringed headdress typical of the Nguni, it represents maturity and social status.

_Women and bead arts

Before the introduction of the glass bead of European origin along the African coasts in the 16th century, the civilisations of South and East Africa produced beads made from ostrich egg shell or, more rarely, metal. Necklaces, bracelets, belts and headbands use a large number of natural plant-based (wood, grain, fibres) or animal-based materials (tendons, teeth, horns, bones). The huge supply of glass beads in the 19th century triggered an unprecedented development in bead art across the region. A means of exchange, glass beads became the common currency for "a fiancée's payment". Each change in status provides an opportunity for changing costumes and adornment. To express their affection, young girls and women make beaded ornaments during the winter months when seduction rites, weddings and initiation ceremonies take place. Worn at community festivals, these often spectacular adornments are an external sign of social success and a source of rivalry between women. Bead art is an expression of identity that has created an authentic art form; different colours and motifs have been integrated over time creating a new fashion language.

Ibheshu
man's skirt
Zulu
South Africa
1940
Leather, glass beads
65.3 x 50.5 cm
Inv. 70.1999.11.206

Headrest
Djimma
Ethiopia
19th century
Wood, beads
18.5 x 16 cm
Donated by Borelli
Inv. 71.1890.28.106

Ijogolo married woman's ceremonial apron
Ndebele
South Africa
1920-1930
Leather, glass beads, brass
65.3 x 50.5 cm
Inv. 70.1999.11.189

_Communicating with Ancestors

While bead art, created by women, may also be practised by diviners, sculpture is reserved for men only. The link between livestock, which increased significantly in the late 19th century giving rise to the wealth and power, and the protection of ancestors, the source of prosperity and knowledge, is achieved through diverse community experiences and the production of objects symbolising the sought-after contact with their forefathers. Group consumption of beer or meat, extending beyond simple hospitality in the home, the sniffing or smoking of tobacco, and sleep have become the vectors of choice for this type of communication, which plays an important social and spiritual role. Headrests, generally offered by women to their husbands, often look like a stylised image of an ox: through dreams, they become a point of convergence and discussion between ancestors from different lineages.

Shona headrest
Zimbabwe
19th century
Wood
19.3 x 25 cm
Donated by
the Forschungs
Institute,
Frankfurt
am Main
Inv. 71.1934.137.6

Container
Swazi
South
Africa/Swaziland
Wood
19th century
58 x 39 cm
Inv. 71.1935.54.95 D

Zoomorphic headrest
Tsonga
Mozambique
Late 19th century
Wood
16.5 x 14.5 cm
Donated by
A. Lombard
Inv. 71.1890.65.11

***Waaga* anthropomorphic funerary pole**
Konso
Ethiopia
Mid 19th century
Wood
198 x 27 cm
Inv. 70.2001.4.1

_Funerary poles

From the south of Ethiopia, to the east of Chad and as far as Madagascar, numerous ethnic groups such as the Konso, Sara, Bongo, Moro, Giriama, Bara and Sakalava, have developed the art of monumental funerary sculpture.

For certain Bongo populations (Sudan and the Central African Republic), the erection of a funerary pole on a chief's tomb appears to be a tradition dating back several centuries.

The Konso (Ethiopia) do not place sculptures near burial sites, however, but group them at the village entrance.

In Madagascar, the influence of the beliefs of the Indian Ocean and Insulindia populations is visible in the funerary poles called *aloalo*.

The tomb is the site for commemorative ceremonies, offerings and zebu sacrifices to ensure the protection of the deceased who, if they are not honoured in this way, may provoke accidents or illness. In the South and West regions of the island, the quadrangular terraces forming the tomb feature wooden poles depicting ancestors or birds.

Funerary statue
Sakalava
Madagascar,
Bosy
19th-20th century
Wood
78.5 x 20.5 cm
Inv. 71.1965.24.3

_Madagascar

Archaeological research has dated the first
settlements in Madagascar to around the
9th century A.D. The gradual and simultaneous
arrival of civilisations from the African continent
(present-day Tanzania and Mozambique)
and Malaysian and Indonesian groups via
the Indian Ocean, resulted in the formation
of small kingdoms on the vast island, making it a
cultural centre with a mix of practices and beliefs.
The way of life of most Malagasy strongly reflects
the influence the deceased have over the world of
the living. The importance attached to funerary
art underscores this concern with the
metaphysical. The Malagasy also fear another
more visible world: the world of the spirits and
supernatural beings, some of which are
malevolent. An amulet, or *ody*, worn at the neck
or waist, is required for protection. The talisman,
made for an individual or for a group, in which
case it is known as a *sampy*, is reputed to
counterbalance adversity and bring success,
power and wealth. A.G.

Mohara amulet
Bara
Madagascar
19th century
Wood, horn,
beads, cotton,
organic materials,
metal
19 x 6.3 cm
Donated by
J. Millot
Inv. 71.1961.60.104

Aloalo funerary
pole
Bara or Sakalava
Southern
Madagascar
19th century
Wood, bovine
skulls, metal
Donated by the
Madagascar
Committee for
the Universal
Exhibition, Paris,
1900
Inv. 71.1901.6.11

/ CHRISTIANITY IN AFRICA
The African churches of
Alexandria, Carthage and
Axoum were prominent during
the first centuries of
Christianity. In the 7th century,
Islam spread and Christianity
declined. However, in the late
15th century, the arrival of the
Portuguese on the West coast
of Africa sparked a revival of the
religion on the continent.
Alfonso, the king of Kongo,
converted to Christianity and
changed the name of his capital
from Mbanza'kongo to San
Salvador. His son Dom Enrique
met with the Pope in Rome. In
the 19th century, Catholics and
Protestants penetrated the
continent and launched an
attack on traditional animist
religions. After 1960, the Church
become more "Africanised"
and the number of Europeans
in its ranks diminished
considerably. At the same time,
numerous syncretic and
schismatic churches began to
develop. The emerging religions
tried to eradicate traditional
beliefs, but animism survived
and symbols of the new
religions, Christian crosses as
well as elements of the Koran,
were integrated, even in
sculpture. G.S.

AFRICAN TEXTILES

Textile arts in Africa make use of the natural resources of local fibres (raffia, linen, cotton, wool, etc.) that are woven and then assembled to make traditional clothing. While weaving and dyeing techniques are similar throughout Africa, decorative motifs are extraordinarily varied. Horizontal loom weaving and dressmaking are the prerogative of men in Sub-Saharan Africa, while the use of vertical looms and dyeing are reserved for women skilled in the techniques of natural dyes (indigo, henna, cola nuts, bark and mud). Embroidery is an essentially male art, although it is also practised by women in North Africa. H.J. and M.-F.V.

1/ *Bogolanfini* hunter's loincloth
Bamana
Mali,
Segou region
Early 20th century
Cotton, clay
136 x 75.5 cm
F. de Zeltner
bequest
Inv. 71.1930.61.908

2/*Hanbel* wall hanging
Berber
Algeria, Ouargla
Late 19th century
Wool, cotton, indigo
338 x 144 cm
Donated by
Parvillée
Inv. 74.1962.0.957

3/Cape
Mangbetu
Democratic
Republic of Congo
Early 20th century
Beaten bark fibre, pigments
174 x 135 cm
Collected by the
Citroen 'Croisière
Noire', 1924-1925
Inv. 73.1963.0.1116

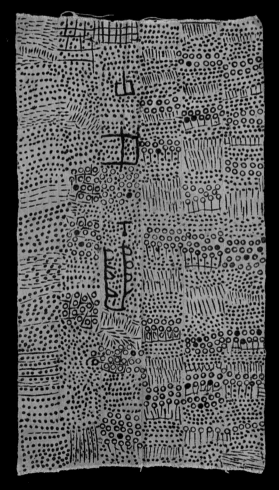

1

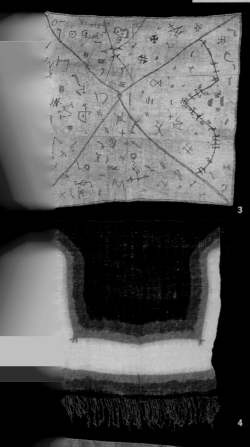

3

4

5

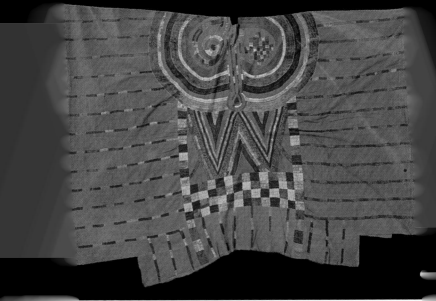

CHRISTIAN ETHIOPIA

In the 4th century, Ethiopia converted to Christianity. For several centuries, churches were dug out in the rock. In the 7th century, they were often built in a circular shape with a central rectangular room, the Saint of Saints, whose outer walls and drum support a ceiling rich in iconography that the faithful could follow during the course of the liturgy. Canvasses mounted on the walls of the church of Abba Antonios, dating back to this period and removed by the Dakar-Djibouti mission in 1931, depict scenes positioned according to the main points of a compass: the Virgin and child (West wall), the childhood and life of Christ (South wall), the holy riders bringing down idols and martyrs (North wall) and the kings and prophets (East wall). Some magical practices, especially the art of protective rolls whose origins lie in an ancient "science", survived up until the 20th century. H.J.

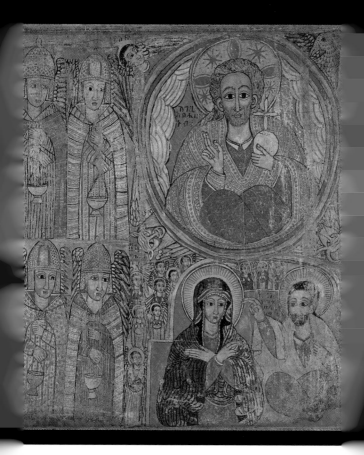

Clan Headdress
Tlingit
Alaska
Circa 1860-1870
Wood, abalone,
leather, sinew,
graphite, copper
oxide, vermillion
31 x 18.5 cm
Inv. 70.2006.1.1

Americas /

American history begins with the final ice age, between 50,000 and 10,000 years B.C., when the continent was peopled by hunters migrating from Asia. Thereafter cut off from the Old World, Native American societies developed rapidly, coexisting with and succeeding one another within major cultural groupings. The European conquest triggered by the voyages of Christopher Columbus wrought radical change in the Native world. Many societies were wiped out, while others resisted, became isolated, or adopted cultural practices from other parts of the world. The museum's oldest American collections were assembled for the "Cabinet du Roi" in the 16th, 17th and 18th centuries, and bore witness to the newly discovered peoples of Brazil and Canada. 19th century explorers concentrated more on pre-Columbian antiquities from Mexico and Peru, while collections made by 20th century archaeologists and ethnologists cover the Americas as a whole. In the museum's exhibition of these collections, the American continent of today and the recent past is presented alongside Pre-Columbian America, in order to highlight the distinctive nature of Native American artefacts, reflecting the unity and singularity of the continent as a whole. The itinerary begins with objects produced by Caribbean and Brazilian peoples descended from the Black slaves brought from Africa, a reminder of the hybrid composition of the cultures and population of the Americas today.

2500 BC
Earliest ceremonial hill sites in North America

1500 BC
Colonisation of the Arctic by the Inuit

1350-500 BC
Olmec culture in Mexico. Beginnings of monumental architecture in Mesoamerica

Between 50,000 and 10,000 BC
Earliest population of the Americas from Asia, via the Bering Straits

7000-5000 BC
Earliest agriculture in the Andes and Mesoamerica

4000-3000 BC
Earliest production of ceramics in Colombia and Ecuador (Valdivia)

1000-200 BC
Chavin culture in Peru. Earliest development of Andean architecture and sculpture

500 BC-900 AD
Zapotec civilisation in Mexico

500 BC-600 AD
Expansion of Saladero style cultures in the Antilles

200 BC-700 AD
Regional developments in the Andes: Paracas, Nasca, Mochica, Tumaco, and La Tolita

0-600
Teotihuacán civilisation in Mexico

300-900
Classical Mayan civilisation in Mesoamerica

5th-10th century
Development of Marajó and Santarem cultures on the Amazon

600-1000
Huari and Tiahuanaco Empires in Peru and Bolivia

700-1400
Mound Builders culture in Mississippi

1000-1400
The Yucatan peninsula dominated by Chichen Itza, then by Maya pan

1000-1400
Later Peruvian kingdoms: Chimú and Chancay

12th-15th century
Taino culture in the Greater Antilles. First Amerindian societies wiped out by European colonization in the first half of the 16th century

1200-1500
Development of the Inca Empire

1345
Foundation of Tenochtitlán, the Aztec capital city

1492
Christopher Columbus reaches the Bahamas and the Antilles. Hispaniola acts as base for Spanish conquest of the New World

1494
Treaty of Tordesillas: division of Spanish and Portuguese possessions

1519-1521
Hernan Cortez conquers the Aztec Empire and founds Mexico

1532-1533
Destruction of the Inca Empire by Francisco Pizarro

1530
Jacques Cartier discovers the Saint-Laurent River

1542
First descent of the River Amazon by Francisco de Orellana

1550
Valladolid controversy: Spanish recognition of the human nature of Indians

1572
Final Inca resistance

1607
First English colony in Virginia

1625-1650
Eviction of Carib Indians from the Antilles by the French and English

Mid 17th-18th century
Numerous Indian uprisings in the face of missionary expansion

1680
Pueblo Indians revolt against the Spanish in New Mexico

1697
Fall of Tayasal, the last independent Mayan city

18th century
Widespread adoption of the horse by the Chacos, Pampas and Plains Indians

1743-1800
Earliest scientific expeditions in South America: Charles Marie de La Condamine, Alexander von Humbolt and Aimé Bonpland

1804
Independence of Haiti, the first black republic

1804-1806
The Meriwether Lewis and William Clark expedition crosses North America to the Pacific Ocean

1813-1830
Independence of Latin American States

1833-1888
Abolition of slavery in the Americas

1838-1839
Deportation of Amerindians from the southeastern United States to west of the Mississippi

1847
Castes War: Mayan peasants rise up against the Yucatan government in Mexico

1853
First Indian reservations in the United States

1860-1914
Rubber exploitation costs the lives of tens of thousands of Amazonian Indians

1876
Defeat of General George A. Custer at Little Big Horn

1910-1920
Mexican Revolution

1950
Aimé Césaire publishes his *Discourse on Colonialism*

1964
Inauguration of the Mexican Museo Nacional de Antropología

1984
Creation in Peru of the Coordinator of the Indigenous Organisations of the Amazon Basin (COICA)

1990
The United States adopts a law imposing restitution of Indian cultural property (bones, funerary and sacred artefacts, etc.)

1992
Nobel Peace Prize awarded to Rigoberta Menchú for her work in promoting the rights of indigenous peoples

1995
The UN set up a work group on the projected Declaration on the Rights of Indigenous Peoples

1999
Creation of the Inuit territory of Nunavut in Canada

2004
Opening of the National Museum of the American Indian in Washington

Map

Ethnology	Archaeology
1. Inuit	39. West Mexico
2. Yup'ik	40. Teotihuacan,
3. Alutiiq	Aztec
4. Tlingit	41. Zapotec,
5. Haida	Mixtec
6. Tsimshian	42. Gulf Coast,
7. Kwakwaka'-wakw	Huastec
8. Blackfoot	43. Maya
9. Sioux	44. Gran Nicoya
10. Comanches	45. Central Costa Rica
11. Pawnee	46. Gran Chiriqui
12. Quapaw	47. Coclé
13. Mandan	48. Taino
14. Huron	49. Suazey
15. Chumash	50. Saladero
16. Hopi	51. Marajoara
17. Huichol	52. Tairona
18. Otomi	53. Mosquito
19. Lakandon	54. Muisca
20. K'iché	55. Quimbaya
21. Koqchikel	56. Cauca
22. Cuna	57. Tumaco-La Tolita
23. Vaudou	58. Jama-Coaque
24. Shuar-Achuar	59. Valdivia, Manta, Chorrera
25. Shipibo	60. Mochica, Chimu
26. Ye'kuana	61. Chavin, Recuay
27. Wayana	62. Chancay
28. Munduruku	63. Paracas, Nasca, Ica-Chincha
29. Karaja	64. Wari
30. Wauja	65. Tiwanaku
31. Bororo	66. Inca
32. Marrons des Guyanes	
33. Candomblé	
34. Quecha	
35. Yuracaré	
36. Toba Pilaga	
37. Mapuche	
38. Tehuelche	

African heritage

European colonisation of the Americas is inextricably linked to the slave trade that brought millions of Africans to plantations in the New World between the 16th and 19th centuries. This mass deportation produced distinctive Afro-American cultures in the vast territory comprising the Caribbean, Brazil and the Southeast United States, where a large majority of the descendants of African slaves now live.

Ceremonial flag, Saint Jacques Major
Voodoo
Haiti
20th century
Fabric, spangles
95.5 x 85 cm
Inv. 71.1987.52.1

Exu, deity of crossroads, and messenger
Candomble,
Nago *ritual*
Brazil, Salvador de Bahia
20th century
Iron
23.2 x 3.2 cm
V. Chiara and N. Guidon Mission
Inv. 71.1971.30.123.1-2

In these areas, the mixing of cultures played a key role in religion, music and language. The African cults and gods survived, often hidden behind a Catholic "mask", such as the candomblé in Brazil, voodoo in Haiti and santería in Cuba.
European crucifixes were integrated into traditional African magic practices and became the "hybrid crosses" used in voodoo rites.
The African divinities Yoruba and Bantu appear in the guise of Catholic saints.

In another form of resistance, runaway rebel slaves managed to form new African communities in the Guyanese forests, and remained relatively untouched by the Creole world. These black fugitives created a distinctive art, decorating everyday wooden objects (combs, paddles, drums, etc.) with engravings and paintings.

Apinti **drum or "talking drum"**
Marrons
French Guyana or Surinam
20th century
Wood, leather
58 x 30.5 cm
Inv. 71.1947.14.5

/ THE MIXING OF MUSIC

Most of today's popular music – such as rock, reggae, rap or rai – has developed from mixed or Creole music. These musical genres, which originated in the Americas between the 17th and 20th centuries have been combined in dynamic and innovative ways, but are rooted in its colonial history. Europeans settled in places inhabited by indigenous populations and imported slaves from numerous African communities originating from places located between Senegal and Angola, Mozambique and Madagascar.

Although sources concerning the musical practices of African slaves in the 17th and 18th centuries are rare, it can be assumed that these populations, brutally uprooted and dispersed in a new land, sought to create music that could be shared among captives as well as with their masters. New musical forms, which drew on elements that were familiar or common to the music in the slaves' regions of origin, as well as those from European popular music, were developed before being reinterpreted, transformed and exported worldwide. M.L.

Magical-religious packet with Christian cross
Voodoo
Haiti, Port-au-Prince Bay
20th century
Fabric, iron
23.7 x 9.8 cm
Donated by K. Fischer
Inv. 71.1950.29.4

AMERINDIAN RITUALS

In order to make the world intelligible, myths established order by separating the earth and the sky, the living and the dead, humans and non-humans (gods, spirits, animals). They were thereby distanced one from the other.
Ever since, rituals have sought to bring supernatural entities and humans together in order to preserve the unity of the world. This is done in two main ways: through offerings, which create a link with the spirits by appeasing them, and through dancing and music, a way of encouraging the spirits to join in and mix with humans, especially during annual ceremonies. Both cases involve deluding the spirits: either in the literal sense – behind a mask, there is a human – or metaphorically – much more is expected in return for an offering than what it was, in fact, worth. F.P. and E.D.

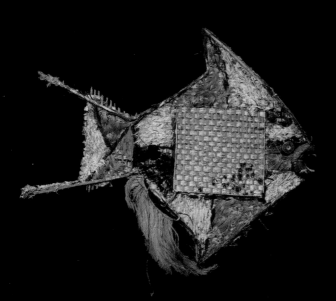

1/**Ant mat in the shape of a fish**
Wayana
French Guyana
20th century
Vegetable fibres, feathers, cotton, ants, resin
57 x 47 cm
H. Coudreau mission
Inv. 71.1890.93.157

2/**Votive bowl**
Huichol
Mexico, Jalisco State
20th century
Calabash, glass beads, wax
11.1 x 5.2 cm
O. Kindl mission
Inv. 71.2000.37.10

3/**Censer**
Lakandon
Mexico, Chiapas State
19th century
Terracotta, lime
14 x 13.5 cm
D. Charnay mission
Inv. 71.1882.17.169

4/*Katsina* **ritual doll**
Hopi
United States, Arizona
20th century
Polychrome wood
27.4 x 13.9 cm
Donated by the Smithsonian Institution
Inv. 71.1885.78.149

5/**Dance paddle**
Hopi
United States, Arizona
20th century
Polychrome wood
52.5 x 13.8 cm
Donated by Wildenstein
Inv. 71.1946.41.7

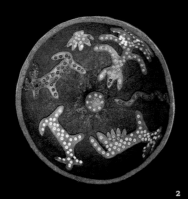

2

3

4

5

6/Rattle
Ye'kuana
Venezuela
20th century
Calabash, wood,
feathers, crystals
44 x 9.6 cm
Donated by the
Société des amis
du musée de
l'Homme
Inv. 71.2001.6.1

7/Mask
Wauja
Brazil, Mato
Grosso State,
High Xingu
20th century
Wood, palm
fibres, cotton,
shells,
fish maxilla
154 x 49 cm
Inv. 71.1967.63.6

6

7

The Yup'ik and Alutiiq Inuits

The Inuits, formerly called Eskimos, are scattered throughout the Arctic, from Siberia to Greenland. In the past, they were a maritime civilisation that relied on seal farming for a living and whose lifestyles were radically different in winter and in summer.

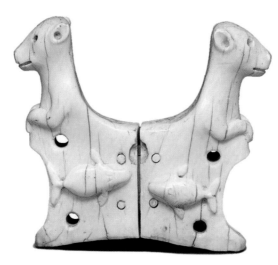

Harpoon support
Inuit
Alaska
18th century
Walrus ivory
Donated by H. de Rohan-Chabot
11 x 12.6 cm
Inv. 71.1978.8.1

***Ulu* woman's knife**
Inuit
Alaska, Nunivak Island
Late 19th-early 20th century
Ivory, iron
15.3 x 12.5 cm
Inv. 71.1949.46.1

In the winter, the Inuits lived in communal houses that, in the Central Arctic, may be igloos, but are usually half-buried dwellings made of wood. Men hunted seals in the ice fields. The animal's carcass, rich in fat, was then shared among the group according to a well-defined code.

In the summer, the groups spread out along the coasts. The women would take their family in a *umiak*, a large boat made of seal hides sewn together and stretched over a wooden frame, while men followed behind in a *kayak*, a single-passenger boat renowned for its seaworthiness. The women would then choose a temporary campsite, while the men went hunting alone in their *kayaks*.

/ CONTEMPORARY RENAISSANCE OF THE ARTS

As a result of contacts with the outside world, North-American artistic practices almost disappeared. At the turn of the 20ᵗʰ century, a number of anthropologists and artists decided to counter the passivity of those who simply wanted to gather together the artwork from the past in museums. They convinced government authorities to encourage indigenous art production. On the Northwest coast, the last traditional sculptor, Mungo Martin, who initiated the younger generation in his art, received financial aid to make new totem poles. The renaissance movement, launched by the Kwakiutl, spread to the Haïda, grouped around Bill Reid. In the 1940s, the Canadian governement encouraged creators of traditional Inuit art to make products that could be marketed and promised to help promote them to the general public. In the Southwest, the school of Santa Fe launched a new look in line with customer demand and based on a naïve realism whose "flat" style is reminiscent of Navajo sand paintings and Pueblo ceramics and, in its figurative aspects, of the art of the Plains. E. D.

According to the Inuits, who are obsessed by demographic balance, the last-born in a community is the reincarnation of the person who last died. Special care is given to try to fashion the child into the image of the deceased so that the community can recognize him. This concern is mirrored in Inuit objects. Whether a ritual object or simple everyday tool, the object, made of leather or ivory, always reflects the highly skilled techniques used to shape it. E.D.

Mask
Yup'ik
Alaska,
Kuskokwim Bay,
Quinhagak
19ᵗʰ century
Wood, feathers,
polychromy
60 x 21 cm
Former A. Breton
collection
Inv. 70.2003.9.3

Mask
Alutiiq
Alaska, Kodiak
Archipelago
19ᵗʰ century
Wood
57.3 x 31 cm
Donated by
A. Pinart
Inv. 70.1881.21.25

The North-West coast

The North-West coast of North America, a region of abundant natural resources, is the cradle of an astonishing civilisation marked by the potlach ritual and the omnipresence of art in everyday objects.

Articulated mask
Haida
Canada, British Columbia
Late 19th century
Wood, vegetable fibres, polychromy, metal
51 x 25.3 cm
Former A. Breton collection,
Donated by A. Elléouët
Inv. 70.2003.9.2

The North-West coast offered its inhabitants a rich, complex and contrasting ecological environment extending from the sea to the west to the wooded mountains of the east. In the spawning season, the rivers overflowed with salmon and other types of fish. The traditional organisation of society was based upon the rhythm of the seasons. Thanks to work carried out by women, the community was able to accumulate considerable reserves of food in the spring. In the summer, the men went hunting for goats in the mountains. They also went to the villages near the sea to make war or take part in potlaches (a ceremonial event in which

Anonymous, *Group of Indians, Sauk and Fox*. United States, 1860-1876.

Clapper
Haida
Canada, British Columbia
19th century
Wood, polychromy
142 x 12.5 cm
Inv. 70.2003.21.1

Ceremonial cloak, known as a "Chilkat blanket"
Tlingit
Canada, British Columbia
19th century
Goat's wool, vegetable fibres
137.7 x 165.8 cm
Donated by the Smithsonian Institution
Inv. 71.1885.78.450

Forehead piece from a ceremonial headdress
Tsimshian
Canada, British Columbia
19th century
Wood, green mother of pearl

Former C. Lévi-Strauss collection
22 x 17.5 cm
Inv. 70.2002.31.1

prestigious goods and food were distributed as gifts to establish political power and enhance status and rank). The winter was devoted to grand, highly dramatised ceremonial cycles spanning several weeks and during which masks played a dominant role.

Villages were established along the coasts, facing the sea. From the open sea, they could often be seem through the mist as irregular lines of sculpted totem poles, behind which the compact gables of the large houses belonging to each lineage could gradually be distinguished. These gables were entirely covered with the paintings of human faces and animals or supernatural beings, half-man, half-beast. From a stylistic point of view, these motifs were based on the principle of duality, i.e. a face rendered by two symmetrical profiles, omnipresent in North-Western coastal art. This principle is applied to numerous materials: fabrics, paddles, boxes, etc. On the North-West coast, all objects, down to the smallest spoon, are perceived as living beings: they have identities that must be revealed. This duality is reinforced by the individual treatment of each filled-in cell: each element of the face or body is separate, becoming an iconic unit in itself, and is juxtaposed to others, with as little empty space as possible between them. This technique gives North-West coastal art the extraordinary visual power that has made it famous. E.D.

The Indians of the Plains

At the end of the 18th century, a brilliant civilisation emerged on the Great North-American Plains. It was crushed by the colonial ambitions of the United States in the latter part of the 19th century, but has continued to haunt the imagination of Europeans ever since.

"Bison dance" coat
Quapaw
United States,
Arkansas
18th century
Painted deerskin
182.5 x 159 cm
Donated by the
Versailles Public
Library,
Former Marquis
de Sérent
collection
Inv. 71.1934.33.4

George Catlin
Portrait of an Indian chief
United States
Circa 1845
Oil on canvas
81 x 65 cm
Inv. 71.1930.54.2006

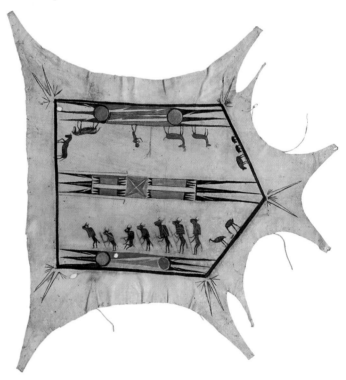

Before settlers cleared the valleys, the Great Plains was a landscape where the famous plateau prairies alternated with wooded areas along the water edges. When the Plains Indians (Sioux, Cheyenne, Comanche, Mandan, Pawnee, Blackfoot, etc.) acquired horses brought from Europe to Mexico, they gained a considerable advantage for hunting their main resource: the American buffalo. Their lifestyle was closely attuned to the seasons. In the winter, the tribes split up into small, scattered groups and set up base in the shelter of the forest. Despite the rigours of the climate, the Indians hunted the buffalo that also found refuge in the valleys. When summer came, things changed and

hunting became a collective and disciplined activity. This was also the season of great tribal gatherings, fellowships and rituals such as the sun dance. In some camps, hundreds of tepees were laid out in concentric circles. Summer was also the favoured season for war. Celebrations were an important part of all these occasions.

The art of the Plains is a mix of figurative art, which is exclusively male, and abstract art, reserved for women. The former relates the past exploits of hunters and warriors, while the latter depicts the role of the mother, with an abstraction that expresses pure creation and the uncertain, *unfigurable* nature of the children still to be born. E.D.

Woman's tunic
Mandan
United States,
Plains region
19th century
Skin, porcupine
quills
81 x 53.5 cm

Donated by the
Bibliothèque
nationale de
France
Inv. 71.1878.32.145

Mon-Ka-Ush-Ka coat, "the earth that quakes" (detail)
Mandan or Hidatsa
United States,
Plains region
Early 19th century
Painted bison
skin, porcupine
quills
111 x 247 cm
Donated by M.
Chaplain-Duparc
Inv. 71.1886.17.1

FROM FASCINATION TO WAR

The spectacular culture of the Plains Indians was highly fashionable at the turn of the 19th century. The region became a destination of choice for the curious. The journey began in Saint-Louis and followed the routes taken by loggers and fur traders. It was undertaken by artists such as Switzerland's Karl Bodmer (1809-1893) and Rudolf F. Kurz (1818-1871) and the American George Catlin (1796-1872), famous at the time and who even toured Europe with his Indian collection. However, from the mid 19th century on, relations between the Indians and the Americans deteriorated, finally ending in war. Abandoning their traditional war practices, the Indians, armed with firearms, entered into a European-type confrontation with the Federal Troops that were forming alliances, concentrating forces and confronting the enemy at the right moment. These tactics resulted in the victory of *Little Big Horn* in 1876. Finally defeated, the Plains Indians were forced to accept the disastrous solution of Reservations. E. D.

Amazonia

**Headdress with
neck covering**
Munduruku
Brazil, Para State,
Rio Tapajós
19th century
Feathers, cotton
75.5 x 32.5 cm
Donated by
P. Broca
Inv. 71.1878.53.3

Amazonia covers an immense geographical
area (more than 6 million km²) but is culturally
homogeneous. Its borders cross the Amazonian
basin to the Guyanas, the Orinoco basin
and some regions of Mato Grosso and Gran
Chaco. This is why it is called "Greater
Amazonia". Today, only about 1.3 million
American Indians live there, one-sixth of the
number originally estimated when the first
contacts were made in the 16th century. More
than 400 languages are still spoken, most
of them belonging to four major families (Tupi-
Guarani, Arawak, Carib and Ge). In spite of
this linguistic diversity, Amazonian societies
share to a great extent the same cultural
and social structure: relative mobility,
politically independent and egalitarian local
groups, division of work according to gender,
importance of hunting, war and Shamanism.

_Amazonia revisited

Breakthroughs in archaeological research were critical in transforming the somewhat limited view of Amazonian cultures. Ceramic remains discovered along the Amazon River and dating as far back as 4,000 years, attest to a political, social and cultural level of organisation far more complex than the apparent simplicity of present-day indigenous societies leads us to believe. 16th century accounts mention hierarchical societies, organised into powerful chiefdoms, with a highly developed ceramic tradition. It was believed for a long time that they had been influenced by civilizations from somewhere in the distant Andes. But the most recent hypotheses attribute an Amazonian origin to South America's multi-coloured ceramic ware. The development of this art, which spanned a period of 2,000 years (1000 B.C.-1000 A.D.), came to a definitive halt with the Spanish Conquest in the 16th century and the progressive invasion of Indian lands, the spread of epidemics and slavery. Nonetheless, a certain stylistic continuation can be noted between pre-Columbian designs and those found on today's pottery. J.-P.C.

_The body and its adornment

It was feather art and body painting that most fascinated the first observers of Amazonian culture. It is still very much alive up to this day and one of the major forms of aesthetic sensibility in these societies. The beauty, richness and composition of feather adornments are dazzling. More than simple decoration, body ornamentation is a way of socialising people and, above all, of establishing their status as human beings. The body is not taken for granted in Amazonia, but is seen as something that is shaped throughout one's life through ritual practices and the use of ornamentation. Among the finest pieces are *mundurucu* headdresses and *wayana* pectoral adornments. Fangs, beaks or claws of wild animals worn on chains sometimes replace feathers. The great ritual traditions also include human trophies which are the spoils of war (*mundurucu* and *jivaro* heads).

Pot
Shipibo
Peru
20th century
Polychrome
terracotta
21 x 13.3 cm
Donated by
S. Monzon
Inv. 71.2000.38.1

Funeral urn
Marajoara culture
Brazil, Para State,
Marajo Island
450-1350
Incised and
painted terracotta
34 x 32.2 cm
Donated by
M. A. Chermont
de Miranda
Inv. 71.1950.64.1

**Ceremonial
pendant**
Bororo
Brazil, Mato
Grosso State,
Rio Vermelho
20ᵗʰ century
Armadillo claws,
feathers,
vegetable fibres,
resin,
mother of pearl,
porcupine quills,
wood, fish fat,
annatto seed
extract
L. 23 cm
C. and D. Lévi-
Strauss mission
Inv. 71.1936.48.181

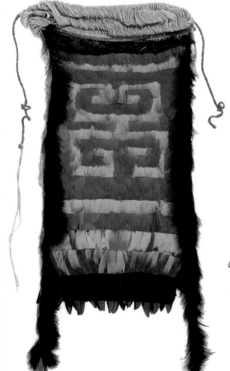

Pectoral
Wayana
Surinam,
High Maroni
19ᵗʰ century
Cotton cloth,
feathers
51.5 x 28.5 cm
Donated by
Dr T. Kate
Inv. 71.1881.107.23

**Woman's
g-string**
Wayana
Guyana
19ᵗʰ century
Cotton, glass
beads
24 x 36.5 cm
H. Coudreau
mission
Inv. 71.1890.93.2

_The world and its contours

Although textile production has declined with the introduction of industrial fabrics, wickerwork is still flourishing. These remarkable flat woven objects with geometric designs have a deep symbolic and ritual significance, such as the tresses decorated with ants applied the bodies of young people during initiation ceremonies in the Guyanas. Beautiful objects have also been created by wood carving, such as the seats reserved for shamans, which are sculpted out of a single block. The image of spiritual entities on masks and musical instruments is common in Amazonia, while figurative representations of humans are more rare. Highly valued by tourists, collectors and art traders, many of these objects are now marketed and exported worldwide. J.-P.C.

Female figurine
Karaja
Brazil, Goias State
Early 20th century
Polychrome
terracotta
10.5 x 5.3 cm
J. Vellard mission,
1929
Inv. 71.1930.32.238

/ BODY PAINTING

Body painting is one of the most original art forms in Amazonian cultures. It is usually applied using roucou and genipa, a plant dye that turns black within a few hours and can become extremely shiny.
Body painting is applied daily or on special occasions (illness, mourning, hunting, war, rituals) by both men and women and covers either part of the body or all of it.
The paintings signify for more than simple decoration; they are an essential human attribute. They provide information not only on the gender and age of their bearer, but also on their social position, ritual status and their relationship with the living and the dead.
With a painted, tattooed or decorated body, the individual acquires a social identity.
This refined decorative art is not only applied to the body, but to other materials as well, such as ceramics, wickerwork and textiles, using the same designs as those painted on the skin. J.-P.C.

Amerindian clothing and textiles

The collections from the 19th and 20th centuries
cover the whole of America from Patagonia
to Canada. They show the diversity of clothing
habits in different areas.

**Woman's blouse
(detail of *mola*)**
Cuna
Panama, San Blas
Islands
20th century
Cotton, synthetic
fibre
60 x 80 cm
Inv. 71.1986.74.4

Leather, hide and beaten bark were among the
first materials fashioned and painted by different
groups such as the Tehuelche from Patagonia, the
Toba Pilaga from Northern Argentina and the
Yuracaré from Eastern Bolivia. The tunics
exhibited show the wide range of Yuracaré
creations, from tunics with very detailed drawings
to others that look as if they were done with brush
strokes. Many other clothes were made from
local fibres that had been spun and woven,
or by transforming industrial textiles using bright
colours.

The Kuna women of the Panama San Blas Islands
focused on the latter technique, the transforming
fabrics purchased from outside. The art of the
molas, layers of fabrics that are cut and then sewn
on top of one another, emerged in the latter half
of the 19th century and is illustrated by a number
of masterworks. *Molas* are often designed in pairs

to decorate both the back and front of smocks. The Andean exhibits, woven in the Quechua communities of Bolivia and Peru, have preserved the main characteristics of the Pre-Hispanic period: they are woven into pieces of fabric with four selvedges that are never cut.

The complementary and symmetrical style is evident in the double-sided fabrics and, for the shawls, in the additional head-to-tail joining of identical sides. The use of sheep's wool, chemical dyes, and motifs from the colonial period are evidence of the rich combination of textile traditions. The clothing forms a mosaic of well-differentiated styles that clearly identify the origin of each individual.

The situation is similar for the Mayan populations in Central America where almost 150 villages with distinctive costumes have been documented. The most characteristic piece is the *huipil*, a type of jacket worn by Mayan women and other ethnic groups in Mexico. The *huipil* is made by joining woven sidepieces with a rich decoration on a belt loom dating from Pre-Hispanic times and is often worn over a skirt woven on a treadle loom imported from Europe. The same tendency can be seen in men's clothing which shows the extent to which indigenous creativity has been enriched by carefully selected outside elements. S.D.

Tunic
Yuracare
Bolivia
19th century
Bark, polychromy
111 x 78.5 cm
Donated by
Mme Mannet
Inv. 71.1898.8.46

Huipil
K'iche, Maya
Guatemala,
El Quiché,
Chichicastenango
20th century
Cotton, silk,
artificial silk
64 x 92 cm
Donated by
H. Lehmann
Inv. 71.1953.96.34

THE SINGULARITY OF AMERINDIAN OBJECTS

The French anthropologist Claude Lévi-Strauss highlighted the unity of American Indian beliefs by showing how myths are related: the same myth can be found in several regions but in different forms. The principle of transformation can also be applied to objects. By comparing objects from different populations over different periods of time on the basis of their similarities, one often finds that, surprisingly, they belong to the same collective source of meaning. For example, all the receptacles have a human or animal form, signifying that the living body is first and foremost a container. E.D.

1/Spoon
Sioux
United States,
Plains region
20th century
Horn
12.8 x 5 cm
Inv. 70.2001.35.1

2/Anthropo-morphic vase
Wari culture
Peru
600-1100
Polychrome
terracotta
18.3 x 9 cm
Donated by the
Société des amis
du musée
ethnographique
du Trocadéro
Inv. 71.1931.33.41

3/Club
Guyana
20th century
Hardwood,
vegetable fibres,
stone head
36 x 13 cm
Inv. 71.1954.19.1 D

4/Club
Huron
Canada, Great
Lakes region
19th-early 20th
century
Wood, shell pearls
58 x 17 cm
Donated by the
Musée de l'Armée
Inv. 71.1917.3.14

5/Drum
United States,
Plains region

1

20th century
Wood and
painted skin
42 x 6.5 cm
Inv. 70.2002.18.2

6/Club
Guyana
19th-early
20th century
Hardwood,
vegetable fibres
44.7 x 10.5 cm
Donated by the
Musée de l'Armée
Inv. 71.1917.3.80

**7/Vase in
the shape of**

a seated lama
Wari culture
Bolivia, Tiwanaku
600-1100
Terracotta
15 x 21.5 cm
Donated by G. de
Créqui-Montfort
Inv. 71.1908.23.461

8/Mortar
Inca culture
Peru
1450-1532
Stone
37 x 13 cm
Donated by
C. Wiener
Inv. 71.1878.2.456

3

4

5

6

7

8

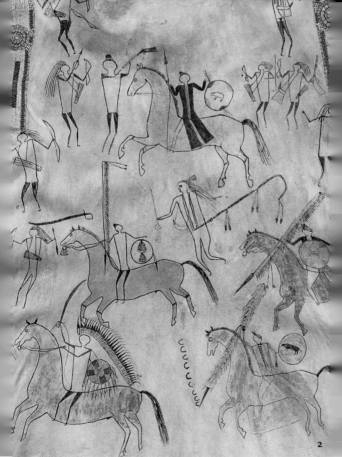

3

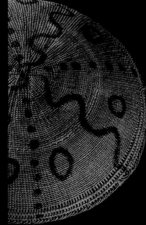

4

5

6

7

7/Basket
United States,
California
18th-early 19th
century
Rushes, feathers,
shell discs
35.5 x 16.5 cm
Inv. 71.1909.19.53 Am

8/Basket (detail)
Yanomami
Venezuela
20th century
Vegetable fibres,
polychromy
34 x 9.3 cm
J. Lizot mission
Inv. 71.1970.42.108

6/Wampum
Huron
Canada,
Saint-Laurent
Valley
18th century
Shell beads,

tendons
5.6 x 114 cm
Donated by the
Bibliothèque
nationale de
France
Inv. 71.1878.32.57

8

Pre-Columbian Antilles

Situated between the two Americas, the Antilles archipelago has an Amerindian history long linked with the Amazonian world. The Taino and their Carib neighbours who inhabited this "gate to the Indies" were among the first populations of the New World to be wiped out by European colonisation.

Anthropo-morphic emetic spatula
Suazey culture
Martinique,
Le Prêcheur,
Anse-Belleville
1000-1500
Bone
6.7 x 2.4 cm
Donated by
E. Revert
Inv. 71.1939.41.190

Shortly before the era of Christianity, groups of Amerindian farmers, originally from the Orinoco basin, settled in the Lesser Antilles as far as Puerto Rico. For almost a millennium, these insular societies produced a Saladero-style ceramic art attesting to their close ties with the continent. Around the 7th and 8th centuries, these ceramic-making groups also occupied the Greater Antilles as well. Socio-political structures became more complex and a number of insular characteristics emerged. Starting in the 12th century, the Taino cultures observed by Christopher Columbus in 1492 also emerged, centred on Puerto Rico and Hispaniola.

/ SACRIFICE AND CANNIBALISM

Christopher Columbus' second voyage brought home the reality of Amerindian cannibalism in the Caribbean to Europeans. In Mexico, the explorers witnessed human sacrifices. These two practices gripped their imagination, justifying, in their eyes, the atrocities they would inflict on the Indians. After being put to death, the body of a sacrificed Aztec was thrown to the bottom of the pyramid and then eaten by dignitaries. Similarly, a captive Tupinamba warrior from Brazil would acquire an almost sacred status after being put to death during a ritual resembling sacrifice, and then being eaten. In fact, the two practices were part of a vast ensemble that also involved head and scalp hunting. Capturing trophies and eating human flesh conferred a social identity rooted in a predatory attitude towards outsiders. It was women who showed the most enthusiasm in taking possession of the scalp or in consuming human flesh: taking the lives of their enemies was seen as a fertility rite. E.D.

Macorix head
Taino culture
Puerto Rico
1200-1492
Basalt
23 x 17 cm
Donated by the Mineralogy Gallery of the National Museum of Natural History
Inv. 71.1930.35.2

Three-cornered stone
Taino culture
Puerto Rico
1200-1500
Stone
15.5 x 36 cm
Donated by
A. Pinart
Inv. 71.1878.1.2697

Necklace or yoke
Taino culture
Puerto Rico
1200-1500
Stone
26.5 x 43.5 cm
Donated by
Dr Montane
Inv. 71.1891.49.1

Organised into chiefdoms under the authority of a *cacique*, these Caribbean societies created art on stone, wood, bone and shells in which *zemi* play a central role. These divinities or supernatural beings are represented in multiple forms, including the so-called three-pointed stones. The *cohoba* ritual, during which shamans ingest a hallucinogenic substance, was practised using vomitory spatulas and inhalers. Stone collars are thought to be linked to a ball game, played in areas marked with engraved stones. A.D.

Pre-Hispanic Central America

The Pacific coast area of Central America is steeped in Mesoamerican tradition, while the Atlantic coast area belongs to the South-American cultural sphere. The Isthmus cultures are very fragmented politically, without towns or stone architecture, but have developed a craftsmanship that is equal in quality to that of higher civilisations.

Representation of a trophy head
Costa Rica, Turrialba region
800-1520
Terracotta
17.5 x 17 cm
Donated by D. Wildenstein
Inv. 71.1967.129.2

_Costa Rica

The polychrome ceramics on a white background dating back to the 9th century in the region under Mesoamerican tradition mainly depict the animals (crocodile, jaguar, birds, monkeys, armadillos) or hybrid animals (snake-jaguar, feathered serpents). These are combined with conventional elements to produce a highly complex design illustrating the battle between the opposing forces of the universe and the earth's fertility. The jaguar embodies the sun, and the crocodile, the earth. Seats or displays for offerings

Composite zoomorphic censer
Costa Rica, Guanacaste province, La Guinea
800-1200
Terracotta
49.5 x 35,2 cm
French archaeological mission to Costa Rica, 1957-1960
Inv. 71.1960.99.85

"Metate" offerings grinder
Panama, Chiriqui
Vesicular basalt
30 x 51 cm
Archaeological mission to Panama
Inv. 71.1902.23.6

are carved out of lava in the shape of a crocodile head. Artists put the emphasis on the crocodile's snout, transforming it into a platform or a loop. This distinctive characteristic can also be found on effigies of the monsters which adorn the lids of large ceramic thuribles.

In regions of South-American tradition, pottery is decorated more by modelling, pastel work or engraving than by paint.

In southern Costa Rica, there are countless painted figurines in animal or human form, almost always in the shape of a whistle or flute with several holes.

Volcanic stone sculpture can be seen on altars and monolithic tables throughout the country, sometimes extended by highly complex openwork panels; the many examples of *metates* (millstones) in the form of a jaguar were used in tombs as surfaces on which offerings were placed.

In the centre and north of the country, sculptures feature people sitting and smoking cigars, as well as crocodile masks (shamans?), standing women holding their breasts (image of fertility), and warriors or "sacrificers" holding an axe in one hand and a trophy head in the other. Almost life-size decapitated human heads are commonly carved in stone, but rarely made in ceramic. The small sculptures, usually carved out of

Alligator-headed altar or seat
Gran Nicoya
Costa Rica, Guanacaste province, Papagayo
1200-1520
Vesicular basalt
43.5 x 43 cm
French archaeological mission to Costa Rica, 1957-1960

Inv. 71.1959.70.3

Anthropo-morphic sculpture, woman holding her breasts
Linéa Vieja
Costa Rica
700-1100
Vesicular basalt
60.5 x 31 cm
Donated by É. Jore

Inv. 71.1902.23.2

sandstone, found in southern Costa Rica are quite different and feature anthropomorphic figures pierced by three slits separating the members; small jaguars with rounded forms, and egg-shaped statues of humans and animals.

The Diquis delta zone is famous for its stone spheres measuring up to 2 metres in diameter; they formed lines that are assumed to have astronomical significance.

Although they had no metal tools, the Costa Ricans have been highly skilled jewellers since the beginning of our times, carving, sawing and drilling jade and other hard stones to make a wide variety of pendants. In southern Costa Rica and Panama, these were gradually replaced from the 6th century on by gold jewellery and *tumbaga* (gold-copper alloy) that could be cast using the lost wax process.

_Panama

The polychrome ceramics of central Panama combine animal motifs with geometric designs, with a double spiral as the basic element. Artists use a wide range of colours: flat reds, mauves and browns outlined in black, all on a light background. Symmetry and the division of space in the friezes or panels are fundamental to their composition. The background is systematically covered with barbed curving lines and spirals. The iconography draws its inspiration from real or imaginary animals – long-beaked birds, fish (hammer-shark or skates), crabs, scorpions, turtles, felines, saurian and reptiles – or composite creatures such as two-headed monsters or a humanised crocodile standing or "dancing". The highly complex whole is combined with an astonishing and elegant blend of curving and angular elements. The forms of Tonosi pottery evoke the fruits of the calabash tree; later on, plates and bowls were put on tall pedestals and placed alongside effigy-recipients, "carafes" and long-necked jars. C.B.

Jar decorated with a crocodile
Gran Coclé, del Indio culture
Panama, Los Santos province, Tonosi district, El Indio
250-500
Terracotta, polychrome decoration
34 x 30 cm
French archaeological mission to Panama, 1967-1970
Inv. 71.1970.28.145

Bowl with pedestal
Gran Coclé, La Canãza culture
Panama, Los Santos province, Tonosi district, El Indio
500-900
Terracotta, polychrome decoration
14 x 26 cm
French archaeological mission to Panamá, 1967-1970
Inv. 71.1970.28.60

Column-statue
Maya culture
Mexico, Yucatan
peninsula
800-1000
Calcitic stone
140 x 50 cm
Donated by the
Galerie J. Bucher
Inv. 71.1967.37.1

Pre-Hispanic Mesoamerica

Mesoamerica is a cultural zone situated
between the North Mexican deserts
and Central America; it is characterised
by its architecturally varied urban centres,
monumental sculptures, and specialised
craftsmen. It followed the same calendar
and had a more or less developed system
of writing.

_The Olmecs

The term "Olmec" refers more to a style
– distributed unequally across Mesoamerica
between 1200 and 300 B.C. – than a civilisation.
However, imposing political and ceremonial
centres, such as San Lorenzo, La Venta and Tres
Zapotes, can be found on the coast of the Gulf
of Mexico. Carefully planned, these immense
collective works involved terracing, the
construction of pyramids and raised earth
platforms, and the burial of monumental
offerings. In this man-made landscape, sculpture,
with colossal heads, altars and stelae, played
a considerable role despite the lack of local
materials. Olmec art excelled in green-coloured
hard stonework, such as jadeite. Large polished
axe blades, often decorated with engraved
designs, were part of the foundation deposits
and offerings. The figurines illustrate the
theme of the baby-jaguar, a mythical creature
symbolising power.

Polychrome plate
Maya culture
Guatemala, Peten department, or Mexico
600-800
Terracotta
30.3 x 6 cm
Inv. 70.2001.36.1

Anthropo-zoomorphic statuette
Olmec culture
Mexico, Oaxaca state
900-600 BC
Schistose stone, traces of cinnabar
12.9 x 5.7 cm

Donated by the Société des amis du musée d'ethnographie du Trocadéro
Inv. 71.1931.33.39

_The Mayas

The Mayan civilisation appeared in the south of Mesoamerica as the great Olmec sites began to disappear. In the lowlands, the architecture of the first centres was colossal, reflecting the new kings' determination to impress both their subjects and their rivals. In the first centuries A.D., small kingdoms sprung up over a vast area around a capital; a king's power was measured by the erection of stelae representing his image, which provided a periodic written record of the important events of his reign and of his ancestors, using a calendar to place him in a historical context. The political landscape changed constantly and the history of the cities is marked by a series of conflicts, victories and defeats, alliances and attempts to dominate that always ended in failure. The highlands, the first to invent writing and the calendar, went through a long period of artistic decline when the lowlands reached their zenith. The two regions are known for their high-quality craftsmanship, in particular

ceramics (containers and figurines) and hard
stonework (jadeite). The green, shiny and
reflective colour of jadeite evoked water, rain,
lush vegetation and fertility and was the preferred
stone for the jewellery, necklaces, bracelets and
pectoral adornments of kings and nobles. Fertility
is also a favoured theme in engraved or painted
representations on ceramic vases; it is expressed
through images of the *bajos,* floodplains with high
agricultural yields. Fish, wading birds, crocodiles
and toads are depicted among water lilies and
a young man symbolising corn springs from
a terrestrial monster like a young shoot from
the wet ground.

**Spherical bowl
in the shape of a
deathshead**
Maya culture
Guatemala, San
Andrès Sajcabajà,
La Lagunita
300-600
Terracotta
12 x 15.5 cm
Inv. 71.1972.4.1

/ WRITING AND CALENDARS

With the exception of Mayan writing, Mesoamerican writings are partial, and combined with varying amounts of narrative pictography and images. The Aztecs, Zapotecs and Mixtecs wrote their own names and dates using a picto-ideagraphic system to which phonetic elements were added. These scripts are found on monuments, but above all on manuscripts (divinatory calendars, historic *codex*, lists of tributes) on bark paper covered with lime. Mayan writing contains both logograms and phonograms and can literally transcribe any form of speech. Mesoamerican calendars used two cycles simultaneously: a 260-day ceremonial or divinatory cycle and a solar cycle spanning 365 days. Writing and calendars appeared and disappeared at the same time. The Mayas, who were the calendar's foremost developers, also had the most complex writing system, which was mainly used to record and date dynastic history. C.B.

God of rain and atmospheric phenomena
Gulf coast culture
Mexico, Veracruz state, Orizaba
300-600
Terracotta
64.5 x 21.5 cm
D. Charnay mission,
1880-1882
Inv. 71.1882.17.41

_The El Tajín and the Huastecs

The civilisation of the El Tajín and the Huastec civilisation thrived to the north of the region of great Olmec sites on the Gulf of Mexico. The former attributed considerable importance to ball games; 13 playing fields were found in El Tajín alone. Some fields were decorated with bas-relief panels depicting scenes of sacrifice by beheading, followed by scenes of hell. Carved stone objects such as "yokes", "axes" and "palms" were part of the players' equipment during game-related rituals. The large hollow ceramic statues representing supernatural beings come from Veracruz. After 900, the Huastecs began sculpting normal-sized anthropomorphic figures out of limestone in a very original style; smaller sculptures show an old man leaning on a stick. Later on, the Huastecs immortalized the divinities of the Aztec pantheon in stone.

/ BALL GAMES

Ball games, which were highly religious as well as sporting events, were widespread in Mesoamerica from 1200 B.C. right up to the Spanish conquest. They pitted two teams against each other on a specially laid-out marked field. Players relayed a heavy solid rubber ball (rubber was an indigenous substance) to one another without using their hands or feet. The plan and layout of the fields, the number of players and their equipment and the rules of the game varied considerably. For the Taino in the greater Antilles, the field was marked out but not enclosed. The Hohokam in Arizona also played ball games but on an even simpler field. There were ball games where the ball was passed by hand, like *pelota mixteca*, or used with bats, like the game illustrated in Teotihuacán. The ball could also be pushed along the ground with sticks, like in the cross game, played in many parts of North America and a forerunner of modern-day hockey. C.B.

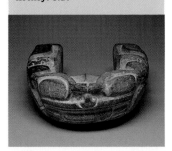

Old man leaning on a stick
Huastec culture
Mexico,
Gulf coast,
Veracruz
600-1519
Sandstone
53.5 x 30.5 cm
Donated by
Mlle Galls
Inv. 71.1887.133.1

Yoke
Gulf coast culture
Mexico, Puebla
state, Cholula
600-900
Porphyroid rock
37.5 x 41.5 cm
Donated by
A. Génin
Inv. 71.1924.13.3401

Teobert Maler, *Palace of the Columns*. Mitla, circa 1875.

Fragment of paving stone
Zapotec culture
Mexico
800-1200
Pink stone
33.6 x 21.5 cm
Donated by
A. Pinart

Inv. 71.1878.1.2698

_The Zapotecs and Mixtecs

The Zapotecs and Mixtecs both inhabited the State of Oaxaca. The Zapotecs were the first to live there, recording and dating their victories in stone as of 600 B.C. Monte Albán is famous for its imposing architecture and numerous tombs, which were often painted and had several rooms containing ceramic urns with human figures, usually representing divinities. Between 400 and 800 A.D., the *ñuñe* culture in the Mixteca Baja became distinct from that of both Monte Albán and Teotihuacán. From 1200, the mixteca-puebla style flourished, and can be seen in the pictographic manuscripts, gold and silverware (tomb 7 of Monte Albán), polychrome ceramic objects and hard stonework in the form of pendants, with the god Tlaloc often as subject.

"Butterfly" vase   champlevé
Teotihuacan   decoration
culture   22.7 x 21.5 cm
Mexico, Mexican   Inv. 70.2000.5.1-2
Basin
150-650
Terracotta with

_Teotihuacán

Located on the central plateau of Mexico,
Teotihuacán, with 100,000 inhabitants, was the
largest planned city of Mesoamerica. Political
power was not embodied by a king or emperor,
but by a council of nobles, warriors and priests.
Murals portraying animal parades, often armed
(jaguars, birds, coyotes), found in residential areas
are a reference to the order of warriors on parade.
The storm god, ancestor of the Aztec Tlaloc, is
identifiable. Certain fantastic creatures (like the
feathered serpent) illustrate cosmic forces, rather
than divinities. Murals depict assemblies and
investitures: symbols and ornaments in various
materials (jade, ceramic, fabric, paper and
feathers) surround a stone mask. Similarly, on
ceramic censers called "theatres", a central mask

is bordered by a large frame with an array of
symbols such as birds, butterflies, fruit and other
plants. The great nude figures in green stone
undoubtedly represent the soul of the figures,
which are dressed and adorned with finery
identifying their nature: the deceased, deified
dead warriors or ancestors. The many masks made
of green stone and often covered with mosaics
symbolize the essence of the model whose body is
mortal. The stone and ceramic figurines are
probably part of compositions representing
collective rituals.

Anthropomor-
phic statue
Teotihuacan
culture
Mexico
150-650
Green rock
70 x 20 cm
Donated by
M. Latour-Allard
Inv. 71.1887.155.113

**Tlaloc, god
of rain and
personification
of the earth**
Aztec culture
Mexico, Federal
District, Mexico
City
1350-1521
45 x 19 cm
Donated by
A. Labadie
Inv. 71.1887.101.16

Sceptre
Aztec culture
Mexico, Federal
District, Santiago-
Tlaltelolco
1350-1521
Stag antler
21 x 11.5 cm
Donated by
A. Labadie
Inv. 71.1887.101.714

_The Aztecs

The Aztecs dominated the political and cultural
scene of Mesoamerica for 150 years prior to the
Spanish conquest. The emperor headed their
highly hierarchical society, with warriors playing
a key role. The triple alliance (with Texcoco and
Tlacopán) meant that in less than a century the
Aztecs were able to take control of most of central
Mexico, as well as a large part of the Pacific coast.
When the Spaniards arrived, Tenochtitlán was a
city of 75,000 inhabitants with a network of
canals and a ceremonial centre. Although the
Conquistadors admired the city, they razed it in
1521 and built their own capital, Mexico City, in
its place. The worship of multiple divinities,
immortalised in stone (andesite, basalt), was

practised regularly. Alongside the goddesses of
water and fertility, the main gods were Tlaloc,
the god of rain, Xipe Totec, the god of vegetation
and patron of craftsmen, Quetzalcóatl-Ehécatl,
the god of wind and Xiuhtecuhtli, the god of fire.
Aztec sculpture abounded with animal
representations, symbols of cosmology and
religion. The gods of the Aztec pantheon are
illustrated by an array of terracotta figurines
for home use, and probably played the role
of protectors.

**Huitzilopochtli,
god of war and
guiding deity**
Aztec culture
Mexico
1350-1521
Green
metamorphic
rock
6.4 x 4 cm
Former Musée
Guimet collection
Inv. 71.1930.100.43

Dog
Aztec culture
Mexico
1350-1521
44 x 20 cm
Former
M. Latour-Allard
collection
Inv. 71.1887.155.18

Hollow 'Mother and Child' figurine
Shaft tombs culture
Mexico, Jalisco state
300 BC-600 AD
Polychrome terracotta
40 x 15.5 cm
Donated by
L. Diguet
Inv. 71.1904.19.137

_Western Mexico

Western Mexico kept slightly apart from the other Mesoamerican civilisations and, even during the Aztec reign, the Purépecha (or Tarasques) resisted their powerful neighbours' ambitions for conquest. This splendid – and relative – isolation enabled the populations of western Mexico to develop highly original styles. In the last centuries B.C. and the first few centuries A.D., in the State of Guerrero, hard stone was carved – in a style called mezcala – into clearly defined figurines with large features and scale models for temples, which could be said to resemble of modern sculpture. Chupícuaro statuettes, painted with geometric designs in vivid colours, triggered the tradition of ceramic art and included standing or seated female figures, mothers, warriors, sorcerers with horn-like headdresses playing the drum, etc. There are also plump hairless dogs (intended for eating), parrots and bird-shaped headrests. The skill of the Western Mexican ceramic artists is also shown in scale models of dwellings, ball game fields and populated ritual sites. C.B.

Pre-Hispanic Andes

Andean culture stretched from the mountain range and the Pacific coast, from Columbia and Equator up to northern Chile. The history of the great civilisations unfolds in the central part, in Peru in particular. It is punctuated by alternating periods of independent regional development and periods of unification, reaching its zenith with the Incan Empire before the arrival of the Conquistadors.

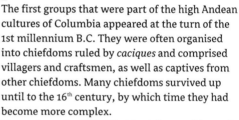

Funeral urn
Mosquito culture
Colombia,
Magdalena
department
1000-1500
Terracotta
88.5 x 31.5 cm
Donated by
G. H. Rivière
Inv. 71.1935.2.1

_Columbia

The first groups that were part of the high Andean cultures of Columbia appeared at the turn of the 1st millennium B.C. They were often organised into chiefdoms ruled by *caciques* and comprised villagers and craftsmen, as well as captives from other chiefdoms. Many chiefdoms survived up until to the 16th century, by which time they had become more complex.

The regions of middle Rio Magdalena and its main tributaries are characterised by secondary burials in funerary urns, dating back to the 8th-10th and 15th-16th centuries A.D.

The Sinu culture flourished in the north, between the Caribbean coast and the foothills of the mountains. Gold and silver workers produced countless objects for adornment and as insignia of power, often decorated with human and animal figures with elements in false filigree wire.

In the centre, the middle Cauca and Magdalena valleys were home to a number of chiefdoms. Gold and silverware attributed to the Quimbaya includes exceptional containers (*poporos*) cast in lost wax with a core. In the Calima region, successive cultural phases left some remarkable gold, silver and ceramic remains. The nearby Malagana culture blends elements from neighbouring cultures in a unique style. In the far south, the region of the high plateaus of Nariño forms an ensemble of cultures related to those that developed in the equatorial region of the Andes (Capuli and Piartal periods, followed by the Tuza period).

Pectoral
Muisca culture
Colombia,
Boyaca Highlands
900-1600
Tumbaga
13 x 13.5 cm
Inv. 71.1935.38.1

Statuette of a warrior seated on a bench (frontal and profile)
Cauca culture
Colombia, Cauca department, Popayán region
1000-1600
Painted terracotta
36 x 24 cm
Bequeathed by G. Valencia
Inv. 71.1947.31.1

Between 1200 and 1500 A.D., two cultural groups can be identified as having reached the "proto-state" stage. The Muisca from the central high plateau were a great power until the 16th century. Their gold and silverware was characterised by small stylised human representations, or offerings, called *tunjos*. They also produced various ornaments and insignia of power. Ceramic art included hieratic figures with coffee grains as eyes and wearing tall headdresses.

The Tairona lived on the Sierra Nevada de Santa Marta and the neighbouring Caribbean coast. Their gold and silverware comprised a wide range of jewellery and ornaments, found in burial sites. Their ceramics includes containers, figurines representing humans or animals and musical instruments (*ocarinas*).

_Ecuador

During the 4ᵗʰ century B.C., on the central coast of Ecuador, the Valdivia culture was the first to carve human figurines out of soft stone or crafted in ceramic. The Chorrera culture emerged around 1500-1300 B.C., producing some exceptional ceramic objects. Human figurines, as well as animal or plant-shaped vases show a great awareness of the environment.

The period between 500 and 300 B.C. was an era of regional developments, with well-differentiated styles that point to a multiplicity of cultures. The Tumaco-La Tolita, straddling Columbia and Ecuador, have left behind some remarkable ceramics, gold and silverware.

Statuette of a chief or a priest
Jama Coaque culture
Ecuador, Manabí province
500 BC-500 AD
Painted terracotta
26 x 10 cm
Inv. 71.1973.48.1

Human head
with cranial
deformity
Chorrera culture
Ecuador,
Esmeraldas
province
1000-300 BC
Terracotta

14.4 x 13.3 cm
Donated by
L. Gómez Alonso
Inv. 71.1936.24.1

Ceremonial seat
Manta culture
Ecuador,
Manabí province
800-1500
Stone
84 x 67 cm
Donated by
C. Wiener
Inv. 71.1878.2.583

Articulated
figurine
Tumaco-La Tolita
culture
Ecuador, El
Carchi province
500 BC-300 AD
Gold, platinum,
silver
15 x 9.3 cm
Donated by
G. Périer
Inv. 71.1945.6.1

Their iconography shows that they maintained
contacts with the neighbouring Jama Coaque
culture. Further to the south, the Bahía de
Caraquez culture was noted for richly
multicoloured ceramic figurines.
The Guangala was another coastal culture and
developed in the areas that had previously been
inhabited by Valdivia groups. This regional
development was also evident in the central
and northern highlands.
The iconography of these cultures shows
significant social diversification. It portrays
prominent figures, as well as individuals carrying
out craft-related or household tasks.
Around 500-800 A.D., on the central coast,
the Manteños-Huancavilcas formed a trade
association involving long-distance maritime
traffic. The Milagro-Quevedo culture developed
along the main river routes between the coast
and the mountains. In the Andes, a variety of
cultural groups prospered: the Carchi, the Cara,
the Cañar, the Puruhuas and the Panzaleo.
Some of these groups, particularly those in
the Sierra, fell under Incan domination in the late
15th century, shortly before the arrival of the
Conquistadors.

_Central Andes: Peru and Bolivia

Ceramics appeared in the Central Andes around 1800 B.C. The remarkable styles of Cupisnique, and Chavin in particular, blossomed.

At the beginning of 1000 B.C., Chavín de Huantar, in the North Sierra of Peru, became a great ceremonial centre and the seat of a theocratic power whose influence spread throughout most of Peru. In addition to monumental architecture and sculpture, art was expressed through ceramic objects and fabrics with an iconography characteristic of Chavín. Recurring motifs include mythical creatures and the main divinities with both human and animal traits: fangs and feline claws, serpent-like spirals, beaks and claws of birds of prey. Around 400-200 B.C., Chavín was abandoned and the Chavin-inspired styles were replaced by a range of regional developments.

Vase representing a mythical fight scene
Mochica culture
Peru, north coast
100 BC-700 AD
Painted terracotta
32 x 16.2 cm
Inv. 71.1887.125.1

Vase, hybrid being holding two trophy heads
Nasca culture
Peru, south coast
200 BC-700 AD
Painted terracotta
15.5 x 16 cm
Donated by
E. W. Titus
Inv. 71.1931.91.1

Vase representing a warrior and a cat
Recuay culture
Peru, Ancash department
100 BC-500 AD
Polychrome terracotta
12.8 x 11.9 cm
Donated by D. David-Weill
Inv. 71.1928.17.4

On the North coast, from about 400 B.C., the Vicus, Salinar and Gallinazo cultures were among the most remarkable. Around 100 B.C., the Moche culture, which united a large part of the north coast of Peru, thrived until about 700 A.D. Sculpted vases depict realistic portrayals of humans and their environment. Ritual scenes were also painted on vases of a simpler shape. Adobe brick architecture can be seen in the large step pyramids and immense platforms made of several million adobe bricks called *huacas*.

The gold and silverware was also exceptional. Burial sites of lord-priests covered with gold adornments and precious stones were recently discovered in Sipan.

On the central coast, large ceremonial centres such as Pachacamac (near Lima), indicate that this was a densely populated area. Further south, in the Paracas peninsula and Nazca region, two major cultures flourished, bearing the names of their locations. In Paracas, splendid funerary fabrics depict images of divinities or mythical beings. The Nasca culture produced exceptional polychrome ceramic ware; it is also linked to the famous geoglyphs on the Nazca Desert.

In the Sierra, the cultures of Cajamarca in the north, and of Recuay, near the region of Chavín, have left behind highly decorated pottery ware. Exchanges of political, religious and artistic influences resulted in a new unification of the Central Andes around 600 A.D. On the *Altiplano* (immense high plateau stretching as far as south-eastern Peru and over most of Bolivia) to the south of Lake Titicaca, in Tiwanaku and in the Central Peruvian Andes, the Waris demonstrated their undisputed dominance in a variety of ways. Tiahuanaco, in Bolivia, became a ceremonial centre with monumental stone constructions. The Gate of the Sun depicts the principal god surrounded by winged divinities, creating a cult that then spread through the Central Andes.

/ HUMANISED LANDSCAPES

Pre-Hispanic populations often worked the environment in which they lived.
In dry regions such as the coast of Peru, farmers expanded the amount of land suitable for cultivation with irrigation canals that captured water upstream for better distribution downstream. In the poorly drained plains, they dug out canals lined with raised slopes (ridges) where they farmed intensively. On the slopes, crop terraces (*andenes*) enabled the farmers to keep the land cultivated by protecting it from erosion, while ensuring better exposure to the sun.
In the Andes, the Incas built a vast network of stone-paved roads and lanes that provided them with a rapid means of access between the major sites of the Empire. Many of these followed the tracks of more ancient routes, modernising and extending them. In addition to their utilitarian role, the roads had a symbolic significance: in the eyes of the Empire's subjects, they represented the power exercised by the Incas over conquered, while the movement of populations was strictly controlled by the Incan armies. J.-F.B.

Kero ritual goblet with cat motifs
Tiwanaku culture
Bolivia, La Paz department
300-1150
Polychrome terracotta
17 x 13.5 cm
Donated by A. de Santa-Cruz
Inv. 71.1953.64.1

Tunic with geometrical decoration
Wari culture
Peru
600-1100
Cotton, feathers
91 x 233 cm
Former G. Halphen collection
Inv. 70.2002.9.1

Ceremonial gauntlet decorated with stylised human figures and birds
Chimu Lambayeque culture
Peru, north coast
1100-1450
Silver
41.6 x 13 cm
Inv. 70.2002.7.1

This image was adopted by the Wari culture that passed it on to others in turn. Planned cities surrounded with high walls also emerged as seats of a political power and administration that ruled over the rural communities.

Around the 11th century A.D., the Central Andes once again entered a period of regional specificity. The Chimú kingdom occupied most of the North coast. Its capital, Chan Chan, covered over 20km². Each king built his own palace on the site; his predecessor's palace was then turned into a burial place. The Chimú covered their kingdom with fortresses and public or religious sites. They irrigated the desert to develop agriculture, and excelled in gold and silverware, using a variety of metals and alloys to make refined ornaments and insignia of power. Ceramic objects were produced in series, generally in just one colour.

On the central coast, slightly to the north of Lima, the Chancay culture predominated. The vestiges

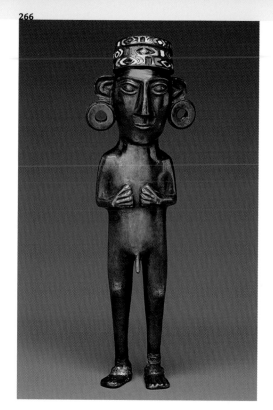

of this culture come from necropolises whose
burial sites were heavily plundered. Pottery was
covered with a cream coating adorned with black-
painted motifs. To the north, on the Amazonian
side of the Chachapoyas site, burial sites laid out
in the cliff sides showed that people once
occupied the eastern foothills about which little is
still known.

In 1438, the Incas set out from the region of Cuzco
and conquered the Central Andes, creating an
empire that marked the final unification of these
regions before the arrival of the Conquistadors.
The Incas left behind not only remarkable legacy of
architecture, but also ceramic objects, textiles,
gold and silverware, and wood and stone
sculpture. Incan gold and silverware, most of which
was melted into bars by the Conquistadors, was also
produced for the Imperial power and state religion.
These indigenous arts disappeared rapidly after
the conquest by the Spanish who imposed their
own aesthetic criteria. J.-F.B.

Male figurine
Inca culture
Peru, South
Andes
1450-1532
Silver, coloured
paste inlays
20.1 x 6.4 cm
Former A. Le
Moyne collection
Inv. 71.1887.114.90

**Paddle for
ceremonial use**
Ica Chincha culture
Peru, south coast
1100-1450
Wood, remains of
polychromy
218 x 21.5 cm
Inv. 70.2000.4.2

Anthropomorphic double vase
Chancay culture
Peru, central coast
1100-1450
Polychrome terracotta
41,2 x 46.3 cm
Donated by É. Colpäert
Inv. 71.1887.53.7

Ritual goblet, *Kero*, in the shape of a cat's head
Inca, colonial period
Peru, South Andes, Cuzco region
18th century
Wood, coloured resin inlays
22 x 15 cm
Donated by the wife of General Mangin
Inv. 71.1933.128.1

/ THE LEGACY OF PRE-HISPANIC AGRICULTURE

From the 16th century on, a large number of agricultural products from America reached the Old World. Some were directly acclimated, and then cultivated on other continents, where they became the main source of food.

Many are very well known today, and even used on an almost daily basis, such as potatoes, manioc, beans and squash, corn and tomatoes. Others, such as cocoa, vanilla, peanuts, various tropical fruits (pineapple, papaya, guava, sour sop, avocado, etc.) or condiments such as chili have also become part of modern gastronomy.

Utilitarian plants, cultivated or wild, are also numerous: calabash, cotton and the rubber tree (from which rubber is extracted) also come from America.

A wide range of medicinal plants have been also been studied for possible pharmaceutical use: not only the famous coca, and tobacco, which are well known, but also plant derivatives such as quinine (an antipyretic and antimalarial drug extracted from quinquina bark) and curare (originally a plant poison), which serves in medical practice as an anaesthetic. J.-F.B.

Textiles from the Pre-Hispanic Andes

The collections cover a period extending from the Paracas culture (Old Horizon, 2000-100 B.C.) to the Incas (Recent Horizon, 1450-1532 A.D.). The textiles, in general, come from burial sites in the coastal deserts of Peru and Chile.

Textiles played an important role in Pre-Columbian Andean cultures. Numerous items attest to their aesthetic quality and technical inventiveness, including the knotted cords called *kipu*, used by the Incas for counting and for recording historic events.
Among the items discovered in tombs are workbaskets containing cotton, cultivated on the coast, and camel wool from the highlands, as well as tools and products in various stages of production. Weavers were highly skilled in a surprising number of techniques. Many masterpieces are woven, or are a variation of weaving specific to the Andes, which uses a discontinuous warp and weft yarn to obtain a design composed of areas of cloth of the same colour. The museum has a rare example made at the beginning of our era, during the time of the Paracas-Nazca transition, two cultures of expert weavers and embroiderers. On the other hand, the basic weaving loom, invented around 2000-1800 B.C., has remained unchanged,

probably because it is the only type able to produce finished pieces with four selvedges. Clothing and accessories were always made with these four selvedges. Their simple forms are produced by assembling squares and rectangles of uncut cloth. Male tunics, with vertical openings for the head and arms, are different from female clothing, which has horizontal openings. Tunics, ponchos, large rectangular pieces for covering the body, loincloths, bags, belts, turbans and head coverings have distinct features indicating their geographical and cultural origin as well as the social status of their wearer. The woven wool tunic in black and white checks topped with a red triangular area, called *collcapata* in Quechua, resembles that of the Incan soldiers who encircled

Textile edging
Nasca culture,
former period
Peru, south coast
100-300
Llama wool
and cotton
8 x 68 cm
Inv. 70.2002.1.1

Tunic decorated with stylised lamas
Nasca culture,
recent period
Peru, central
coast, near Lima
300-700
Cotton, llama
wool
58 x 71.5 cm
Captain P.
Berthon mission,
1903-1908
Inv. 71.1911.21.447

Atahualpa when the Spanish captured it at Cajamarca in 1533. In contrast, the fine white cotton tunic with sleeves, embroidered with people with raised arms, seems better adapted to the coastal climate. Although found in Pachacamac near Lima, this tunic was probably woven on the north coast of Peru, in a Chimú kingdom already annexed by the Incas.

The textiles from the Pre-Columbian Andes have highly varied designs, some of them so realistic that one can identify the animal or plant species or ritual scenes depicted. On the other hand, some

Strip of tapestry work:
Person being carried on a litter
Peru, north or central coast
1100-1450
Cotton, llama wool
33.5 x 14 cm
Donated by C. Wiener
Inv. 71.1878.2.557

cultures established complex codes that are difficult to decipher. The figures on the Wari-style woven tunics (600-1100 A.D.) are often stylised and distorted by the dimensions of the background. The most difficult to decipher, however, are the fabrics decorated with single strips whose width, colour and positioning had a special meaning for the many inhabitants of the Bolivian highlands, perhaps from as early on as 600-1000 A.D.

S.D.

Unku shirt
Peru, north or central coast
1100-1450
Cotton, llama wool
90.7 x 126.3 cm
Donated by the Bibliothèque nationale de France
Inv. 71.1878.5.39

Tunic with chequered decoration
Inca culture
Peru, coastal region
1450-1532
Cotton, llama wool
90.5 x 78 cm
Captain P. Berthon mission, 1903-1908
Inv. 71.1911.21.448

THE MUSICAL INSTRUMENTS COLLECTION

THE PRESENTATION OF MUSEUM'S ETHNO-MUSICOLOGICAL
COLLECTIONS IS BUILT ON THE KNOWLEDGE AND ACHIEVEMENTS OF
THE PAST AND IS BASED ON A RIGOROUS BUT HARMONIOUS APPROACH
THAT TAKES IN BOTH THE ARTISTIC AND SCIENTIFIC POINT OF VIEW.

Drum
Kuba
Republic
of Congo
20th century
Incised and
carved wood,
metal nails, hide
H. 75 cm
Inv. 70.2001.15

**Guimbarde
(Jew's harp)**
Papua New
Guinea, Southern
Highlands, village
of Kambre
20th century
Bamboo, vegetal
fibres, opossum
jaws, insect's nest
L. 20 cm
Inv. 72.1993.1.39

_THE COLLECTION

*The musical instruments collection at the musée du quai Branly is com-
posed of approximately 9,000 musical instruments. It brings together
items once housed in the various geographical departments of the
musée national des Arts d'Afrique et d'Océanie and in the ethno-musicological department of the musée de l'Homme, as well as a number of
recently acquired pieces.*

*The collection began in 1878, when around 150 musical instruments,
most of them archaeological objects, were assembled at the musée
d'Ethnographie du Trocadéro. The collection's subsequent development
was largely the result of the extensive scientific research carried out in
the fields of art history, ethnology and anthropology at these institu-
tions. Its growth was also spurred by the unfolding of events in French
colonial history.*

*Today, the collection is made up of around 3,700 musical instruments
from Africa, 2,100 from Asia, 2,000 from the Americas – among which
650 are of pre-Hispanic origin – and 600 from Oceania and another 600
from Insulindia. It is representative of the four major musical instrument
families, which are named after the element in the instrument that
vibrates to produce sound: aerophones (air), chordophones (the plucking,*

bowing or striking of strings), membranophones (the striking of scraping one or two stretched membranes) and idiophones (the clashing, striking, shaking, plucking, rattling or scraping of rigid materials).

The permanent exhibition area

Musical instruments bear witness to both a culture and its art. They have specific formal and aesthetic characteristics, and the mechanisms that produce certain pitches or multiply and amplify sound are an integral part of a culture's system of representation.

Over a hundred instruments are exhibited in the permanent exhibitions area. In the sections devoted to the arts and cultures of the Americas, Asia, Insulindia and Oceania, and in some of the Africa display cases, these pieces are displayed alongside other types of objects for an enhanced extra-musical museographic scenography. Five musical instrument displays highlight the African itinerary, alternating with another transversal theme, that of textiles. These displays include a total of around 50 pieces, and present a range of instruments commonly used in the Maghreb and Sahel regions, along with a number of items representing the main instrumental families. Four of these displays are

Rattle played at female ritual ceremonies
Kayapo
Brazil, village of Moppo
Turn of
20th century
Calabash, feathers, wood, cotton threads
H. 34 cm
J. Vellard
Expedition
Inv. 71.1930.32.12

Six-stringed lute
Nepalese culture
Tibet
20th century
Carved wood, hide, strings made from horse hair
L. 91 cm
Inv. 71.1986.20.2

**Garamut
wooden drum**
Sawos
Papua New
Guinea,
Sepik, village
of Nogosop
20th century
Carved wood
L. 109 cm
Inv. 72.1963.5.35

Rattle with bells
Benin
20th century
Calabash, strings,
snake vertebrae
H. 32 cm
71.1931.4.6

accompanied by sound extracts enabling visitors to sample a variety of
musical repertoires. The exhibition areas devoted to Madagascar and
Ethiopia are equipped with sound systems: music acts as a sound reference, enticing visitors to explore and savour this part of the museographic
itinerary. Two audiovisual programmes based on the music of the Peul
and pygmy peoples draw visitors into the artistic and cultural world of
these communities.

The musical instruments reserve
*The musical instruments reserve is at the very heart of the museum's
public areas, forming part of the museographic environment. One of
Jean Nouvel's most spectacular and original architectural concepts in
the museum design is a tall glass tower that rises 24 metres from ground,
reaching the very top of the building. It can be seen from the museum's
reception hall, and forms a partially visible six-level reserve area in*

which the musical instruments collections are housed. Visitors can take
a peek at what goes on behind the scenes in a museum, and learn more
about what these different groups of instruments look and sound like.
The instruments have been divided up among the six levels of the reserve
according to historical and scientific considerations. Their geographical
origin and organological characteristics are taken into account, enabling
visitors to identify the major series at a glance. They have been mounted
in different ways, depending on their shape, material, size and condition.
Some of the more fragile items are stored in cardboard boxes or placed
in drawers. Special air-conditioning and lighting systems control hygro-
metry, temperature and luminosity.

**Nedundu
wooden drum**
Mangbetu
Democratic
Republic of
Congo, around
the Uelle river
Late 19th century
Wood, cloth strap
L. 102 cm
Donation R. du
Bourg de Bozas
Inv. 71.1903.33.500

_EXHIBITING MUSIC

The exhibition takes a dual approach: music as an art form in its own
right, and as a part of other social forms of expression. It incorporates
different types of music, the musicians themselves, dance, and song.
Musical museography has developed in parallel with new sound and
image broadcasting technology. Multimedia systems are located in the
musical instruments reserve, in the permanent exhibition area, and on
the central mezzanine containing the museum's anthropological database. They are independent from one another yet complementary, both in
content and technique.

**Six-piped Ding
Nam mouth
organ**
Vietnam
20th century
Calabash,
bamboo,
wax seals
H. 90 cm
Donation Mme
de Chambure
Inv. 71.1960.73.1

Around the reserve
The six levels of the instruments reserve include a total of nine audiovisual systems. The programmes illustrate techniques, playing positions,
while a sound montage with isolated recordings and extracts from musical repertoires, acquaints visitors with the sounds made by the instruments. The music's beat rhythms the image of instruments, which appear

**Imelda Sharup
and family,
Kukush
and family,
Rafael Tseremp**
Shuar
Ecuador, Taruka
1994
(photo Pierre-Jérôme Jehel)

*then disappear, enveloping the glass tower in a haze of murmurs and a
perfume of sound. The technique highlights the relationship between the
functional architectural structure of the reserve, which is plunged into
semi-obscurity, and the musical nature of its contents.*

The two "music boxes"

*The music boxes provide an opportunity for experiencing music collec-
tively through a system that combines sound spatialisation equipment
with the projection of immersive images.*
*The first box is located to one side of the collections area, and has four pro-
grammes illustrating how certain kinds of musical events determine or
qualify a given geographical area, or how geographical space becomes a
determinant factor in analysing the way a type of music is perceived.*
*The second box is located at the western end of the museum and presents
five programmes demonstrating the connections formed between partic-
ipants in the same musical event, whether they are musicians, dancers,
or other. Each programme shows the way in which musicians practice
their art and presents them performing.*
*The music boxes offer a shared experience, a direct contact and a total
immersion in music, with the art form played out in a dynamic three-
dimensional space.*

The *Listening to music of the world* programme

Another area specially designed for listening can be found on the central mezzanine housing the museum's anthropological databases. It offers a glimpse of the diversity of musical aesthetics across the five continents, and its computerised soundtrack is based on a choice of a dozen musical repertoires, and then on selection of particularly representative pieces of vocal or instrumental music. While listening, visitors are provided with information on the circumstances in which the piece of music was played, the musicians who performed it, and the instruments that brought it to life. The audio and the visual are juxtaposed in a presentation highlighting the form and nature of various musical materials, with the image giving new meaning to sound, and vice versa.

Applying this type of museology to ethno-musicology means coordinating three different fields: research, conservation and mediation. The various museographic areas, including the partially visible musical instruments reserve and the multimedia systems, provide an opportunity to observe, through sound and image, the playing techniques required for different instruments, to share in a unique musical experience in areas offering exceptionally high sound quality, and to become acquainted with some of the fundamental aspects of musical practices in the context of the performance that gives them their raison d'être. M.L.

Choir of female singers during a ritual for the supreme spirit Jèngi
Baka
Cameroon, Messea
2002
(photo Susanne Fürniss)

Musicians in the pinpeat orchestra during a village ceremony
Cambodia
2005
(photo Stéphanie Khoury)

P. P. Narayanan, Low-caste pulluvan musician, playing a kutam (pot)
India, Kerala
2000
(photo Christine Guillebaud)

THE TEXTILE COLLECTIONS

FROM CONTINENT TO CONTINENT, REGION TO REGION,
VILLAGE TO VILLAGE, THE SKILLED HANDS OF MEN
AND WOMEN HAVE PRODUCED AN ASTONISHINGLY
WIDE RANGE OF TEXTILES. THE CHOICE OF MATERIALS,
TECHNIQUES, FORMS AND DECORATIONS, MIRROR THE
RELATIONSHIPS FORGED BETWEEN MANKIND AND
THE NATURAL WORLD, BETWEEN MANKIND AND THE
GODS, AND BETWEEN THE LIVING AND THE DEAD.

**Arkilla kerka
Wedding blanket**
Peul
Mali
Early of
20th century
Wool, cotton
Various
techniques
481 x 177 cm
Inv. 70.2002.19.1

**Length for
woman's
mola blouse**
Appliqué decor
"myth of the
clinging tortoise"
Cuna
Panama,
San Blas islands
Cotton
35.5 x 43.5 cm
Inv. 70.2004.38.1.88

Although the museum's textile collections include examples from
archaeological and historical collections, in particular from America,
they mainly date from the 19th and 20th centuries. They reflect the main
focus of interest of individual collectors whose different approaches
provide a collection that is richly varied, and which reveals the technical,
social and aesthetic values of different times and places.

The raw materials – animal, vegetable and mineral fibres and dyes –
come from nature, and peoples tended to favour one over another for a
specific purpose according to their physical or symbolic qualities – seeds,
porcupine quills, shells, feathers, metal strips, spangles, glass beads, etc.
– inserted or applied at a certain stage in the manufacturing process.

Weaving and dyeing techniques produce very varied and sometimes
highly complex forms of decoration, as is the case for Amerindian fabrics,
whether pre-Columbian or contemporary. Decoration can be achieved by
inserting extra wefts, or, as in tapestry work, by limiting weft yarns of a
single colour to the outlines of a motif, which can produce a wide variety
of effects depending on raw materials used: wool for carpets and
garments created in the Maghreb and in Central Asia, the finest silk for
Chinese clothing, as well as other materials. Width of fabric lengths is

also turned to good use, as in West Africa, where very narrow, contrastingly dyed strips of cloth are stitched together to create a truly vibrant form of decoration.

Alongside weaving come a whole range of plaited fabrics, and "nonwoven" textiles like woollen felts and beaten bark cloth – use of the latter being particularly widespread in Oceania.

Ikat weaving is a technique practised on all continents, producing spectacular results, especially in continental and insular Asia. Hanks of yarn are dyed different colours before weaving. Sometimes it is the warp yarns that are dyed different colours, sometimes the weft, and sometimes both, to create highly diverse decorative styles.

Dyeing carried out on finished fabrics and combined with resist procedures protecting certain areas from the dying process can produce other forms of decoration. Every region of the world has used these techniques to produce its own specific style, in addition to appliqué and even more especially, embroidery.

Fabrics are used in every aspect of life, whether for everyday use or for special occasions, from the sacred to the profane. Different cultural groups use textiles artistically to adorn the exterior and interior of their

Wincha head-band (detail)
Quechua
Bolivia, La Paz department
Sheep's wool, glass beads
Double woven fabric
61 x 7 cm
L. Giraud expedition
Inv. 71.1965.41.48

Man's coat (detail)
North Syria
Late 19th-early 20th century
Wool, cotton, silk, silver thread
Tapestry
140 x 143 cm
Inv. 71.1989.25.7.2

Length of fabric
Kuba
Democratic
Republic of
Congo
Raffia
Cloth weave,
"brushed"
embroidery
63 x 56.5 cm
Inv. 73.1988.1.6

dwellings, especially in nomadic societies. Knotting and tapestry work create identifying motifs on dividing curtains, blankets, bags and carpets, as do appliqué, embroidery and dyeing. Examples include marriage coverlets decorated with motifs of good omen from such far apart regions as China and the Sahel. Expression is also given to religious feelings, as in the ikat hangings offered to temples in Cambodia.

The relationships between fabric and clothing, from draped garments to the most sophisticated tailoring, and between garment and body, as well as a person's individual status and social position, are also significant. Clothing signals social category, age group, and rites of passage, which are reflected in styles, colours and motifs specific to each culture. It also indicates power and prestige, and expresses the connections between men and their gods and between the living and the dead. The Tlingit ceremonial cloak from the northwest coast of Canada, the Sudanese

lawo butu
**noble woman's
ceremonial
tubular skirt**
Ngada
Indonesia,
Flores island
Late 19th century
Cotton cloth,
warp ikat,
glass beads
appliqué
and shells
83.7 x 165 cm
Donated by J. P.
Barbier-Mueller
Inv. 70.2001.27.89

**Woman's shawl
(detail)**
Senegal
20th century
Cotton, indigo
Damask satin,
resist dyeing by
sewing
126.5 x 262 cm
Donated by
Cooperation
Ministry
Inv. 71.1962.59.102

Mahdist army tunic, the shawl with its woven or dyed religious inscriptions from India, and the long scarf worn by the men of Sumba are but a few examples of this.

All these fabrics, whether precious and richly ornamented for festive occasions or designed for everyday use, whose inventive decoration often more than compensates for the rustic simplicity of materials, show the skills of professional workshops or the family circle that are handed down from generation to generation. Throughout history there have been many contacts, borrowings, abandoned techniques and "transfers of technology". Changes in styles and functional use have always been influenced by trends in fashion. F.C.

Johnston
and Hoffman
No title
India
1870-1880
Printed on
albumin paper
19 x 11.7 cm

THE PHOTOGRAPHIC COLLECTIONS

THE PHOTOGRAPHIC COLLECTIONS AT THE MUSÉE
DU QUAI BRANLY COME FROM AN INHERITANCE
COMBINING THE EXTENSIVE COLLECTIONS HOUSED
AT THE MUSÉE NATIONAL DES ARTS D'AFRIQUE ET
D'OCÉANIE AND THE MUSÉE DE L'HOMME, WITH
ADDITIONAL ACQUISITIONS MADE BY THE MUSÉE
DU QUAI BRANLY OVER THE PAST FEW YEARS.

_FROM SOUVENIR ALBUM TO SCIENTIFIC COLLECTION

Théodore Bocourt
**Native belonging
to a tribe in Laos
and Cochinchina**
Laos
1862
Printed on
albumin paper
21.2 x 15.5 cm

*"I've brought you back some pictures" will long remain the typical
greeting of any returning traveller, and it is easy to imagine the
excitement of those who first set out armed with a camera. What to
photograph? What to bring back? And, a little later on, What to bequeath?
And to whom? To a museum, to a learned society, to the family? Museums
often find themselves at the end of the chain, entrusted with a collection,
and with a history that leaves many gaps to be filled.*

*The further off a region, the more important it was to bring back
photographs. Consequently, Europe and the Near East, although not
totally absent from the exhibits, are not overly represented. On the other
hand, there is a significant collection of pictures pertaining to the
historical territories of French ethnological research: Africa, Latin
America, Oceania, Asia, and the Polar regions. But colonial history
overtook research, and new maps were drawn: Asia is the subject of the*

largest group of photographs, but it is an Asia where Vietnam figures a
great deal more than China. And, not surprisingly, former French colonial
territories in Africa are heavily represented.

The collection, however, far exceeds the fields to which logic might wish
to limit it, and contains photographs taken or given by a very diverse
range of travellers. In almost chronological order, we can cite soldiers,
amateur photographers, doctors, and professional photographers – then,
as scientists increasingly became fieldworkers, archaeologists and
anthropologists. Each set off with his camera, and each, methodically or
otherwise, took photographs to accompany projects or ideas ranging from
the most trivial to the most ambitious.

Subjects and instruments varied according to era, but cameras were in
use from 1841 onwards. Initially employed as a humble "servant of arts
and sciences", photography was used to create visual records of collected
objects such as skulls and skeletons. Its use soon extended to travellers on
sea voyages – undertaken for purposes of coastal reconnaissance,
exploration of archaeological sites, or hydrographical mapping. In the
1870s the rapid proliferation of professional studios offered travellers
ready-made photographs to include in their souvenir album or scientific

S. B. Toumanoff
**Rich Buryat
woman**
East Siberia,
Republic of
the Buryat-
Mongols
1860-1879
Printed on
albumin paper
15.8 x 10.8 cm

Johnston
and Hoffman
No title
India
1870-1880
Printed on
albumin paper
19 x 11.7 cm

Bernardt Hagen
**Singles' house
In Bogadjim**
Papua New
Guinea,
Astrolabe Bay
1893-1897
Printed on
aristotype paper
17.1 x 22.6 cm

collection. Finally, travel was not all that Europeans did, and the diplomatic visits of the 1850s served as the pretext for taking so-called ethnographic portraits.

At the close of the 19th century, the extension of trade networks and ease of trade, as well as simplified photographic techniques, led to a veritable explosion in the art of photography. The earliest pictures (daguerreotypes, negatives on collodion-coated glass, and prints on albumin paper) were succeeded by smaller format photographs (silver brome gelatine negatives, firstly on glass, and then on paper). Industrial processes made taking pictures easier than ever, even in unfavourable conditions, and human activities came to be photographed in ever greater detail.

In parallel to this, photography was becoming more and more professional. In France, the 1920s and 1930s saw the rise of a generation of ethnological researchers many of whom applied Marcel Mauss' descriptive methods to photography to record techniques used in body decoration, carrying and transport, preparation, ways of dressing, eating, hunting, fishing, building, trading, dancing, etc. This was the period when researchers believed in exhaustiveness, as they had in the mid-19th century, and strove to document an unattainable universal (the Dakar-Djibouti mission, along with other French missions of the time). In the years between the First and Second World Wars, where scientific

Claude
Lévi-Strauss
**Bororo in
composite dress**
Brazil, Kejara,
rio Vermelho
1935-1936
Printed on baryta
paper
7.5 x 11 cm

Frank Christol
**Bamileke chief
surrounded
by his personal
entourage**
Cameroon,
Bafang region
1930
Printed on
baryta paper
22.8 x 16.6 cm

Richard Buchta
**Murchinson
Falls,
the Nile**
Uganda
1875-1880
Printed on
albumin paper
15 x 20 cm

*interest went hand in hand with a growing taste for the exotic,
photographic collections grew considerably. Since then, photographs
have mainly been acquired through researchers donating the results of
their fieldwork.
Acquisitions made since the start-up of the Musée du quai Branly project
reflect once more the many different backgrounds of their authors – a
mixture of professional photographers, amateurs, scientists and artists.*
Ch.B.

THE HISTORY COLLECTIONS

THE HISTORY COLLECTIONS COMPRISE CLOSE TO 10,000 WORKS
RELATING TO VOYAGES OF EXPLORATION AND DISCOVERY AND COLONIAL
HISTORY. PRINTS, WATERCOLOURS, PAINTINGS, SKETCHES AND
NOTEBOOKS, AS WELL AS SCULPTURE, FURNITURE, MAPS AND
MEDALLIONS, SHOW THE KNOWLEDGE AND DIFFERENT VIEWS THAT THE
WESTERN WORLD HAD OF "OTHER" FROM THE 16TH CENTURY UP UNTIL
THE MID 20TH CENTURY.

_A GENEALOGY OF VIEWS OF THE OTHER

Antoine-Jean Gros
Negro head
Turn of
19th century
Oil on canvas
46 x 38 cm
Inv. 75.8946

*16th and 17th century works largely concern the New World, and are a mix of
fantasy and reality: images of the American Indians underscore the role
imagination played during that period. The Enlightenment changed the
way in which "otherness" was viewed, with scholar-travellers who brought
new objectivity to bear but who also propagated the belief in the idea of the
"Noble Savage" as symbolised by the peoples of the Pacific islands. Prints,
sketches and watercolours depict species of plants in meticulous detail, but
also idealised scenes in which Tahitian dancers are a primary feature. The
idea of the Pacific islands as a Garden of Eden was well entrenched throughout the 19th century, as shown by the works of Paul Gauguin.*

*The Enlightenment is also represented by a major iconographic collection
on the subject of slavery. The works depict ships arriving at the coasts of
Africa, and the capture, transport and life of slaves on plantations, as well
as its abolition in Haiti and later on other French islands. Scenes from*

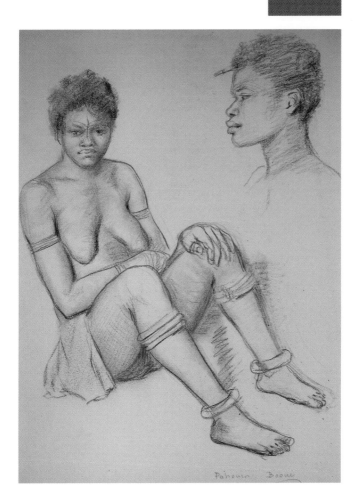

Bernardin de Saint-Pierre's novel Paul et Virginie, *which played a major role in turning public opinion against slavery, are featured on pottery and landscape wallpapering, as well as in works of embroidery and numerous engravings. Trans-Saharan slavery is above all represented by paintings from the late 19th century.*

Although the Pacific islands continued to attract attention until the 1830s, the focus turned to North Africa with the conquest of Algeria and the taking of the Smala of Abd el-Kader, a favourite theme of Orientalist painters such as Horace Vernet, Eugène Fromentin and Prosper Marilhat. Oriental dancers, winding alleyways and desert and oasis landscapes became key features in the imagery of North Africa.

In the final quarter of the 19th century, interest shifted to sub-Saharan Africa, as major explorations of the continent's unmapped interior were launched. A large number of engravings on the subject of colonial

Edmond Laethier
**Travel journal:
young Fang
woman**
1887-1888
Charcoal and
pastel
17 x 24 cm
Inv. 75.15209.1-3

Michel Géo
**Main
productions of
plant origin,
Madagascar**
1931
Oil on canvas
308 x 276 cm
Inv. 75.2005.0.724

Louis Bâte
**Sorcerers' dance,
Ubangi-Shari**
1920s
Watercolour
drawing
53 x 40 cm
Inv. 75.12769

conquest, as well as books of drawings made by military personnel and artists (Edmond Laethier, André Coffinieres de Nordeck) during these expeditions are conserved in the History collections. Although the heroic figure of the soldier-explorer was a central theme in 19th century colonial painting, the importance of portraits of chiefs and local kings is not to be underestimated as they played an important part in European imagery of the times – figures such as Abd el-Kader, Queen Pomaré of Tahiti, the West African resistance leader Samory Touré, the Béhanzin kings of Dahomey and Bao Dai of Vietnam.

Iconography from the early decades of the 20th century mainly linked to colonial life, with the colonist as the central figure. Economic benefits are also highlighted, in the products supplied to France from the colonies, as in the providing of medical care and the creating of infrastructures (Michel Géo and André Herviault) by the French. Dioramas glorifying the French colonial empire came to an end with the Second World War. A more personalised vision is offered by a number of Africanist artists from between the Wars, such as Louis Bâte, Marcelle Ackein, Jeanne Tercafs and Alexandre Iacovleff.

Although the works largely mirror Western viewpoints, there also exists a substantial number of paintings by local artists trained in French schools of fine arts in the early 20th century. These paintings, in particular those of the Hanoi and Antananarivo schools, take a far more intimist approach, putting the individual and household life in the foreground. Whether it is a canvas by Paul Gauguin painted during his stay in the Marquesas Islands or a sketch by an anonymous soldier in Morocco, these works give us a valuable insight into the various Western visions of the Other through the ages. This precious historical testimony enables us not only to establish a genealogy of viewpoints on the Other, but also to better understand the strong hold that these images have on our imaginations today. N.S.

Louis Canuet
Portrait of an Algerian woman
Late 19th-early 20th century
Oil on canvas
104 x 77.5 cm
Inv. 75.1507

Charles Giraud
Portrait of a young Tahitian girl
1846
Black lead with white gouache highlights
48 x 31 cm
Inv. 75.10122.1

INSULAIRES ET MONUMENS DE L'ÎLE DE PÂQUE.

RARE BOOKS AND DOCUMENTS

THE MUSÉE DU QUAI BRANLY MEDIATHEQUE IS A RESOURCE CENTRE
DESIGNED TO PROVIDE USERS WITH THE WIDEST POSSIBLE RANGE OF
DOCUMENTATION ON THE MUSEUM COLLECTIONS. IT DRAWS ON A WEALTH
OF MATERIAL LARGELY ORIGINATING FROM THE LIBRARIES, PHOTOTHEQUE
AND ETHNOLOGICAL LABORATORY OF THE MUSÉE DE L'HOMME AND THE
MUSÉE NATIONAL DES ARTS D'AFRIQUE ET D'OCÉANIE, ALONG WITH A
NUMBER OF MORE RECENT ACQUISITIONS FROM SPECIALIST LIBRARIES.

Easter Island
In *Voyage de La
Pérouse autour du
monde*, published
in accordance
with the decree
of 22 April 1797,
and edited
by M.L.A. Milet-
Mureau
Atlas, pl. n° 11,
drawn by
Duché de Vancy,
engraved
by Godefroy
Paris, Imprimerie
de la République
Cote F-R-C-000001

*The Musée de l'Homme library, set up in 1937, was gradually enlarged by
donations from such eminent anthropologists and ethnologists as Marcel
Delafosse, Alfred Métraux, Paul Rivet, Marcel Mauss, Michel Leiris,
Claude Lévi-Strauss, and Paul-Émile Victor. This rich national heritage
(over 3,000 documents) includes accounts of the travels of great explorers
from the 16th century onwards (Léon l'Africain, Cook, La Pérouse,
Bougainville, Dumont d'Urville, etc.), and the earliest publications on
French and foreign anthropology covering every continent from the mid-
19th century to the present day.*

*After the Musée de l'Homme was founded in the mid-19th century, French
and foreign ethnological expeditions benefited from the rapid developments in photography. Over the years, fieldworkers (scientists and amateurs alike) amassed a collection of 700,000 photographs using every type
of processing technique (a large number on glass plates), including Prince
Roland Bonaparte's albums, the Désiré Charnay collection, and the collec-*

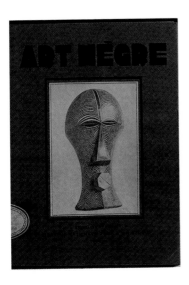

tion of the anthropological laboratory of the *Musée national d'Histoire naturelle*. Scientific archives, field notebooks, sketches and a whole range of documentation from these expeditions provide a wealth of information on the illustrations and artefacts collected from all over the world.

The Library of the *Musée national des Arts d'Afrique et d'Océanie*, created at same time as the former *Musée des Colonies* in 1931, contained over 400 rare documents, including the Georges-Marie Haardt collection (photographs of the "Croisière Noire") and the archives and photographs of the 1931 Colonial Exhibition and the *Musée de la France d'Outre-Mer*. Its collection also included over 200 different editions of Bernardin de Saint-Pierre's novel Paul et Virginie.

More recent acquisitions and gifts have added specialist collections to the mediatheque's rich heritage, including the Hubert Goldet collection (auction catalogues), and those of Françoise Girard (Oceania), Georges Condominas (South-East Asia), and Jacques Kerchache (art history), along with the Faublée-Guérin donation (the archives of Thérèse Rivière and Germain Tillion's mission in the Aures Mountains).

Given the fragile condition of some of the documentation, the *Musée du quai Branly* took steps to ensure maximum public access by financing a digital sound archive collection (Gilbert Rouget), a database of 200,000 photographs (albums and glass plates), 70,000 archives and documentary pages containing information on the collections, along with the flagship reviews of the four learned societies housed within its walls: the Journal de la société des africanistes, *the* Journal de la société des américanistes, *the* Bulletin des océanistes and Eurasie.

Negro Art at the exhibition of the Palais des Beaux-Arts from 15 November to 31 December 1930
by J. Maes and H. Lavachery
Brussels-Paris, Librairie nationale d'art et d'histoire
1930
31 p., 48 boards, 25 cm
Cote F-L-A-003194

Idols found in San Juan de Teotihuacán
Claude-Joseph-Désiré Charnay
Teotihuacán (State of Mexico)
1880-1882
Photograph, single-coloured positive
21 x 14.5 cm
Cote 1998-20156

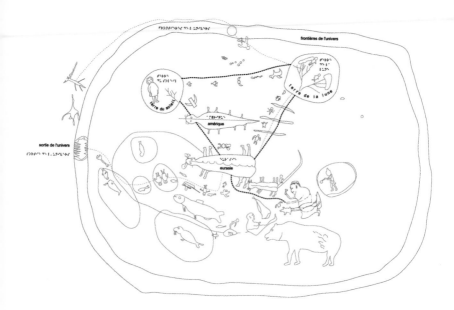

THE RIVIÈRE

LOCATED AT THE CENTRE OF THE COLLECTIONS AREA, THE RIVIÈRE
("RIVER") INVITES VISITORS TO TRAVEL THROUGH SPACE AND TIME AS
THEY ARE PERCEIVED AND EXPERIENCED BY NON-EUROPEAN PEOPLES.
IT IS A THEMATIC, TRANSVERSAL SPACE, IN CONTRAST WITH THE
GEOGRAPHIC ORGANISATION OF THE COLLECTIONS AREA ITSELF,
AND IS DESIGNED TO ACQUAINT VISITORS WITH THE REMARKABLE
PLACES INHABITED BY HUMAN SOCIETY, AND MANKIND'S MANY
DIFFERENT VISIONS OF THE WORLD.

Installation model for the Rivière
Shamanic map

The series of displays bordering the banks of the Rivière bring both our minds and senses into play. The displays are there to be looked at, interpreted, listened to and touched. The itinerary follows three themes, each broken up into three sections. The first presents the West's gradual mapping of the world and the history of the collections; the second, the ways in which different human societies organise space; and the last, man's relationships with the Beyond and the world of the spirits.

_DISCOVERING - COLLECTING

As is the case with any ethnographic collection, the one at the musée du Quai Branly is by no means exhaustive. It is the result of historical events, some peaceful, others violent, and of different theories and views of the world. From the Renaissance up until the present day, the collections have been enriched and enlightened by items that illustrate man's spirit of curiosity, drive for conquest or for scientific knowledge, interest in ethnographical research, or simply the love of "primitive objects" and

/ IN THE WORLD OF THE SHAMANS

While in trance, shamans project their spirits outside their physical bodies to give them clairvoyant and healing powers, and to accompany the spirits of the dead. In doing so, they travel in a parallel world with a specific geography, peopled with creatures with which they must do fierce battle. The journey is fraught with danger and requires ritual precautions and the wearing of a magical garment. The shamanic world presented here was drawn for a Russian anthropologist in 1929.

/ LANDMARKS

The Canada, the Inuit built stone cairns known as *inuksuk* – literally, "human form". Protruding above the snow, whatever depth it may be, these landmarks guide hunters on their wanderings. They indicate good observation points, caches of meat or major fishing grounds. Inuksuit are also erected to make traps for caribou hunting, or to mark the spot where a death occurred from starvation or accident – thus turning them into places where offerings are made.

unfamiliar cultures. Western civilisation's discovery of the world, and the history of the collections, is synthesised in a map and through variety of multimedia supports.

Behind every collection lies a story of human adventure. Some of these tales are illustrated by portraits and first-hand accounts. All the discoveries and contacts with unknown peoples were spurred by the quest for lands of marvels and riches, wonders evoked by such figures as El Dorado ("the Man of Gold") and such places as the South Polar Region. These displays serve as an introduction to the collections themselves. They provide a historical perspective, and highlight the complexity of the collection process itself, which is always a reflection of a specific period and way of thinking.

_TRAVERSING - INHABITING

The central section of the Rivière is devoted to the territories inhabited by men. In order to explore or take advantage of their surroundings – whether extending to the far horizon or hidden from view – human societies must map out and delimit their territory to establish landmarks and find their way around.

This practice is evident in the icy stretches populated by the Inuit of Canada, and in the arid Australian outback. These regions show how areas are demarcated and qualified by structures that indicate places essential to a people's survival (for gathering, fishing or hunting), for

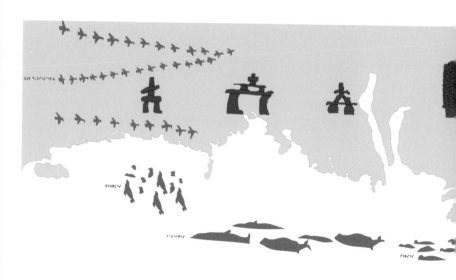

**Installation
model for the
Rivière**
Inuksuit
Canada, Nunavut,
Baffin

example. But the organisation of space is often an expression of power struggles and hierarchical relationships as well. This is true of the city of Mexico, whose central square was the centre of religious and secular power and of the Aztec Empire, or of the palace of the King of Foumbam, in Cameroon, where spaces were governed by strict rules, and special areas within the compound assigned to groups close to the monarch.

Houses are, without doubt, the place most familiar to men. The arrangement of rooms and relationship with natural surroundings are fixed by rules that cover both kinship (within and between families) and social codes: fortified dwellings such as those found in Africa accommodating several families at once; the enclosed residences of the Middle East, where several generations live together protected from the outside world; or Japanese houses, whose sliding doors open it to the world. Many populations are still nomadic and carry their dwellings around with them, like the Plains Indians whose tepees can be put up or taken down at a moment's notice, and whose organisation is strictly codified. Territorial markings are also traced directly on the skin: the Tabwa in East Africa have scars indicating the route their ancestors took to reach the lake where they settled and their descendents now live.

_JOURNEYING - HONOURING

All societies pray to, honour, and at times visit their dead. Similarly, the souls of the deceased travel down a path that leads to the world of the ancestors. The Dayak of Borneo enable us to journey along one such road, thanks to a map based on folk tales and traditional songs drawn up by a missionary. In Siberia, shamans, through trances, follow the paths that lead them to the "kingdom of souls".

Many cultures consider the place where their founding ancestor first emerged or appeared to be the centre of the world, a centre that serves as an absolute reference point when its people live far from one another. The Yoruba, for example, have large communities on the American continent, but always refer back to the pillar of Ile-Ife in Nigeria. The centre of the world can also be a place visited through meditation, such as the Kunlun Mountains in Tibet.

The link with the Beyond is also expressed by projecting the sky on to the earth, or even into houses. The ceilings of houses built by the Wayana people of Guyana are decorated with paintings of animals that watch over them – one example among many of a people seeking the protection of heavenly powers. P.P.

THE PAVILLON DES SESSIONS

THE PAVILLON DES SESSIONS AT THE LOUVRE MUSEUM
IS DEVOTED TO THE ARTS OF AFRICA, ASIA, OCEANIA
AND THE AMERICAS. IT STANDS AS A PERMANENT
"BRANCH" OF THE MUSÉE DU QUAI BRANLY MORE
THAN IT FORESHADOWS IT.

_A COMPLEMENT TO THE MUSÉE DU QUAI BRANLY

*It was inaugurated on 13 April 2000 by Jacques Chirac, who had long
wanted to bring recognition to these cultures, hitherto little represented
in French museums, by housing their works in a proper 'temple of the
arts'. In 1990, Jacques Kerchache, exhibition commissioner, collector and
specialist in world sculpture, had launched the project by publishing a
manifesto entitled "Masterpieces from the world over are born free and
equal", in which he advocated the opening of a department at the Louvre
devoted to the cultures that represent "three-quarters of humanity".
Many illustrious predecessors had been animated by the same desire and
had expressed a similar wish, including Guillaume Apollinaire, Félix
Fénéon, Claude Lévi-Strauss and André Malraux.*
*Although the Musée Dauphin, a marine and ethnographic museum
founded in 1827 by royal decree and housed in the Louvre, had enabled
the public to view a large number of "exotic artefacts", it took many years
before the Louvre opened its doors to these masterpieces of world cultur-*

Zulu spoon
South Africa,
province of
Kwazulu-Natal
19th-early
20th century
Wood
H. 57 cm
É. Saint-Paul
bequest
Inv. 71.1977.52.14

Transformation mask
Kwakwaka'wakw (kwakiutl)
Canada, British Columbia
19th century
Painted wood, graphite, cedar, cloth, rope
34 x 53 cm closed, 130 cm open
Former collections Heye Foundation, New York;
C. Lévi-Strauss
Inv. 71.1951.35.1

al heritage. It was decided in 1996 that they would be housed in the Pavillon des États, which is located between the Flore and the Denon wings, and was renamed the Pavillon des Sessions on this occasion.

Its architecture, designed by Jean-Michel Wilmotte, largely takes the building's historical dimension into account. It is understated and elegant, and it enables visitors to circulate with ease, while the works themselves stand out in uncluttered space. An indirect lighting system complements the area's natural light sources, in order to cast a subdued aura over the sculptures in a play of light and shadow.

_AN ANTHOLOGY OF EXEMPLARY WORKS

Following on from the galleries which present European paintings, Greco-Roman sculptures and the art of Ancient Egypt, the sculptures housed in the Pavillon des Sessions are of impressive power and plastic diversity. In his selection, Jacques Kerchache was not seeking to be encyclopaedic or exhaustive, and instead, he concentrated on the identity of the works and, through them, on the artist's stamp. The resulting anthology illustrates Paul Valéry's formula that "form becomes emotion", so much do the works echo one another, despite their great variety in age, size and materials.

The sculptures, which are grouped by geographical area in four rooms without any apparent partitioning, come from French public collections, mainly from the ethnology laboratory of the Musée de l'Homme and Musée national des Arts d'Afrique et d'Océanie. It is complemented by a number of gifts, State acquisitions and long-term renewable loans from

Ancestor statue
Indonesia, North of Nias Island
19th century
Wood, rough red patina
H. 55.7 cm
Former collections
A. Breton, H. Rubinstein, A. Schoffel
Inv. 70.1999.3.1

Akati Ekplékendo
Sculpture dedicated to the God Gou
Fon
Benin, Abomey
1858
Iron, wood
H. 165 cm
Donated by capitaine E. Fonssagrives
Inv. 71.1894.32.1

Female statuette
Chupícuaro culture
Mexico
600-100 B.C.
Slip terracotta
H. 31 cm
Former collection
G. Joussemet
Inv. 70.1998.3.1

the countries the collections come from, as well as French regional museums (including overseas French territories).

The exhibition space, which covers a total of 1,400 square meters, opens with Africa, continues on to Asia and Oceania, and ends up with America (from South to North).

African works include a sculpture of the deity Gou, the god of iron and warfare, made by Akati Ekplékendo from the Republic of Benin, who was active in the 1850s, and whose style is extraordinarily modern, recalling Picasso's daring uses of form. Also on exhibition are a Zulu anthropomorphic spoon from South Africa and a Yangere drum from the Central African Republic, which both illustrate the close connection between beauty and function.

Asian exhibits include a wooden statue from the Nias Island, which represents an ancestral spirit. This hieratic and highly structured sculpture once belonged to André Breton.

The Oceania section presents an astonishing Uli hermaphroditic statue from New Ireland, structurally complex and mocking in attitude, which was acquired by the State. Such artefacts were associated with funeral rites. In contrast with this item, a sculpture from Nukuoro, in Micronesia, is noticeable for its minimal ornamentation and its refined lines.

Statuette
Caroline Islands,
Nukuoro Atoll
Late 18ᵗʰ century
Wood
H. 35 cm
Donated by
G. H. Rivière
Inv. 71.1933.2.1

Duho
ceremonial seat
Taino
Haiti
1200-1500
Guayac wood
42 x 30.3 cm
Donated by
D. Weill
Inv. 71.1950.77.1

Uli **statue**
New Ireland
18ᵗʰ-early
19ᵗʰ century
Wood, red ochre,
charcoal,
limestone,
small roots, resin,
turbo opercula
H. 150 cm
Former
collections
Museum für
Völkerkunde,
Leipzig;
A. Schoffel
Inv. 70.1999.2.1

*The American section, which covers a large geographical as well as chrono-
logical span, presents the visitor with a more intimate atmosphere. Here
are exhibited a Taino ceremonial wooden seat from the Greater Antilles,
created between 1200 and 1500, and a Chupícuaro sculpture, which has
become the emblem of the Musée du quai Branly. This generously propor-
tioned Mexican terracotta item wears its two thousand years with incom-
parable grace. In North America, a 3.25 metre high ogress, in the form of
the central pillar from a British Columbian kwakwaka'wakw meeting-
house, stands not far off from a curious transformation mask, half man,
half crow. They both bring to an end this enchanted journey populated
with myths and silent voices. M.D.*

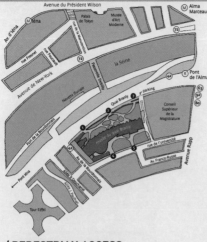

/ PEDESTRIAN ACCESS

There are entrances to the museum
on the rue de l'Université and the quai Branly.
Université entrance: 218 rue de l'Université
"Bassins" (Ornamental Pools) entrance:
206 rue de l'Université
Alma entrance: 27 quai Branly
Debilly entrance: 37 quai Branly,
opposite the Debilly footbridge
Branly entrance: 51 quai Branly

BY THE MÉTRO (PARIS UNDERGROUND)
RER C: Pont de l'Alma
Line 6: Bir Hakeim
Line 9: Alma-Marceau, Iéna

BY BUS
Line 42: Tour Eiffel
Lines 63, 80, 92: Bosquet-Rapp
Line 72: Modern Art Museum-palais de Tokyo
River shuttle (Batobus, Bateaux parisiens and Vedettes
de Paris): get off at the Eiffel Tower

/ BY CAR
Paying car park entrance at 25 quai Branly. Pedestrian
access via the rue de l'Université, just outside
the garden. 520 parking spaces, including 12 parking
spaces for the disabled.

/ INFORMATION
telephone: 01 56 61 70 00
E-mail: contact@quaibranly.fr
Website: www.quaibranly.fr
Ticket counter: in the garden
Information: in the entrance hall

practical information

/ SERVICES

Pushchairs, walking frames and wheelchairs
are available for loan in the cloakroom.

/ AUDIOGUIDE

Suitable for all types of visitors, the audioguide
proposes an initial selection of exhibits to view
and provides a soundscape in harmony with the
objects on display. Audioguides may be hired at
the ticket counters in the garden and collected
in the entrance hall.

/ BROCHURES AND PROGRAMMES

Detailed guides to the Musée du Quai Branly
programmes are available at the reception desk.

/ VISITORS WITH STATION NEEDS

Reception in the museum foyer.
The visits and workshops are accessible to the
hearing-impaired (videoguides and sign language
conferences), and are also adapted to people
with learning disabilities.
The "Rivière" (River) multisensory tour is a specially
designed exhibition which winds its way through
200 metres of the collections area, and features
Braille texts, touchable low relief displays and
multimedia screens.
Wheelchairs are available on loan.

**OPENING
HOURS**
_TUESDAY TO
SUNDAY FROM 10.00
AM TO 6.30 PM.
_GROUP ENTRY
ONLY FROM 9.00 AM.
_LATE NIGHT
OPENING ON
THURSDAYS UNTIL
9.30 PM.

TILLS CLOSE AT
5.45PM, AND 8.30PM
ON THURSDAY

_CLOSED MONDAYS.

RESERVATIONS
_BY TELEPHONE:
01 56 61 71 72
_BY E-MAIL:
RESERVATIONS
@QUAIBRANLY.FR
_AT FNAC
OR TICKETNET
POINTS OF SALE

/ TARIFS

_ADMISSION TICKET TO THE MUSÉE DU QUAI BRANLY (COLLECTIONS AREA AND SUSPENDED GALLERIES)

_Full price: 8,50 €
_Reduced price: 6 €

This gives access to the permanent collections, special "theme" exhibitions, the anthropological exhibition, the multimedia gallery, and the Jacques Kerchache reading room.

_TICKET FOR THE TEMPORARY INTERNATIONAL EXHIBIT (GARDEN GALLERY)

_Full price: 8,50 €
_Reduced price: 6 €

This is purchased separately from the entrance ticket to the museum.

_THE "UN JOUR AU MUSÉE" TICKET (COLLECTIONS AREA, SUSPENDED GALLERIES AND THE GARDEN GALLERY)

_Full price: 13 €
_Reduced price: 9,50 €

This gives access to the museum and the temporary exhibits.

_THE MUSÉE DU QUAI BRANLY PASS

(Valid for one year starting from the purchase date)
Pass Quai Branly: 45 €
Pass Quai Branly Duo: 70 €
Pass Quai Branly Collectivité (Group): 35 €
Pass Quai Branly Jeunes (Young people's): 15 €

These passes give unlimited access to all areas of the museum, eliminate the need to queue for entrance to the museum during busy periods and entitle their holders to reductions on admission to shows in the theatre.

_Admission to the museum and to temporary exhibitions is free on the first Sunday of each month.

FREE ENTRY

_UNDER 18S, THE UNEMPLOYED, PEOPLE ON INCOME SUPPORT, DISABLED EX-SERVICEMEN AND CIVILIANS, JOURNALISTS, HOLDERS OF THE CULTURE CARD, FRIENDS OF THE MUSEUM, HOLDERS OF THE QUAI BRANLY PASS, PLUS ICOM AND ICOMOS MEMBERS.

/ PERFORMING ARTS, CONFERENCES AND DEBATES, CINEMA

The theatre and cinema are situated on the niveau Jardin bas (Lower Garden level).
Access via the stairs or lift in the entrance hall, niveau JB (Lower Garden level).

The Claude Lévi-Strauss Theatre offers a varied performing arts programme of performances, popular traditions and special events (epics, rites and songs). The Outdoor Theatre (Théâtre de verdure) with its terraced seating built into the slopes of the garden hosts open air performances and conferences.

_CONFERENCES AND DEBATES
Free access. Through its programme of conferences which are open to all visitors, the Université populaire du quai Branly (Quai Branly Public University) aims to broaden the public's knowledge of non-Western arts and civilisations, inviting historians, researchers, philosophers and artists from all nations to take the floor.

_CINEMA
The museum screens fiction films and documentaries in connection with scheduled performances and specific topics.

/ VISITS, WORKSHOPS
Familiarise yourself with the collections of exhibits and the cultures which created them... The museum offers a variety of ways for visitors to meet up with different cultures.

_Introductory visits and activities provide a first contact with the museum and are designed to help the visitor develop a better understanding of the range of collections on display.
_Narrative visits use oral traditions from around the world as a vehicle for understanding different ethnic groups.
_Question and answer visits in the cinema feature discussions led by lecturers before or after the visits.
_Cross-cultural visits set out to break down

PERFORMANCE PRICES
_RATE A (SOUTH TIER)
_FULL PRICE: 20 €
_REDUCED PRICE: 14 €

_RATE B (NORTH TIER)
_FULL PRICE: 14 €
_REDUCED PRICE: 10.50 €

PERFORMANCE PRICES FOR CHILDREN
_NORMAL PRICE: 8 €
_REDUCED PRICE: 5.50 €
(FOR GROUPS WITH A MINIMUM OF 10 PEOPLE)

CINEMA PRICES
_FULL PRICE: 5 €
_REDUCED PRICE: 3,50 €

INDIVIDUAL PRICES (EXCLUDING ADMISSION FEE)
VISIT WITH COMMENTARY, NARRATIVE VISIT
_FULL PRICE: 8 €
_REDUCED PRICE: 6 €

QUESTION AND ANSWER VISIT
_FULL PRICE: 5 €
_REDUCED PRICE: 3.50 €

geographical barriers by weaving together visual and
thematic parallels between objects from different
continents.

_**One-day voyages of discovery** offer a unique
experience and are intended to familiarise the visitor
with a future travel destination. These involve a tour
of the museum's collections, a performing arts
workshop (music, storytelling or dance) and
a conference-debate with an ethnologist or
an introduction to the dialect spoken in the area.

_**Conferences** take place in the workshop rooms
and consist of introductions to traditional art forms
(storytelling, music, dances and puppet shows)
and contemporary art conferences-performances.

_**Major popular or ritual festivals** provide opportunities
for the different groups to meet for a varied
programme of events: special "Melting Pot" evening
performances, the Journées du patrimoine (Heritage
Days) or the Nuits blanches (White Nights).

/ THE MEDIA LIBRARY

The museum's media library has four independent
access areas for visitors:

_ THE STUDY AND RESEARCH MEDIA LIBRARY
_250,000 documents and 3,000 review titles
_5th floor, access via a dedicated lift in the entrance hall
_Free access, registration required, 180 places, room
equipped with a computer workstation suitable for the
visually-impaired
_Tuesday to Saturday from 10.00 am to 6.30 pm
and Thursday evenings until 9.30 pm. Closed Sunday
and Monday.
mediatheque@quaibranly.fr

_THE RARE BOOKS COLLECTION
_Rare and precious books
_5th floor, access via a dedicated lift in the entrance hall
_By appointment only
_ Tuesday to Saturday from 10.00 am to 6.30 pm
and Thursday evenings until 9.30 pm. Closed Sunday
and Monday.
cabinetdesfondsprecieux@quaibranly.fr

_THE COLLECTIONS ARCHIVE AND DOCUMENTATION

**ONE-DAY VOYAGE
OF DISCOVERY**
_FULL PRICE: 30 €
_REDUCED PRICE:
21 €

**WORKSHOP
FOR ADULTS**
_FULL PRICE: 10 €
_REDUCED PRICE:
7 €

**WORKSHOP
FOR CHILDREN**
_FIXED PRICE: 8 €

GROUP PRICES
**VISIT WITH
A LECTURER**
_10 PERS.: 190 €
_15 PERS.: 220 €
_20 PERS.: 250 €
_SCHOOL GROUPS:
70 €

**WORKSHOP
FOR ADULTS**
_FULL PRICE: 200 €
_REDUCED PRICE:
134 €

**WORKSHOP
FOR CHILDREN**
_FULL PRICE: 130 €
_REDUCED PRICE
AND SCHOOL
GROUPS: 100 €

CONSULTATION ROOM
_3rd floor of the Université building, access via a dedicated lift in the entrance hall
_By appointment only
_Monday to Friday from 10.00 am to 6.30 pm.
Closed Saturday and Sunday.

_THE JACQUES KERCHACHE READING ROOM
_Documentary collection of 5,000 publications, including 500 for children from age 7; continually updated, featuring exhibition catalogues, art books, atlases, information and cultural news journals and multimedia programmes
_Ground floor, access via the entrance hall
_Free access for all visitors with an admission ticket to the museum, 50 places, room equipped with a reading machine for the visually impaired
_Tuesday to Sunday from 10.00 am to 6.30 pm and late nights Thursday until 9.30 pm. Closed Monday.

All visitors of these rooms may:
_ Consult the collections (independent access)
_ Obtain bibliographical assistance
_ View a film
_ Listen to music and sound recordings
Visitors to the research and study media library may:
_ Copy documents (fees charged for photocopies and printouts)
_ Consult collections that are kept in storage
_ Learn how to search for resources online

/ THE MUSEUM BOOKSHOP
Situated on the ground floor, 220 rue de l'Université, the bookshop sets the standard for all primal arts retail outlets in France. Beneath its high ceilings painted by Australian aborigine artists, the shop offers a wide choice of publications, along with postcards and posters, magazines, CDs, DVDs and objects from countries featured in the museum.
Easy access for people with reduced mobility.
Tuesday to Sunday from 10.00 am to 7.00 pm and late nights Thursday until 10.00 pm. Closed Monday.
librairie.Musee-Branly@rmn.fr

DIFFERENT WAYS TO EXPLORE THE MUSEUM

If you have a couple of hours to spare, why not try an introductory visit? To enjoy browsing in the bookshop at the end of the visit, opt for an audioguided visit of the collections area.

If you can allow half a day for your visit, try an exploration of the museum. Discover the collections at your leisure, along with the temporary exhibitions in the Suspended Galleries; stop off at the Jacques Kerchache Reading Room to learn more about what you have seen during your visit and then treat yourself to a break in the café Branly!

If you can set aside a full day. The "un jour au musée" formula is the ticket for you! It allows access to the collections area and all of the temporary exhibitions, enough time for you to savour your visit and wander around the museum to your heart's content... before rolling up your sleeves and participating in an arts workshop. For lunch, simply take your choice: the restaurant "Les Ombres" or the café Branly. Sit down, relax and let yourself be tempted!

/ BEFORE AND AFTER THE VISIT
_The museum on the Web
www.quaibranly.fr
Suitable for all types of Internet users (with "Accessiweb" standards for the visually-impaired), the website is both a learning tool and a novel way to exchange views and engage in creativity. It includes:
_ Practical advice for your visit and museum news
_ Information about all of the collections
_ A directory of scientific web sites with comments
_ Blogs, forums, comments area

/ THE SOCIÉTÉ DES AMIS DU MUSÉE
Since 2002, the Société des Amis du musée du quai Branly has provided support and fostered public interest in the museum as a place to discover and share knowledge about the cultures of the world.
E-mail: amisdumusee@quaibranly.fr
Website: www.amisquaibranly.fr

REFRESHMENTS AT THE MUSÉE DU QUAI BRANLY
ON THE TERRACE
THE RESTAURANT "LES OMBRES" (SEATS 130 PEOPLE)
FACING THE MOAI STATUE: THE CAFÉ BRANLY (SEATS 80)

Photography: collections
Patrick Gries
Bruno Descoings
Valérie Torre
Benoît Jeanneton
Vincent Chenet
Hugues Dubois

Photography: building
Antonin Borgeaud
Nicolas Borel

Head of the publishing section
Clair Morizet

Head of the paper division
Muriel Rausch

Editors
Sophie Chambonnière
Juliette Solvès

Graphic design
Fouin + Zanardi

Copy editing
Valor

Translation
Tradutours

Graphics for maps
Aurélie Pallard

Graphics for site plans
Polymago

Photoengraving
MCP-JOUVE

Printed in July 2006 by Imprimerie Moderne de l'Est,
Baume-les-Dames